DECODING THE SECRETS OF

EGYPTIAN
HIEROGLYPHS

Bob Brier, Ph.D.

THE
GREAT
COURSES®

PUBLISHED BY:

THE GREAT COURSES
Corporate Headquarters
4840 Westfields Boulevard, Suite 500
Chantilly, Virginia 20151-2299
Phone: 1-800-832-2412
Fax: 703-378-3819
www.thegreatcourses.com

Copyright © The Teaching Company, 2016

Bob Brier, Ph.D.

SENIOR RESEARCH FELLOW
LIU POST

D r. Bob Brier, recognized as one of the world's foremost experts on mummies and Egyptology, is a Senior Research Fellow at LIU Post (formerly the C.W. Post Campus of Long Island University). He earned his bachelor's degree from Hunter College and his Ph.D. in Philosophy from The University of North Carolina at Chapel Hill.

Dr. Brier has twice been selected as a Fulbright Scholar and has received LIU's David Newton Award for Excellence in Teaching in recognition of his achievements as a lecturer. He has served as director of the National Endowment for the Humanities' Egyptology Today program.

In 1994, Dr. Brier became the first person in 2,000 years to mummify a human cadaver in the ancient Egyptian style. This research was the subject of a National Geographic television special, *Mr. Mummy*. Dr. Brier was also the host of TLC's series *The Great Egyptians*.

Dr. Brier is the author of *Ancient Egyptian Magic*; *Egyptian Mummies*; *Encyclopedia of Mummies*; *The Murder of Tutankhamen: A True Story*;

Daily Life in Ancient Egypt; *Egyptomania*; *Cleopatra's Needles: The Lost Obelisks of Egypt*; and numerous scholarly articles.

Dr. Brier has taught two other Great Courses: *The History of Ancient Egypt* and *Great Pharaohs of Ancient Egypt*. ■

Table of Contents

Introduction

Professor Biography i
Scope 1

Lecture Guides

Lecture 1
Why Egypt Needed Hieroglyphs...3

Lecture 2
The Ancient Egyptian Alphabet..23

Lecture 3
How a Language Becomes Lost..41

Lecture 4
Napoleon in Egypt 63

Lecture 5
Early Attempts to Decipher the Rosetta Stone 86

Lecture 6
William Bankes and the Keys to Decipherment...........................107

Lecture 7
Jean-François Champollion
Cracks the Code..130

Lecture 8
Suffix Pronouns and the Hieroglyphs of Ptah.............................153

Lecture 9
  The Immortal Scribe 176

Lecture 10
  Hieroglyphs and the Bible...202

Lecture 11
  Dependent Pronouns and the Passive Voice 226

Lecture 12
  Past Tense and Adjectives..252

Supplemental Material

How To Draw Hieroglyphs 278
English to Hieroglyph Dictionary....................................287
Hieroglyph to English Dictionary....................................304
Biliteral Chart...320
Triliteral Chart 324
Dependent Pronouns..325
Suffix Pronouns 326
Vocabulary..328
Bibliography..343
Image Credits 347

This guidebook uses the following typographical conventions:

- Quotation marks are used for English words cited as words (rather than used functionally; e.g., The word "ginormous" is a combination of "gigantic" and "enormous").

- Italics are used for all Egyptian words, word parts, and phrases that are not in hieroglyph form.

- Slashes are used to indicate sounds (e.g., /b/).

- Often, hieroglyphs and English appear in the same sentence. Here's an example: At the top, the scepter also has a *djed* pillar, 𓊽, representing the backbone of the god Osiris and meaning "stability." (Note that the commas are English and not part of the pillar hieroglyph. The same applies to any English punctuation mark appearing next to a hieroglyph.)

- In pronunciation transliterations involving suffix pronouns, the suffixes are technically part of the word they are attached to. This is indicated by periods. Here's an example: The sentence 𓇋𓅱𓏭𓐍𓂋𓉐𓏭 is pronounced something like *Yew.i em per.i.* (Note that the final period ends the sentence as a whole and has nothing to do with suffix pronouns.)

- If the pronunciation of a complete transliterated sentence is embedded in a full English or English/hieroglyph hybrid sentence, it will start with a capital letter, as in the example in the previous bullet point. ▪

This course is for everyone who has wondered what the mysterious hieroglyphs carved on ancient Egyptian temples say. The course's goal is to give you the ability to read ancient Egyptian texts. You'll start slowly by learning the ancient Egyptian alphabet and by writing names in hieroglyphs. Once you see that all those birds, feet, and snakes are not just pictures, you will be on your way to translating ancient texts.

The early lectures will introduce some hieroglyphic words, but will also tell the story of how hieroglyphs were deciphered. Decoding ancient Egyptian writing was one of the great intellectual adventures of all time, and it was not easy. The early lectures follow this story's heroes as they struggle to decipher the Rosetta Stone, a feat that took the greatest minds of Europe two decades to complete.

With a thorough understanding of how hieroglyphs were deciphered, you will be ready to learn the language itself. First you'll learn vocabulary words and then the basic rules of grammar. Soon you'll be working on simple sentences from papyri and temple and tomb walls.

In addition to learning how to read hieroglyphs, you will also learn how to write them, enabling you to think like an Egyptian. Hieroglyphs serve as a doorway into ancient Egyptian culture. When you learn to read and write the names of the gods, you will also learn the mythology associated with them. The course focuses on the myth of Isis and Osiris, which was central to the Egyptian belief in resurrection, and also on how Ptah created the world with words.

You will use your hieroglyphic knowledge to understand royal jewelry of Middle Kingdom queens in a new way. With your new translating skills, the jewelry becomes texts to be read.

By the end of the course, you will have learned the various ways that hieroglyphs can be used. You will know hundreds of ancient Egyptian words and understand the order of these words necessary to form sentences. You will be ready to translate the Hotep-di-nesu, a prayer for the dead carved on tomb walls. And in the final lecture, you will pull it all together and translate a lengthy inscription of the lid of Tutankhamen's sarcophagus. ■

Why Egypt Needed Hieroglyphs

Learning ancient Egyptian is easier, in some ways, than learning Spanish or French. One reason for this is that Middle Egyptian, the phase of the language that will we learn, is not spoken; thus, we can devote most of our efforts to learning to read it. Further, we don't have to conjugate verbs in ancient Egyptian or worry about masculine and feminine nouns. By the end of the course, you will understand how the language works and be able to translate rather complex sentences from real texts. And when you go to museums that have Egyptian collections, you will have a much better understanding of what you are looking at. Hieroglyphs will be your doorway into the culture.

Helpful Hints for Our Course

- The word *hieroglyph* comes from Greek. When the Greeks entered Egypt around the late 4th century B.C., they saw the carvings on temple walls and called them, in Greek, *hiero* ("sacred") *glyph* ("carvings"). Note that *hieroglyph* is the noun form of the word and *hieroglyphic* is the adjectival form.

- In each lecture of this course, we will learn new vocabulary words, which is the most important part of learning a language. This guidebook has a small dictionary of the words we will need, but you should also make your own handwritten dictionary to give yourself extra practice in writing.

- To write hieroglyphs on your computer, you can download a free program called JSesh. You may also want to get a copy of Sir Alan Gardiner's book *Egyptian Grammar*. The book contains a rather complete dictionary; it lists all the hieroglyphs, explaining what they are and the sounds they represent; it has sequential lessons that teach grammar and vocabulary; and it has homework assignments at the end of each lesson.

- Probably the best way to view this course is to watch just one lecture per day. That way, you can let the hieroglyphs sink in, have time to think about them, and spend 20 minutes or so writing them.

Egypt's Invention of Writing

- The Nile is one of the main reasons that Egypt had to have writing.

- Egypt is bounded on the east and west by desert and, on the north, by the Mediterranean. These are not easy boundaries to

After visiting Egypt around 450 B.C., the Greek historian Herodotus said, "Egypt is the gift of the Nile."

cross, especially because Egyptians feared the desert and were not particularly good sailors.

- The last natural boundary is the southern one, which in ancient times was at the city of Aswan. Here, there is a cataract—large boulders in the river—making passage difficult, both into and out of Egypt from the south.

- Each year, monsoons in Ethiopia bring torrential rains that wash rich topsoil into the Nile. In July, the Nile overflows its banks and deposits this soil on both sides of the river. For us, this is a natural phenomenon, but for the Egyptians, it was a magical event.

- The Egyptians fully appreciated the importance of the Nile. They made offerings to Hapi, the Nile god, who was shown as having both male and female traits. He's clearly male, but he has a female breast. The idea is that by himself, he gives life to Egypt.

- The annual inundation from the Nile fertilized the land of Egypt every year, allowing it to grow more food than it needed. But when there are surpluses, people want to keep track of

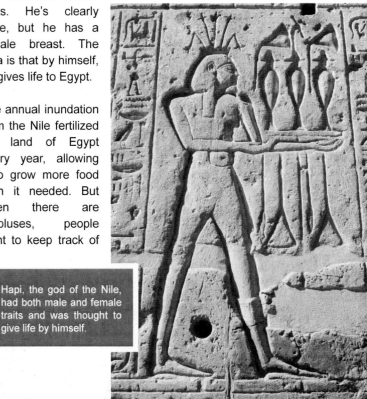

Hapi, the god of the Nile, had both male and female traits and was thought to give life by himself.

them, especially if there is a system of taxes. That's where writing came in. The Egyptians needed writing to keep track of the taxes that were due and the taxes that were collected.

The Narmer Palette

- Another reason that Egypt had to have writing relates to the fact that the Egyptians had a pharaoh as a ruler. To understand this, let's look at one of the oldest historical documents in the world: the Narmer Palette.

- In ancient Egypt, both men and women wore eye makeup. This makes sense in a desert country, to reduce the glare from the sun. The ancient Egyptians made these cosmetics by mixing duck fat and ground malachite. Palettes were used for combining these materials.

- The Narmer Palette is thought to be a ceremonial palette, created to celebrate the unification of Upper and Lower Egypt. Interestingly, Upper Egypt is in the south because when you went south, against the current, you were going "up the Nile." Thus, Upper Egypt is below Lower Egypt.

- One side of the palette has a large figure in the center. We know this figure is the king because he is wearing the tall white crown of Upper Egypt. In his hand is a mace, with which he is about to smash a captive. This king's name is Narmer, perhaps the first king of unified Egypt.

- Above the captive is a falcon holding the head of another captive by a nose ring. The falcon is the symbol of the pharaoh. The six papyrus plants that come out of the stylized body of the captive may be hieroglyphs for 6,000; each plant is 1,000 in hieroglyphs. Narmer may have taken or defeated 6,000 of the enemy. Narmer is wearing a kilt, and coming down its back is a bull's tail, a symbol of his power. He also wears a false beard, another symbol of authority.

- Behind Narmer is a smaller figure, his sandal bearer, and behind that figure are the hieroglyphs for the word *servant*. He is not, however, just a lowly servant but an important official. Around his neck is a cylinder seal on a cord, which shows that he is high up in the hierarchy.

- Behind the captive may be the name of the town he comes from. Beneath Narmer's feet are two fleeing enemies, with their towns apparently indicated by the hieroglyphs above them.

- How do we know that the king's name is Narmer? The palette shows a rectangular structure called a *serekh* that represents the façade of a palace. Inside that rectangle are two hieroglyphs. The one on top is a catfish, which was pronounced *nar* in ancient Egyptian. Beneath it is a chisel, pronounced *mer*, forming the word *Narmer*.

- The second side of the palette has the same top, with the name of Narmer in the palace façade. Beneath this is a victory procession. Narmer is now wearing the short red crown of Lower Egypt. He came from the south, conquered the king of the north, and now rules both north and south, unifying Egypt.

- In the procession that precedes him is a figure that's larger than the others. The hieroglyphs above him mean *vizier*, or prime minister. His posture is stooped because he is wearing a heavy leopard skin, the sign of a high priest. The smaller figures hold standards, perhaps the divisions or towns from which the army came. They are walking toward decapitated bodies that have their hands tied.

- Beneath this procession are two mythological animals with their necks intertwined. This may well represent the unification of the two lands. At the very bottom of the palette is a bull, breaking down a walled city while trampling the enemy. The bull is yet another symbol of the pharaoh.

- The Narmer Palette is important because of its historical content and because it is very early writing and describes the beginning of Egypt as great nation. But it's also important to ancient Egyptian art. It set conventions that would be followed for 3,000 years.

  - The palette depicts hierarchical proportions. The more important people are shown larger.

  - The "smiting the enemy" pose would become the logo for Egypt, appearing on temples for the next 30 centuries.

  - The falcon and the bull also reappear as emblems of kingship.

  - Also important is the practice of placing the action on registers. In other words, the palette is divided into sections, which makes it easier to read.

- As mentioned, the Narmer Palette is an early example of Egyptian writing. The hieroglyphs on the palette are not sentences but more like labels. They give Narmer's name, the vizier's title, and perhaps the captive's name. Because they don't tell a full narrative, we have to fill in the blanks, and it's possible that we don't have the right story.

  - The "handwriting" on the two sides of the palette seems different. For example, on one side, the *serekh* (the palace façade) is almost crudely drawn, while on the other side, it's much more complete. Even Narmer's name is different on the two sides.

  - It seems likely that the two sides were carved by two different artists. Perhaps one side was carved, then some time elapsed, and it was decided to carve the second side. But which side was carved first?

  - It may be that the side with the intertwined mythical beasts was carved first. After all, the object is a palette, and where the necks intertwine is the only suitable place for grinding cosmetics. Sometime later, the second side was carved. That would mean that what is generally thought of as the front is the reverse, and we may be telling the story backwards.

The Egyptian Pharaoh

- In Egypt, the pharaoh was viewed as a god. He had absolute power and owned all the land. With such centralized power, the pharaoh was capable of marshaling all the manpower of Egypt for his purposes.

- For example, just before the inundation of the Nile, the pharaoh could organize farmers to begin digging irrigation canals so that more crops could be grown. Then, the pharaoh could collect even more taxes, which required writing.

- As a pharaoh, if you grow more crops than you need, you can support a large class of people who don't contribute to the economy and can serve in an army. You no longer need to call out the farmers when invaders are coming because you have a trained and equipped army that can easily defeat them.

- You can also march out with your professional army and invade other countries, such as Palestine, Syria, and Turkey. After your enemies are defeated, you can demand an annual tribute. At this point, the army is not a drain on the economy but contributes to it.

- The Egyptians had the first professional standing army in history, and because they had to keep track of thousands of soldiers in different divisions, once again, they needed writing.

- Egypt was the world's first great bureaucracy. It had surpluses that had to be recorded, taxes to be collected, and armies to keep track of, and all this required writing. We have looked at one of the first historic documents in the world, the Narmer Palette, not only as an introduction to hieroglyphs but also as a statement about the importance of the king.

Why Egypt Needed Hieroglyphs

Hi. I'm Bob Brier. Let me begin by telling you how delighted I am that you want to learn hieroglyphs. In some ways, it will be like learning any other language. There are vocabulary words to be learned, grammatical rules to be followed, and some homework will be necessary—but not too much. In these ways, learning ancient Egyptian is like learning Spanish or French, but I think it's actually easier.

One reason for this is that we will not be learning to speak it. Middle Egyptian, which is the phase of the language that we'll be learning, is a dead language. No one speaks it, so most of our efforts can be devoted to learning to read it. There will be no "Bonjour, je suis Bob Brier" or "Me llamo Bob Brier." We don't have to divide the lesson into reading and conversation. You're not going to encounter any talking mummies. That will save a lot of time. Something else that makes learning hieroglyphs relatively easy is that we don't conjugate verbs. No "je suis," "tu es," "il est." Again, this saves lots of time and memory space in the brain.

Unlike romance languages, we don't have to remember which nouns are masculine and which are feminine. We won't have to worry if "boat" is masculine or feminine, or what gender "pen" is. The reason is that almost every feminine noun ends in a *t* sound. If it has a *t* at the end, it's feminine; if not, it's masculine. So there are a lot of features built into the language that makes it learner-friendly.

We only have 24 lectures together, but I think we'll be able to make considerable progress. By the end of this course, you will pretty much understand how the language works, be able to translate some rather complex sentences from real texts, and when you go to museums that have

Egyptian collections, you will have a much, much better understanding of what you are looking at. Hieroglyphs will be our doorway into the culture.

Let me point out that I have been saying hieroglyphs, not hieroglyphics. The carvings and drawings of birds, feet, gods, and boats that we'll be studying are hieroglyphs, not hieroglyphics. Hieroglyphic is the adjectival form of the word. Indeed, we will learn a hieroglyphic script, but the symbols that make up that script are hieroglyphs. OK? So I don't want to hear anyone saying hieroglyphics anymore.

The word "hieroglyph," comes from the Greek. When Alexander the Great entered Egypt around 332 B.C., they saw the carvings on temple walls and called them sacred carvings. *Hiero* for "sacred" or "priestly" and *glyph* for "carving."

We won't be doing any carving in this course, but we will be learning to write the hieroglyphs on paper. I think you will find this especially enjoyable. There is something calming and rewarding about writing hieroglyphs. It is an end in itself. I will show you how to draw many hieroglyphs step by step. Even if you have bad handwriting, you can learn to write reasonable hieroglyphs.

I have poor handwriting in any script. I'm old enough that when I was a kid, it was considered wrong to be left-handed, and we were forced to become righties. In kindergarten, I wrote with my left hand, then was switched in first grade, and I never had a decent handwriting in any script. When I learned Greek, I had poor Greek handwriting, and it was the same with hieroglyphs.

Later, when I was teaching hieroglyphs, and writing on the blackboard, my poor students wound up copying my terrible handwriting. When they would go to graduate school, my colleagues would see their handwriting and say, "Oh, you're Bob Brier's student." This was not a compliment. Then something happened.

Many years ago an old friend, the Egyptologist Geoffrey Martin, was staying with me in New York, and he sat in on one of my classes. I was going over a homework assignment and Geoffrey, dear soul that he is, was appalled by my handwriting. He walked up to the board, took the chalk from my hand, and said, "Bob, this will not do," and proceeded to show the students how to properly draw the hieroglyphs. Geoffrey and I are very close, so this was just fine with me, and my students thought it was hilarious. He convinced me I had to change.

Fortunately for me, at this time, my secretary, Sheila Martinez, was an artist who had been to Egypt with my students and had a beautiful hieroglyphic handwriting. She began teaching me how to change mine. It took an hour a day for quite a while, but today it's decent—not wonderful—but my students are not singled out for their poor handwriting anymore. If I could change my hieroglyphic hand at the age of 40, I am sure you will be able to draw excellent hieroglyphs and take pride in your achievement.

In the next lecture I'll show you how to draw the primary hieroglyphs, and in our exercise-book are step-by-step instructions for each one. Drawing the hieroglyphs will be a significant aspect of this course, and I think you're going to have a lot of fun with it.

Each lecture, I will introduce new vocabulary words, which is the most important part of learning the language. If you know your nouns and verbs, you will usually be able to make sense of a sentence. So vocabulary is very important. Again, our exercise-book has a small dictionary of the words we'll need, but I suggest you make your own handwritten dictionary. This will give you extra practice in writing, and will also help you remember the words. We'll talk about your dictionary a bit later in the course, so don't worry about it right now.

Often you will see printed hieroglyphs on the screen. I used a program called JSesh to produce these hieroglyphs. *Sesh* is the ancient Egyptian word for "scribe." I am not sure what the J means; it may stand for the computer language Java. JSesh is a program created by Egyptologists, and it is free online. So if you want to write hieroglyphic notes to your friends or on your computer, or print hieroglyphic birthday cards, download JSesh.

Now, a word about books. As we go along, I will suggest some books that I think you might enjoy. The one I want to mention here is very highly recommended. It is Sir Alan Gardiner's *Egyptian Grammar*. It's big and imposing, but don't be deterred. It is wonderful, and you'll love it.

It is the book that most of us learned our hieroglyphs from, and it's still a standard. It has many exceptionally useful features. First, it contains a rather complete dictionary, so you can look up any words you don't know. Second, it lists all the hieroglyphs, explaining what they are, what sound they represent. These are organized according to what they depict, so all the birds are together, all the people hieroglyphs together.

Then Gardiner tags each hieroglyph with a letter—according to subject—and a number. So a particular bird hieroglyph is A-1, and another is A-2. A hieroglyph of a particular god might be C-11, and so on. So if you see a hieroglyph you don't know, you look it up in the sign list, get its number, and then go to a longer hieroglyph list, look up A-22 and you get an explanation of what it is, how it is used, what its sound is; it's really great fun. JSesh uses Gardner's system of numbering hieroglyphs to call up the hieroglyphs.

The Gardiner book also provides sequential lessons that teach grammar and vocabulary, and at the end of each lesson are homework assignments—sentences to translate not only from hieroglyphs to English but also from English to hieroglyphs. Unfortunately, the answers are not in the back of the book.

This is the kind of book that you will love to thumb through just looking for new words and texts. In this course, I try to follow Gardiner's lessons closely enough so that after you have completed all the lectures, you will have a good enough background to continue your studies in Gardiner's book. I like the idea that Gardiner's exercises use texts from real monuments; most are not made up. I've had to change his examples because we don't have all the vocabulary he assumes, but still, it's close enough that you will feel at home in Gardiner's book. So, I strongly suggest you get a copy of Gardiner's *Egyptian Grammar*, which you can find online or order through a local bookseller.

Let me make a suggestion about how you should watch this course. No binge watching. For some courses that's just fine, you become fascinated with the subject, and just want to keep going. My hope is that you will be fascinated with this course, too, but it will be better to do just one lecture per day. That way you can let the hieroglyphs sink in, have time to think about them, and then spend 20 minutes or so writing them while doing the homework.

Now, that's enough housekeeping for today. I want to leave time to explain why Egypt had to invent writing. It's not an accident that Egypt invented writing, and the native tribes of North America didn't, even though those tribes lived much later. You have to have a certain kind of society to need writing. Let's see what made Egypt that kind of society.

"Egypt is the gift of the Nile." At least that's what Herodotus said around 450 B.C. when he visited Egypt. Herodotus was a Greek tourist who was blown away by Egypt's wonders. The pyramids, the temples, the mummies, they all astounded him. Herodotus traveled everywhere, and when he retired to write his history of the world he devoted an entire book to Egypt. It's great reading, and I recommend it highly—you can get it in paperback— but the important thing for us is that he is the first to mention, in print, the importance of the Nile.

I believe the Nile is one of the main reasons why Egypt had writing. Let's look at a map. Ancient Egypt was bordered on the east and west by desert, which isolated it from other countries. It was not easy to cross a desert in the ancient world. You had to dig wells, make preparations, and so on. The Egyptians were not desert dwellers; they feared the desert. Remember, they didn't have camels in ancient Egypt. Camels were introduced later, around Roman times.

On the north, Egypt was bounded by the Mediterranean. Again, not an easy boundary to cross, especially since Egyptians were not good sailors. They knew how to sail on the Nile, which was a piece of cake. You didn't have to navigate; you could see both banks at all times. Also, the winds were almost always from the north, so if you were going south, you just put up the sails and off you went. When you wanted to return, once again, it was easy. The current flows from south to north. So, take down your sails, steer with your oars and tiller, and you were on your way home. Our last natural boundary is the southern one, which in ancient times was at the city of Aswan. Here we have a cataract—large boulders in the river. Again, making passage difficult, both into and out of Egypt from the south.

So, Egypt to a great extent was isolated, deserts on two sides, Mediterranean in the north, cataracts in the south. How did it survive? Indeed, not only survive, thrive. Here is where Herodotus's statement about Egypt being the gift of the Nile is so important. It isn't a metaphor; it's literally true. Let me explain.

Once a year, in July, the Nile overflowed its banks and deposited rich black soil on both sides of the river. For us, this is a natural phenomenon. Each year monsoons in Ethiopia, to the south, bring torrential rains that wash rich topsoil into the Nile. We can understand this easily, but for the Egyptians, it was a magical event. What they saw was that the Nile first turned dark brown from the topsoil suspended in the water. Then the river turned green, from the slower-moving vegetation being washed north into Egypt, and then the river rose 30 feet. Pure magic.

You see, the Egyptians didn't know the source of the Nile. They never went that far south. And the reason Herodotus's statement is literal is that when the Nile overflowed its banks and inundated Egypt, it deposited the fertile topsoil. The rich, black land of Egypt is indeed the gift of the Nile.

The Egyptians fully appreciated how important the Nile was to them. They made offerings to Hapi, the Nile god, who was shown as simultaneously having both male and female traits. He's clearly male, but he has one female breast. The idea is that, by himself, he gives life to Egypt.

Now for the connection between the Nile overflowing and writing. The annual inundation fertilized the land of Egypt every year. There was no soil depletion, no need for fertilizers, and Egypt could grow more food than it needed. When you have surpluses, you want to keep track of them, especially if you have a system of taxes. And, boy, did Egypt have a system of taxes. And that's where writing comes in. You need writing to keep track of the taxes that were due and the taxes that were collected.

But there's another reason why Egypt had to have writing—they had a pharaoh as ruler. To explain this, let's look at the world's oldest official document of an event—the Narmer Palette. Let me first explain what a palette is and how they were used in ancient Egypt.

Both men and women wore eye makeup. This makes sense in a desert country, to reduce the glare from the sun, very much like football and baseball players today smear black paint under their eyes. Now, how did the ancient Egyptians make cosmetics? Pretty much the same way we do today.

I'll tell you a funny story. Years ago, I was at a local fast food place called Pudgey's Chicken. In spite of its unfortunate name, it served chicken without skin, which is much more healthful for you. As I was waiting to pick up my order, I asked the kid behind the counter, "What happens to all the chicken skins?" He told me that every night a cosmetic company picked them up. That's how some cosmetics are made, with chicken fat as a base. It was the same in ancient Egypt. You took a little duck fat—there were no chickens in the old world—mixed in a bit of ground malachite, and presto, eye makeup. Palettes were used for grinding these cosmetics. So you took a nice piece of slate, carved it into a pleasing shape, and you had a surface on which to grind your makeup.

Now let's look at the Narmer Palette. We are looking at what is traditionally believed to be the front side of the Narmer Palette. You'll notice that it is very large and not a nice smooth surface, not really practical for grinding cosmetics. We think it was a ceremonial palette, created to celebrate a historical event, and that event is the unification of Upper and Lower Egypt.

Originally, Egypt was divided into two kingdoms, Upper and Lower. Upper is in the south because when you went south, against the current, you were going up the Nile. So, Upper Egypt is below Lower Egypt. I know, it's confusing, but you'll get used to it.

Now let's see what's happening on the palette. The first thing you notice is the large figure in the center. He's the king, and we know that because he is wearing the tall white crown of Upper Egypt. In his hand he holds a mace, basically a rock on a stick, and he is about to smash his captive, whom he holds by the hair. I can tell you the king's name; it's Narmer, perhaps the very first king of unified Egypt. You'll see how I know that in a minute.

Above the captive is a falcon holding the head of another captive by a nose ring. The falcon is the symbol of the pharaoh. The six papyrus plants that come out of the stylized body of the captive may be hieroglyphs for 6,000— each plant is 1,000 in hieroglyphs. So Narmer may have taken 6,000 of the enemy and defeated them.

That's the headline, but there's lots more to say. Look at what Narmer is wearing. A kilt, and coming down its back is a bull's tail, a symbol of his power. He also wears a false beard, another symbol of authority. You can even see the chin strap holding it on.

Now look behind Narmer at the smaller figure. It's his sandal-bearer. And I think he is carrying a pot of water for when the pharaoh gets thirsty. Behind that little guy are the hieroglyphs for the word "servant." The hieroglyph on top is traditionally called a rosette, but it appears to be flower petals of some sort. The hieroglyph beneath it is a small club.

These are very early hieroglyphs—carved at the beginning of the written ancient Egyptian language, so we aren't exactly sure what they mean, but we have a good idea. The rosette appears in front of other king's names, so my bet is it means "king." The little club, in later Egyptian texts, means "servant," so the little guy with the sandals is the "King's servant." But don't think he is just a lowly servant. He is actually an important official. Around his neck, he's got a cylinder seal on a cord. This shows he was high up in the hierarchy. Also, just being represented on the palette must have been a great honor.

Behind the captive may be the name of the town he comes from, we're not sure. Remember, these are very early hieroglyphs, carved around 3100 B.C., right at the beginning of writing. Beneath Narmer's feet are two fleeing enemies, with their towns apparently indicated by the hieroglyphs above them.

Now, how do I know the king's name is Narmer? Look at the top. Two representations of a cow goddess look down on the scene, perhaps in approval. But between them is a rectangular structure called a *serekh* that represents a façade of a palace. There are doors and windows. Inside that rectangle are two hieroglyphs. The one on top is a catfish, which was pronounced *nar* in ancient Egyptian. Beneath it is a chisel, pronounced *mer*—Narmer. That's how the first king's name was pronounced.

Now let's look at the second side of the palette to see the end of the event commemorated. The second side of the palette has the same top, with the cow goddesses and the name of Narmer in the palace façade. Beneath it, however, we have something different, a procession, a victory procession. Narmer is now wearing a different crown, the short, red crown of Lower Egypt. He came from the south, conquered the king of the north and now rules both north and south. Egypt is unified. His name is very prominent in front of him, Narmer.

In the procession that precedes him is a figure that's larger than the others. The hieroglyphs above him are not his name—they mean *vizier* or prime minister. I think you can see his stooped posture. That's because he is wearing a leopard skin. It is a sign of a high priest, and it is not an easy garment to wear; it's not tailored, so he is bent over, holding the heavy garment on.

The smaller figures hold standards, perhaps the divisions or towns from which the army came. They are walking towards decapitated bodies that have their hands tied. Don't mess with Narmer.

Beneath this procession, we see two mythological animals with their necks intertwined. This is unusual, they appear only in a few other times in Near Eastern art, and we don't know exactly what the beasts represent. Here they may well symbolize the unification of the two powerful lands.

At the very bottom of the palette is a bull, simultaneously breaking down a walled city while he tramples on the enemy. The bull is yet another symbol of the pharaoh.

The Narmer Palette is important for several reasons, because of its historical content, and because it's very early writing describing the beginning of Egypt as a great nation. But it's also important to ancient Egyptian art. It sets standards, conventions that would be followed for 3,000 years.

First, it shows hierarchical proportions. The more important people are shown larger. Just look at Narmer on the front compared with everyone else.

Second, the "smiting the enemy" pose will be the logo for Egypt, the very symbol of the country. It appears on temples for the next 30 centuries.

Third, the falcon and the bull will also reappear over and over again as emblems of kingship.

Fourth is the practice of placing the action on registers. People don't just float around. They stand on something. The palette is divided into sections, which makes it easier to read.

As I mentioned before, the Narmer Palette is a very early example of Egyptian writing. If you think about the hieroglyphs on the palette, you will see that they are not sentences; they are really more like labels. They give Narmer's name, the vizier's title, perhaps the captive's name. They don't tell a full narrative; we have to fill in the blanks, guess at the full story. Everyone always assumed that both sides were carved at the same time to commemorate a single event. This may not be correct.

Let me tell you about something I noticed on the palette that suggests that possibly we don't have the right story. Years ago I was waiting for someone at the Egyptian Museum in Cairo, and he was late. We were supposed to meet at the Narmer Palette, and since I knew he would be late, I decided to use the time to take a very close look at the Narmer Palette's hieroglyphs. As I looked at both sides, I became convinced that I recognized two distinct handwritings—one on one side of the palette, one on the other.

Let's look at the rosette next to the sandal bearer. See how it's drawn on two sides. One side has seven petals and on the other only six. This is a handwriting. The same person isn't going to write this hieroglyph so differently. Two different people did this.

Also look at the *serekh*, the palace façade. See how simply, almost crudely, it's drawn on the reverse side. Compare that with the other side. Much more complete. Even Narmer's name is drawn differently on the two sides. The catfish in his name is quite different from side to side.

I am absolutely convinced that the two sides were carved by two different artists. The question is why? I don't know. Perhaps one side was carved and then some time elapsed, and it was decided to carve the second side. Now for the even bigger question. Which side was carved first?

I have an idea. It's a half-baked idea, but I think it's interesting. My guess is that the side with the intertwined mythological beasts was carved first. After all, it's a *palette* and where the necks intertwine is the only suitable place for grinding cosmetics. Some time later the second side was carved. So, that would mean that what we've been calling the front is the reverse. We may be telling the story backward. I'm far from sure about this, but what is clear is that if you know a bit about hieroglyphs, you will look more closely at them and see things that others miss.

Anyway, the Narmer Palette definitely shows us just how important the king is in Egyptian civilization. This also led to the development of writing.

In Egypt, the pharaoh was viewed as a god. He had absolute power, owned all the land, and didn't have to worry about committees approving his decisions. With such centralized power, the pharaoh was capable of marshaling all the manpower of Egypt for his purposes. If you have a great king, you can do amazing things, like building pyramids.

Also, you can organize the farmers so that just before the inundation comes —you need a calendar for this—they begin digging irrigation canals so that more land is irrigated and more crops can be grown. Then you can collect even more taxes, and this requires writing more than ever. And this surplus leads to yet another reason why Egypt had to have writing.

If you grow more crops than you need, you can support a large class of people who don't contribute to the economy and who can serve in an army. Now you don't just call out the farmers when invaders are coming, you have a trained army, equipped, that can easily defeat them.

Wait, even better—you can march out with your professional army and invade other countries—like Palestine, Syria, Turkey. Then you beat them up, take home everything that isn't nailed down, and tell them that if they don't send an annual tribute, you'll be back. Now the army is not a drain on the economy; it contributes to it.

Egypt had the first professional standing army in history. They loved war; it was good business. But they had to keep track of the thousands of soldiers in different divisions, so once again they needed writing.

The idea is that Egypt was the world's first great bureaucracy. It had surpluses that had to be recorded, taxes to be collected, armies to keep track of, and all of this required writing. We've looked at the first historic document in the world, the Narmer Palette, not only is it an introduction to hieroglyphs, but it's a statement about the role of the king and how important he was. We also saw how Narmer wrote his name. Next time we will learn how to read and write our own names in hieroglyphs.

For now, though, I want to leave you with your first hieroglyph assignment. I don't want you to do any research. Just look at the following hieroglyphic sentence and see what you think it says.

I know you don't know much about hieroglyphs yet. All we've seen are the few early hieroglyphs on the Narmer's Palette. Pretend you are a medieval scholar trying to decipher a language that has been lost for more than a thousand years. See what you come up with.

See you next time.

The Ancient Egyptian Alphabet

Consider this ancient Egyptian sentence: 𓅮𓃀𓏏𓈖𓇳 𓂋𓂝𓇳 𓅓 𓊪𓏏𓇯. Almost everyone guesses that the sentence concerns birds and going somewhere, which is reasonable given that we see birds, feet, and so on. However, if you made that guess, you're making the same "Big Mistake" that scholars trying to decipher the inscription on the Rosetta Stone made: assuming that the hieroglyphs are completely ideographic, that is, picture writing. It seems as if the depiction of a bird would mean that the text is related to birds. But in fact, this sentence translates to "The sun is shining in the sky." In this lecture, we'll learn why that's true.

Translating 𓅮𓃀𓏏𓈖𓇳 𓂋𓂝𓇳 𓅓 𓊪𓏏𓇯

- For the most part, hieroglyphs are phonetic and represent sounds. The bird in the sentence above is a quail chick and represents the sound *w*, the foot has the sound *b*, and the wavy line is *n*. The small circle at the end, though, is ideographic. It represents the sun and helps make clear the meaning of *wbn* (pronounced *weben*— it's sometimes easier to spell these with vowels for pronunciation) clear. It is the word for "shine." Thus, we note two things about our first Egyptian word. It is mostly phonetic, with no vowels, and an ideograph provides a clue to its sense.

- The second word in the sentence is made up of three hieroglyphs. A mouth sign (*r*), an arm (*eh*), and the sun circle again, which has no sound but helps make the meaning clear. The sound is *reh*, and the meaning is "sun."

- Next comes an owl. That's pronounced *m* and means "in." The last word has a rectangle (*p*) and a semicircle (*t*); it is pronounced *pet*.

The hieroglyph under it represents the sky, and the word means "sky." (The Egyptians viewed the sky as a canopy held up by four pillars.)

- Notice how the word for sky is formed, with two small hieroglyphs above a longer one. The ancient Egyptians were concerned with aesthetics. They wanted their words and sentences to look good, and stringing out the three hieroglyphs on one line wouldn't look nearly as nice.

- Thus, the sentence means, "The sun is shining in the sky." We should also notice that the verb *shine* comes at the start of the sentence. Verbs came first in ancient Egyptian.

- In this sentence, hieroglyphs are actually used two ways: phonetically, to represent sounds, but also as pictures to help us determine the meanings of phonetic words, such as the sun and sky hieroglyphs. These signs are called *determinatives*.

- Hieroglyphs can also be used as *ideograms*. These are hieroglyphs used pictorially but not at the end of a word. Rather, ideograms stand alone. To help you recognize that they are standing alone, they are usually flagged in the ancient Egyptian language with a stroke. Thus, for "sun," we could write ⊙| .

- To summarize, hieroglyphs can be used in three ways:

  ○ Phonetically, representing a sound.

  ○ As a determinative, coming at the end of a word to clarify its meaning.

  ○ As an ideogram, in which the picture represents a concept all by itself.

The Egyptian Alphabet

- The following bullets show the Egyptian symbols for English letters. For full words, see the dictionaries located at the end of this guidebook.

- Egyptians didn't write vowels, and their A is not exactly the sound of our A. Philologists call it semivocalic, as in the Arabic ʿayn. For this sound, we draw a vulture.

- B is a foot.

- There is no real C, but there is a CH, as in the Scottish *loch*. It's a placenta: ⊖. Note that this course will use the transliteration *kh* because this fits more closely with many conventional spellings of ancient Egyptian words.

- D is a stylized hand.

- E is an arm.

- F is a horned viper.

- G is a jar stand.

- There are two different Hs in the Egyptian alphabet. The reed hut H is a simple structure made of reeds to give farmers some shade from the blistering sun. ⊓ The other H is twisted flax. It represents two strands of the flax plant twisted together. The difference between the two Hs is that the reed hut is more emphatic, as in "hot," where you expel your breath forcefully. The flax H is not so emphatic and is more like the /h/ in "hello."

- I is a reed leaf, the kind that flowers by the seashore.

- J is a snake. It is really a /dj/ sound, as in "judge."

- K is a basket with a handle.

- There's no L in the ancient Egyptian alphabet. Note that the Greeks later added a lion for L.

- M is an owl.

- N is simple up-and-down peaks. The word for water was *nun*; thus, it is not surprising that the ideogram for water also represents the /n/ sound. The water sign may have been the first hieroglyph.

- There is no O in the ancient Egyptian alphabet.

- P is a rectangle (not a square) and represents a woven reed mat.

- Q is a hill.

- R is a mouth. ⬯

- The letter S looks like a cane, but it's a bolt of folded cloth. ⎮

- T is a loaf of bread. ⌒

- The U is a quail chick. 𓅱

- There is no V in the Egyptian alphabet, but the horned viper, F, can be used as a substitute. ⌇

- W is also the quail chick. 𓅱

- There is no X is in the Egyptian alphabet.

- Y is the reed written twice. It has the sound of a long /e/ as in "merry." 𓇌

- Z is a bolt on a door. ⎯

- Two more hieroglyphs complete the alphabet. They are for sounds for which English doesn't use a single letter.

  - /Sh/ is really one sound, but in English, we use two letters to represent it. The ancient Egyptians used a pool of water the for /sh/ sound. ⬭

  - Last is the sound /tch/. This is represented by a tethering ring. ⬭

Writing Your Name in Hieroglyphs

- When we write our names in the Egyptian alphabet, note that we are not translating our names. We are not working at the level of meanings. We are simply transcribing our names from one alphabet to another. This is called *transliteration*.

- Let's say that your name is Andrea Schwartz. 𓄿𓄿𓈖𓂋𓄿

  - ○ Notice that you have to be careful with the positioning of hieroglyphs. If you have two signs that are long and narrow, they would go one over the other; in this case, the water sign goes on top of the hand. 𓈖 Then the mouth hieroglyph 𓂋 goes on top of the arm sign. 𓂝

  - ○ Only hieroglyphs in the same word are stacked. The Egyptians didn't usually merge words.

Lecture 2's Homework

1. Practice writing one line of each hieroglyph on lined paper. In other words, do a line of vultures, then the foot, and so forth. To improve your hieroglyphic penmanship, use a fine-point felt-tipped pen. Hieroglyphs were intended to be drawn with a brush. A felt-tipped pen will approximate the brush.

The Ancient Egyptian Alphabet

Welcome back. Today we're going to begin our study of hieroglyphs by learning the Egyptian alphabet and how to write our names in hieroglyphs. But first I have to give you the answer to the homework question. What does this ancient Egyptian sentence say?

I've been teaching this course for 40 years, and I'm always surprised at how consistent the guesses are. Almost everyone thinks it is about birds and going somewhere, which is perfectly reasonable since we see birds, feet, and so on. But reasonable is not necessarily correct. The sentence has nothing to do with feet, walking or birds.

Everyone is making the same mistake that the scholars trying to decipher hieroglyphs were making—assuming that the hieroglyphs are 100 percent ideographic, that is, picture writing. That when you have a bird, the text is talking about birds. It's not. This is what I call the Big Mistake. In fact, this sentence translates to "The sun is shining in the sky." Let me explain why.

Hieroglyphs, for the most part, are phonetic and represent sounds. The first bird is a quail chick and represents the sound w, the foot has the sound b, and the wavy line is an n. This little circle at the end, though, is ideographic. It represents the sun and helps make the meaning of wbn clear. It is the word for "shine."

So, two things to note about our first Egyptian word. First, it's mostly phonetic, with no vowels. The Egyptians did not write vowels and often we don't know which vowels were used. Second, an ideographic sign at the end provides a clue to the word's meaning.

The second word in our sentence is made up of three hieroglyphs. A mouth sign—*r*—an arm—*eh*—and our sun circle again, which has no sound but helps make the meaning clear. So the sound is *reh*, and the meaning is "sun." Next, comes an owl. That's pronounced *m,* and it means "in." Our last word has a rectangle—*p*—and a semicircle—*t*—so it is pronounced *pt.* The hieroglyph under it represents the sky. The Egyptians viewed the sky as a canopy held up by four pillars—and the word means "sky."

Note how the word for "sky" is formed. Two small hieroglyphs together above a longer one. The ancient Egyptians were very concerned with aesthetics. They wanted their words and sentences to look good. If you strung out the three hieroglyphs on one line, it wouldn't look nearly as good.

So, our sentence means, "The sun is shining in the sky." Nothing about birds, feet, or arms. We should also notice that the verb "shine" comes at the start of the sentence. Verbs come first in ancient Egyptian. I should point out that sometimes in Egyptian—just as in English—there is some ambiguity. The word *wbn* "to shine" also means "to rise." So your sentence could also be translated as "The sun is rising in the sky."

In our sentence, hieroglyphs are actually used two ways. Phonetically, to represent sounds, but also as pictures to help us determine the meanings of phonetic words, like the sun and sky hieroglyphs. These signs are called determinatives because they help determine the meaning of a word. There is one more way that hieroglyphs can be used, and that's as ideograms.

Ideograms are hieroglyphs used pictorially but not at the end of a word. Rather, ideograms stand alone. To help you recognize that they're standing alone, they're often flagged in the ancient Egyptian language with a stroke. So we could do some speed writing and for "sun" we could write this,

So to summarize, hieroglyphs can be used in three ways. First, phonetically, representing a sound. Second, as a determinative, coming at the end of a word to clarify its meaning. And third, as an ideogram, where the picture represents a concept all by itself.

We will get lots of practice with all three uses of hieroglyphs, and they'll become familiar with repetition, so don't worry.

Now it's time to learn the ancient Egyptian alphabet. I'll show you how to write each hieroglyph step-by-step. Just a heads-up, There's no letter L, O, V or X in Middle Egyptian. I'll show you how to draw an L lion that was used much later, during the Ptolemaic period. But don't be surprised when we skip right over some other letters. Now, get some paper and a pencil or pen.

Let me give you one tip to improve your hieroglyphic penmanship. Use a fine-point felt-tipped pen. Hieroglyphs were intended to be drawn with a brush. A felt-tipped pen will approximate the brush.

Let's start with A. I know I said that the Egyptians didn't write vowels and now I'm showing you an A. It's not exactly the sound of our A. Philologists call it semivocalic, like the Arabic *ayn*. It may have sounded a bit like the O in "Otto" even. For this sound, we're going to draw a vulture.

Watch the steps and then follow along when I draw it a second time.

We start with the beak, something like that. Next, we go with the front of the body. then give him front legs. We come down for the back, giving the back wings, come up for his leg, give him something to stand on, and you got a vulture.

Now, let's do it again. I'll do it slowly; you'll see the sequence. Start with your beak, do the front, give him his front legs, come down with the back, back wings, come over, up with the leg, and always the bird stand on something. That's our letter A. This is one of the most difficult of the alphabetic hieroglyphs. Don't worry if you are having trouble; you'll get it. Everyone does. Remember, our exercise book also shows you how to draw it step by step.

B is a foot.

Start with a line down, then you just need a triangle coming over here, come back and then you got the back of a foot—B. Line down, triangle, come back, and bring it down, then you got a foot. It's very stylized.

There is no real C. But we have a CH like in the Scottish *loch*. It's a placenta.

You just draw a circle, and with three lines across, and you got it. Sometimes there are four lines across; it doesn't matter which, and that's our CH sound.

D is a hand.

It's stylized, not realistic. Start with an oval, then draw the wrist like that, and now comes the thumb. It almost looks like a mitten. So you do the oval, the wrist, and the thumb. And that's D.

E is an arm.

It's one of those semivocalic sounds. Not quite a vowel. Now, start with the fingers of the hand, like that. Then go with the arm, and then the shoulder. The shoulder isn't a square; it's got a little bit of a down like that. And that's the E. So remember, you just do the thumb, you do the hand underneath it, you bring the arm all the way out, and then you go up, and you got the shoulder. And that's the E sound.

F is a snake, the horned viper.

Start with the head and body, like that. And then just give him the two horns. And that's it; he's very stylized. So you just give him a body, and then two horns, and you've got it, the F.

G is a jar stand.

It's not a teepee. It's a hard *g* sound as in "guarantee."

Often desert civilizations created round-bottomed pots that could be set upright in the sand. Indoors, you needed a stand for the pot, usually made of clay. The bottom of the pot would rest in it. The triangle cutout is to allow a breeze to go through and cool your water in the jar. Now let me show you how to draw the jar stand.

Start with two vertical lines, like that. Now the curved bottom; it's a little bit of prospective, put in the top, and then your little triangular, so you get the breeze to cool your water. And that's the jar stand. Once again, two vertical lines, the nice curved bottom, do the top straight across, and your triangle, so you have cool water. And that's your letter G.

Now for H. There are actually two different Hs in the Egyptian alphabet. The reed hut H, ⌐⊔ is a simple structure made of reeds so the farmer can get out of the blistering sun for a while. It's all straight lines. Let me show you. We go up, across, down, across, and up. Again, like that, simple straight lines. And that's one of the Hs.

The other H is twisted flax ⎘ and is surprisingly difficult to draw. It represents two strands of flax twisted together. It looks like three loops, one on top of the other, but don't draw it that way. It just doesn't come out right. Let's do it the way the ancient scribes did it. Start with a curve at the top, bring another one down, and then finish the bottom. That's your twisted flax H. Start with a curve at the top, ring another one down, and finish your bottom.

The difference between the two Hs is that the reed hut is more emphatic, as in "hot" where you expel your breath forcefully. The flax H is not so emphatic and is more like the *h* in "hello." Now on to I, another semivowel.

I is a reed leaf. ⎗

The kind that flowers by the seashore. It probably was vocalized like the *i* in "it." Start with a straight line. Then give it a rounded top, like that. Then come down parallel, and then finish it off with another curved line. Let's do it one more time. Down, curve the top, straight down, and then give it another curve, and that's it.

For J we have a snake.

It is really a *dj* sound, as in "judge." First, start with the head, come down across and down, and that's it. The key is getting the angles. It's really right angles, almost. So start with a head, come down, across and down. And that's your J or *dj*.

K is easy. It's a basket with a handle.

Draw a slice of a circle, and then just do the handle at an angle coming down like that. And that's your K. Let's try it again. Just do your slice of a circle, and the handle coming down. Looks like a coffee cup, but it's a basket.

As I've said before, there's no L in the ancient Egyptian alphabet. This would be added later. We are studying Middle Egyptian, the language spoken around 2000 B.C. Later the Greeks would use a lion for their Ls in their names, like Ptolemy and Cleopatra. If your name is Lilly, you'll want to know how to draw it, so let me show you one now.

For the lion, start with a rectangle for the head. Then do the mane. Next, you can do the body, give him a tail, and then you can do hind quarters, front legs, and if you have time, you can give him a nose. It's kind of cartoony, but you can do it quickly that way. Let me show you one more time. Start with a rectangle for the face, then his mane. Next the body, tail, back legs, front legs, and you can even give him a nose. And that's your lion L.

M is another bird, an owl.

The key thing is to start with the head, which looks like this. It's an unusual bird because it's looking frontally at you. Usually the bird you can't see frontally. Now we do everything exactly the same as the A, the vulture. We start with the front, we give him his front legs, we come down with the back feathers, the back, we come up for the leg, and give him something to stand on. And, if you have little time, give him his distinctive beak, and you have an owl.

Let's try it again. Start with the rectangle up here, the unfinished rectangle, then go to the front of the body, the front leg, now come down just like the vulture for the back, come across and up for the tail feathers, and give him something to stand on and we'll give him his beak. That's your owl.

Sometimes instead of the owl, Egyptian scribes used another hieroglyph. ⟨⟩

It's a base upon which a statue stood. We will see it later in the course, and I will remind you about it, but let me show you how to draw it. It's very simple. You just come across, and front and back. And that's the statue base. So it's just across, down at an angle, and back. Either the owl or the statue base, same thing.

Now for N. ⟨⟩

It is simple up and down peaks. The word for water was "nun," so it is not surprising that the ideogram for water also represents the sound n. Now let's do it here. Up and down, up and down. There's no specific number of peaks, you can do four or five, but the important thing is, the ends have to go down. So let's do it one more time, and that's your n.

I believe that the water sign may have been the first hieroglyph. There are early water jars with the wavy-line designs. It's the first label ever. From this, we can go on to create the Narmer Palette. Remember? It's all labels. For Narmer, the servant, the vizier.

And now back to our alphabet.

Like L, there is no O in the ancient Egyptian alphabet, so we'll skip over O and go straight on to P.

P is a rectangle—not a square— and represents a woven reed mat. ⟨⟩

It's simple, just do a rectangle and you've got it. Let's do it one more time. You may be wondering how we know that this rectangle is a reed mat.

Well, on tomb walls, when the hieroglyph is drawn in detail, we often see the weaving.

Q is just a hill. △

It has a slightly different sound from the basket *k* we just learned. Think about the difference in the initial sounds of "queen" and "kid." The Q is almost a *kw* sound. Let me show you how to do it. Draw the bottom line of the hill, then the top, and then it's curved down to the bottom like that. That's Q. So again, just do the bottom, come up, and curve it down to the bottom, that's your Q.

R is a mouth. ⬭

First, just do the top, and then the bottom. And that's it. Just the top, and then the bottom, and you got R.

The letter S looks like a cane ⌐ but it isn't. It's a bolt of folded cloth. Don't try to draw it in a single line. It just doesn't come out well that way. Do it in three strokes. We know the scribes did it that way because we can see brushstrokes and even where the ink in the brush began to run out.

So, start with a vertical line, then a shorter parallel line, and then connect the two. And that will always come out nicely. Again, your vertical line, your parallel, connect the two, and you got it.

T is real easy. It's just a semicircle. It's a loaf of bread. ⌒

Start at the bottom and just do the top, and that's your letter T. One more, that's your letter T.

The U is our third and last bird in the alphabet. 🐦

He's a quail chick. Now start with the head, and then when you do the body, the thing about the quail chick is, it's mostly straight lines. So when you come down, do it like that. You can come across for here, do it here. And now you've got the feet, put in a wing, give him his beak, and you got your quail chick. Let's try him again. Start with the head, then we can come down here. Now if you want you can draw the parallel line here first, then connect. Now you give him feet; he's going to walk, put him on something, complete the face with the beak coming down and give him his wing. And that's your quail chick.

There's no V in our alphabet. So we go to W, but W is also the quail chick that we used for U.

Now there's also no X.

Y is the reed written twice.

It has the sound of a long e as in "merry." So just with our I, we give it a straight line, we give him a curve at the top, come down, and then give it the other curve. And we're going to do it twice. Straight line, curve, come down, and that's the Y sound. We'll do it one more time. Straight line, curve, curve at the top, come down, like that. Straight line, up at the top, come down, curve, and that's the Y sound.

Z is a bolt on a door.

The kinds that slides. When written, it's simply this. Do it again, just so you'll see. It's a line like that. Now, when you actually see it, you'll see that it's much more complicated, but for writing it, they just did it this way.

Now, there are two more hieroglyphs to complete our alphabet. They are for sounds for which English doesn't use a single letter.

The sound sh is really one sound, but in English, we have to use two letters to represent it—S and H. The ancient Egyptians used a pool of water for the sh sound.

Just draw a rectangle. And that's your pool of water. So just a long thin pool, and once in a while, they put two lines in it to indicate water. So that's the *sh* sound.

Last is the sound *tch*. This is represented by a tethering ring.

It was used to keep animals from running away. Put each loop over a hoof and your donkey isn't going anywhere. Let me show you how to do it. Start by drawing the two loops. This is what's going to fit over the donkey's hooves. And then the string. And that's your tethering ring. So, two loops, and then, that's it. That's *tch*.

Now let's write our names in the Egyptian alphabet. Note that we are not translating our names. We are not working at the level of meanings. We are just transcribing our names from one alphabet to another. This is transliteration.

Let's say your name is Andrea Schwartz. Well, for the *a* sound we start with the vulture.

Then *n* is the water sign.

Then we have the hand *d*.

We start with the oval, do the wrist, the thumb.

Next, we have an R. I put one sign on top of the other. If you have two short signs they can go one over the other because remember, the Egyptians liked it to look good.

⌒

So now we have mouth hieroglyph

⌒

which is easy. And then we need the arm for the *a*; we're going to stack them again.

⌐

There's our *an dre a*. And then we have an A at the end, maybe.

𓅂

That's the "Andrea."

𓅂 ⌒ ⌐ 𓅂

Now for the "Schwartz," let's go by the sound. Now Schwartz is a *sh* sound, really, so I think we can use something like the *sh*, good. Now we can have a quail chick, maybe—A. Now next we're going to have an R-T-Z. So we're going to have three short signs, let's stack them up. Sometimes the Egyptians will do that. So we have the *sh- wa*. Now, we have the R, the T, and the Z together.

⌷ 𓅱 𓅂 ⌒

That would be your "Schwartz." There you can see I have stacked three hieroglyphs, just because they would like because it looks better that way.

That's how we write Andrea Schwartz in hieroglyphs.

Well, it's been a big lesson. We've learned the three ways that a hieroglyph can be used, the hieroglyphic alphabet, how to write hieroglyphs, and how to position them. That's quite a lot. We just have to practice a bit to let it all sink in.

Let me give you a homework assignment. On lined paper, practice writing one line of each hieroglyph. Do a line of vultures, then the foot, and so forth. Don't rush it; enjoy it. Our exercise book will show you how to draw the alphabetic hieroglyphs. Just follow the step-by-step instructions for each one. I think you'll really enjoy the process. I find drawing hieroglyphs to be a therapeutic escape from a frantic day. When I'm stuck listening to a not-so-interesting lecture, I take out my felt-tipped pen, and I draw hieroglyphs. I have a hunch that I am not the only one among my colleagues who does that.

I'll see you next time.

How a Language Becomes Lost

I n the last lecture, we learned the Egyptian alphabet, practiced how to draw the hieroglyphs, and wrote our names in hieroglyphs. In this lecture, we'll review what we've learned so far. But first, we'll look at the issue of lost languages. How it is possible to lose a language that was written for thousands of years by the greatest power in the world? The answer lies in Egypt's long and unique history.

The Prehistoric Period and the Old Kingdom

- The Egyptian civilization lasted for 3,000 years. In fact, its history is so long that Egyptologists divide it into segments that are more manageable to conceive.

- The Prehistoric Period includes everything before writing. Egypt started writing down its history around 3100 B.C., with the Narmer Palette. Thus, while Egypt was in the historic period around 3100 B.C., all of Europe was still prehistoric and would be for thousands of years to come.

- The Old Kingdom follows the Prehistoric Period (3100 B.C.–2181 B.C.). The first date is an approximation, but the important point is that this is the beginning of Egypt's greatness as a nation. Although it comes at the beginning of Egypt's historic period, this is the period Egypt attained some of its greatest achievements, such as building the pyramids.

  ○ A king named Zoser built the first pyramid ever: the step pyramid of Saqqara. For more than a century, people had been buried under mud-brick *mastabas* (Arabic for "bench"),

Many people think that the pyramids were the culmination of Egyptian civilization, but in fact they came at the beginning, although it took two centuries to get them right.

so named because of their shape. Then, Zoser's architect, Imhotep, built a mastaba for the pharaoh out of stone, creating the first stone building in the world. But when it was completed, Zoser was still alive; thus, Imhotep decided to place a smaller mastaba on top of the first, and he kept going as long as Zoser was alive. The result was the step pyramid.

○ For the next two centuries, Egypt was caught up in pyramid mania, building larger and more elaborate pyramids, culminating with the Great Pyramid of Giza, the only one of the seven wonders of the ancient world still in existence.

○ The base of the Great Pyramid base covers 13.5 acres. It's made out of about 2 million blocks of stone averaging 2.5 tons each, and it's all done with remarkable precision. The inside is a maze of rooms and passageways also requiring great precision. To create something like this, writing was necessary, along with mathematics, architecture, and the ability to coordinate thousands of workers.

○ The pyramids weren't the only amazing achievements during the Old Kingdom. Some of the greatest masterpieces of art come from this early period of Egypt's history, including the fabulous pair of statues of Rahotep and Nofret, son and daughter-in-law of the pharaoh Khufu, and the great statue of Kephren with the falcon on his shoulder.

● After five centuries of amazing civilization in Egypt, there was a governmental collapse that has still not been fully explained. One theory is that the last pharaoh of the Old Kingdom, Pepi II, may have lived too long. He ruled for about 94 years. According to the theory, toward the end of his reign, he became unable to control the country; the governors of various districts, or nomes, then vied for power, and the centralized government collapsed.

● For more than 100 years, Egypt experienced a period of decentralization of power. This is called the First Intermediate Period (2181–2040 B.C.).

The Middle Kingdom

● The Middle Kingdom lasted from 2040 to 1782 B.C. Once again, there was a strong central government centered on the pharaoh. After about 400 years, there was another collapse, this time, because of an invasion by a people called the Hyksos.

● The Hyksos may have been able to conquer Egypt because they had superior weapons, as well as the horse and chariot. They ruled Egypt for more than 100 years; this is now called the Second Intermediate Period (1782–1570 B.C.). But a mighty ruler expelled the Hyksos, and once again, an Egyptian pharaoh took the throne. This began the New Kingdom.

The New Kingdom

- The New Kingdom (1570–1069 B.C.) was the period of some of the greatest and most famous pharaohs. Queen Hatshepsut took the throne and ruled as king; Akhenaten briefly changed the religion of Egypt to monotheism and almost destroyed the country; and Akhenaten's son, the boy-king Tutankhamen, ruled for 10 years.

- Toward the end of the New Kingdom, Ramses the Great took the throne. He ruled for 67 years and engaged in many construction projects, including his mortuary temple, the Ramesseum. Perhaps the most famous temple he built is Abu Simbel, carved into the rock just past Egypt's southern border.

Tutankhamen's tomb shows that Egypt in the Middle Kingdom was a country of incredible wealth.

Abu Simbel, built by Ramses the Great

Loss of the Language

- With all these temples and tombs and an incredibly stable, powerful nation, how is it possible to lose the ability to read the language? Texts are everywhere in Egypt: on temple walls, papyri, and coffins. The answer to how a language can be lost lies in Egypt's last 1,000 years of history.

- Once again, Egypt would collapse, but this time, it wouldn't recover its glory. About 100 years after Ramses the Great, the priests had become quite powerful. They had been given large tracts of land by the pharaohs for centuries; they were now as powerful as the king himself and took over control of Egypt. The 21st Dynasty was a dynasty of priest-kings, but it was not a strong government, and soon, Egypt was invaded and ruled by foreigners. This is the Third Intermediate Period (1069–525 B.C.)

- There would be Libyans, Nubians, and other rulers, and in the end, even more powerful countries took over. This is called the Late Period (525–332 B.C.). The brutal Persians invaded and destroyed temples and tombs. The priests, the literate class, were not supported, and fewer people could read hieroglyphs.

- In 332 B.C., Alexander the Great entered Egypt and expelled the Persians. The Persians were so cruel that Alexander was probably viewed as a savior rather than a conqueror of Egypt. Alexander's entry into Egypt began 300 years of Greek rule. This is called the Ptolemaic Period (305–30 B.C.) because when Alexander died, his kingdom was divided among his generals. Ptolemy got Egypt, and all subsequent Greek rulers were named Ptolemy.

Alexander the Great (356 B.C.E.–323 B.C.E.)

- The queens have only three names. They are: Berenike, Arsinoe, or Cleopatra. There were seven Ptolemaic queens named Cleopatra and the famous one was the last, Cleopatra VII.

- As far as we know, Cleopatra VII was the only one of the Ptolemies who ever learned to speak Egyptian, and that is how the loss of the language began.

- The Ptolemies lived in Alexandria and almost never left. The Ptolemies still conducted business, collected taxes, and permitted the priests to build temples, but most transactions were conducted in Greek. Smart young men in Egypt who wanted to rise in the bureaucracy learned Greek. But Egyptians still spoke Egyptian. To some extent, the final loss can be attributed to the Romans.

- Led by Octavian, the Romans defeated Cleopatra and Mark Antony at the Battle of Actium, ending three centuries of Greek domination over Egypt. The Romans ran Egypt like a business, wanting only to ship grain back home to feed Rome's growing population. The priesthood was not supported, the Egyptian religion declined, temples closed, and the ability to read hieroglyphs was gradually being lost. The final blow was Christianity.

Octavian (63 B.C.E.–14 C.E.)

- Christianity entered Egypt in the middle of the 1st century A.D., spread by Saint Mark. In the early 4th century, monasticism began in Egypt, with Saint Anthony preaching that asceticism brings one closer to God. The caves of Egypt became filled with hermits.

- There was a conscious effort to stamp out the old religion and the use of hieroglyphs. Hieroglyphs were considered a pagan script and could not be permitted in the new religion. Given that the Egyptians had been familiar with the Greek alphabet for three centuries, Greek letters were chosen to replace hieroglyphs.

- People still spoke the native Egyptian language, but they wrote the sounds using Greek letters, along with a half dozen new letters to supply sounds that the Greek alphabet didn't have. This final form of the ancient Egyptian language is called Coptic because the Egyptians who converted to Christianity were known as Copts.

- In 391, Emperor Theodosius I closed all non-Christian churches. Just three years later, in 394, we have the last known hieroglyphic inscription. It was scratched on a wall at Philae temple by a scribe in the house of records of Isis by a scribe named Esmet-Akhem.

Practicing Hieroglyphs

- Let's begin this practice session by reading a few names of famous people written in hieroglyphs.

    o 𓂝𓃀𓅱𓈖𓇌𓏏𓐰 means George Washington.

    o 𓆓𓃀𓎛 means Beethoven.

    o 𓃀𓅱𓈖𓃀 means Madonna.

- Next, we'll add some vocabulary words to the few we already know. To keep track of these new words, keep a notebook that will serve as your own personal dictionary. In the front, reserve a page for each letter of the hieroglyphic alphabet. You won't need a page for O or L, because the Egyptians didn't have them. As we learn a new hieroglyphic word, add it on the appropriate page. (Vocabulary words are also listed in Dictionary at the back of the book.)

- We already know the words from the sentence "The sun is shining in the sky," 𓏤𓏤𓏤. Add *shine*, *sun*, *in*, and *sky* to your list.

- If we make a slight change to the word for *sun*, we can have the name of the sun god, Re: 𓏤. Simply substitute the sun determinative for the god determinative. This shows us something important about the ancient Egyptian religion. The Egyptians used different words for the sun and for the sun god. This shows that the Egyptians didn't worship the fiery globe in the sky. Although the sun was associated with the god, it was not the god himself. This is a much more sophisticated position than the worship of inanimate objects.

- The owl, 𓅓, is pronounced *m* and means "in," "from," and "out of." It's a one-letter word, similar to our words *a* and *I*.

- 𓇌𓅓, a variant, means "there in." Here, a reed appears before the owl. Put this word on the reed or I page of your homemade dictionary.

- The water hieroglyph, ⌇, is pronounced *n* and means "to" but only with regard to persons. As in, "I gave it *to* Alice."

- If we want to go to a place or do something to a thing we use the mouth sign, ⌒. It is pronounced *r*, and it means "to" with regard to places, as in, "I went *to* the city." Here, the mouth *r* would be used for "to."

- Remember, because the ancient Egyptians often didn't write the vowels, we say *r*. It could have been pronounced *ir*, *ar*, *ru*, or in other ways. The same is true with the owl for "in," "from," and so on. It could have been pronounced *am*, *im*, *mu*, or in other ways.

Practicing Pronunciation
- For the next exercise, try to figure out how the following word was pronounced: ⌒. The answer is *ten*, meaning "this." We insert the

short *e* to make the word easier to say. It is the feminine form, which is easy to remember because almost all feminine words have a *t* at the end. (The word *ten* doesn't have a *t* at the end; it is an oddity.) The word "this" comes at the end of the word it modifies, like most adjectives in Egyptian. Thus, "this sky" would be [hieroglyphs]. We know that *sky* is feminine because it ends in a /t/. Thus, we would say *pet ten*.

- The masculine form of *this* is the rectangular reed mat and a water sign, pronounced "pen," [hieroglyph]. Notice how it is written. Because they are both short hieroglyphs, one is on top of the other. The two demonstrative adjectives for *this* are placed after the nouns. This is usual; almost all adjectives follow their nouns.

- A pair of adjectives that is the exception to the rule is [hieroglyphs], pronounced "key." The basket is /k/, and the double reed leaf is /y/. This word means "another." This is the masculine form, and unlike most other adjectives, it goes before the noun. The feminine form is "ket," [hieroglyph]; this pronunciation makes sense because the word is feminine and ends in /t/.

- The pronunciation of [hieroglyphs] is "bew." The foot is /b/, and the chick is /w/. The word is the noun for "place."

- The pronunciation of [hieroglyph] is *khet*, which means "thing."

Lecture 3's Homework
1. Translate the phrase "to another place."

How a Language Becomes Lost

Welcome back. Today I'd like to explain how it's possible to lose a language that has been written for thousands of years by the greatest power in the world. The answer lies in Egypt's long and unique history.

I can remember when America celebrated its bicentennial in 1976—200 years, and we went crazy. Egypt lasted for 3,000. It is difficult to imagine a civilization lasting that long. The history is so long that Egyptologists divide it into segments that are more manageable to conceive. Let's look at them.

The Prehistoric Period includes everything before writing. Prehistoric doesn't refer to a particular date in the history of the world. It refers to a civilization's time before it wrote down its history. It is a relative term. Egypt started writing down its history around 3100 B.C. with the Narmer Palette. Everything before that is prehistoric. So while Egypt is in the historic period around 3100 B.C., all of Europe was still prehistoric, and would be for thousands of years to come.

The Old Kingdom follows the Prehistoric Period. It's around 3100 B.C.– 2181 B.C. The first date is just an approximation, but the important thing is that this is the beginning of Egypt's greatness as a nation. Although this is the beginning of Egypt's historic period, this is when Egypt pulls off some of its greatest achievements. Indeed, this is when Egypt builds the pyramids. Many people think that the pyramids were the culmination of this great civilization, but no, they came right at the beginning. Still, they didn't come quickly. It took two centuries to get them right.

It started with a king named Zoser who built the first pyramid ever—the step pyramid of Saqqara. That was a development that didn't happen overnight. Previously, pharaohs and nobles had been buried under mud brick *mastabas*—Arabic for "bench," so named because of their shape, they look like benches. Then Zoser's architect, Imhotep, got the great idea to build a *mastaba* for the pharaoh out of stone, not mud bricks. So he created the first stone building in the world. But when it was completed, Zoser was alive and well, so Imhotep decided to place a smaller *mastaba* on top of the first, and then he kept going, as long as Zoser was alive, and that's how we get the step pyramid of Zoser.

For the next two centuries, as long as America has been a country, Egypt was caught up in pyramid mania, building larger and larger, more and more elaborate pyramids, culminating with the Great Pyramid of Giza, the only one of the seven wonders of the ancient world still standing. It's huge. Its base covers 13½ acres. It's made out of about 2 million blocks of stone averaging 2½ tons each, and it's all done with remarkable precision. For example, one corner to the other, the elevation is level to within a quarter of an inch. The inside is a maze of rooms and passageways also requiring great precision. To create something like this you need writing.

Zahi Hawass, the former Egyptian Minister of State for Antiquities Affairs, used to say, "Egypt didn't build the pyramids, the pyramids built Egypt." What he meant was that to build something as complicated and large as the Great Pyramid of Giza you needed mathematics, architecture, the coordination of thousands of workers. All these skills had to be developed for the construction of the pyramids of Egypt.

The pyramids weren't the only amazing achievements during the Old Kingdom. Some of the greatest masterpieces of art come from this early period of Egypt's history—the fabulous pair of statues of Rahotep and Nofret, son and daughter-in-law of the pharaoh Khufu, or the great statue of Kephren, with the falcon protecting him from behind. These are masterpieces of art by any standard, and they come at the beginning of Egypt's recorded history. So for five centuries Egypt is doing great, building pyramids, creating fantastic art, and then the music stops. There is a governmental collapse. We're not sure why.

One theory is that the last pharaoh of the Old Kingdom may have lived too long. Pepi II is the longest-reigning monarch in the history of the world. He may have ruled for as long as 94 years. He took the throne when he was just a kid, but still, that's an amazing reign. The theory is that he became too old to rule, to control the country, and the governors of various districts, or *nomes*, vied with each other for power and the centralized government collapsed.

So for more than 100 years we have a period of decentralized of power, and Egypt goes downhill. We call this period the First Intermediate Period—it's from around 2181 B.C.–2040 B.C.—because it comes between stable periods, it's intermediate. But don't be sad, Egypt will rise again and be great, and this begins the Middle Kingdom.

The Middle Kingdom lasted from 2040 B.C.–1782 B.C. Here we once again get a strong central government focused around the pharaoh. We get masterpieces of art such as the head of Sesostris. Look at it closely. It's uniquely Middle Kingdom. Only then are the kings shown as human. He's tired, weary from the responsibilities of leading a great nation. It's a wonderful portrait; it's not idealized.

So life is good for around 400 years during the Middle Kingdom. But at the end, we get another collapse, this time, because of an invasion by a people called the Hyksos. How could anyone conquer mighty Egypt? The answer may be superior weapons. The Hyksos had the horse and chariot, and the Egyptians didn't. So for more than 100 years the Hyksos rule Egypt, and this is the Second Intermediate Period—about 1782 B.C.–1570 B.C.

But Egypt rises again. A mighty ruler expels the Hyksos, and once again we have an Egyptian pharaoh on the throne. This begins the New Kingdom. The New Kingdom runs from about 1570 B.C.–1069 B.C. This is when we get some of our greatest, most famous pharaohs. This is when Queen Hatshepsut took the throne and ruled as king. She didn't hide the fact that she was a woman; she took the title king and ruled as a pharaoh, not a queen.

This is also the period when Akhenaten briefly changed the religion of Egypt to monotheism and almost destroyed the country. During the New Kingdom, we get Akhenaten's son, the boy-king, Tutankhamen, and all his treasures. He was only a minor king, ruling for only 10 years, but think of all the gold in his tomb. Later in this course, we will translate some of the inscriptions on Tutankhamen's treasures. This was a country with incredible wealth.

Towards the end of the New Kingdom, we get pharaoh Ramses the Great. He rules for 67 years and has plenty of time to build. His mortuary temple, called the Ramesseum, is beautiful, and he builds loads of temples up and down the Nile. Perhaps his most famous is Abu Simbel, carved into the rock just past Egypt's southern border. It will play a crucial role in the decipherment of hieroglyphs, as you'll learn in a later lecture.

But at this point, we have to ask the question. With all these temples and tombs, with this incredibly stable, powerful nation, how is it possible to lose the ability to read the Egyptian language? Texts are all over the place, on temple walls, on papyri, on coffins. How do you lose a language? The answer lies in Egypt's last 1,000 years of history.

Once again, Egypt would collapse, but this time, it wouldn't recover its glory. A hundred years after Ramses the Great, the priests were becoming very powerful. They had been given large tracts of land by the pharaohs for centuries, and now they were as powerful as the king himself and took control of Egypt. The 21st Dynasty was a dynasty of priest-kings, but this was not a strong government, and soon Egypt was invaded and ruled by a series of foreign powers. This we call the Third Intermediate Period—it's about 1069 B.C.–525 B.C.

There would be Libyans, Nubians, and others, and in the end, even more powerful countries took over. This the Late Period; this is from 525 B.C.–332 B.C. Egypt is ruled by superpowers. The brutal Persians invade and destroy temples and tombs. The priests, the literate class, are not supported, and fewer and fewer people can read hieroglyphs. Later it will get even worse for the Egyptian language.

In 332 B.C., Alexander the Great enters Egypt and expels the Persians. The Persians were so cruel that Alexander is probably viewed as a savior rather than a conqueror of Egypt. Alexander's entry into Egypt begins three hundred years of Greek rule. We call this period the Ptolemaic Period, from about 305–30 B.C. because when Alexander dies, his kingdom is divided among his generals and General Ptolemy gets Egypt.

All the subsequent Greek rulers will be named Ptolemy. The queens have only three different names. They are either Berenike—we get our Bernice from that—Arsinoe, or Cleopatra. There were seven Ptolemaic queens named Cleopatra, and the famous one was the last, Cleopatra VII. As far as we know, she is the only one of the Ptolemies who ever learned to speak Egyptian, and this is the start of how you lose a language.

The Ptolemies lived in Alexandria and pretty much never left it. Alexandria was called The City, and all the rest was Egypt. They were still conducting business, collecting taxes, even permitting the priests to build temples, but most transactions were conducted in Greek. If you were a smart young Egyptian man in ancient Egypt during this period and wanted to rise in the bureaucracy, then you learned Greek. But still, Egyptians were speaking Egyptian, too. So what happened? To some extent, the answer is the Romans.

Led by Octavian, the Romans defeat Cleopatra and Mark Antony at the battle of Actium, ending three centuries of Greek domination over Egypt. The Romans run Egypt like a business, wanting only to ship the grain back to feed Rome's growing population. The priesthood is not supported, the Egyptian religion declines, temples close, and the ability to read hieroglyphs is being lost. The final blow is Christianity.

Christianity enters Egypt in the middle of the 1st century. It's being spread by Saint Mark, and it really took hold. In the early 4th century, monasticism began in Egypt, with Saint Anthony preaching that asceticism brings one closer to God. Now the caves of Egypt are filled with hermits. Even today Egypt is home to many monasteries. St. Catherine's on the Sinai Peninsula is the longest continuously inhabited building on the planet.

With the introduction of Christianity, there is a conscious effort to stamp out the old religion, and the use of hieroglyphs. Hieroglyphs are a pagan script and must not be permitted in the new religion. But what should replace them? Well, the Egyptians had been familiar with the Greek alphabet for three centuries, why not use Greek letters?

Now remember, people are still speaking the native Egyptian language, they are just going to write the sounds of their language using Greek letters and a half dozen other new ones to supply sounds that the Greek alphabet didn't have. This is the last form of the ancient Egyptian language, and it's called Coptic because the Egyptians who converted to Christianity were called Copts.

"Copt" comes from the Greek *Aygptios*, for "Egyptian," which became *Gupt*, which became *Copt*. So the Copts are all Egyptians; it's redundant to say the Egyptian Copts.

In 391 A.D. Emperor Theodosius I closes all non-Christian churches and temples. Just three years later, in 394, we have the last known hieroglyphic inscription. It's scratched on a wall at Philae temple by a scribe in the house of records of Isis. His name was Esmet-Akhem, and he probably knew that he was the end of a 3,000-year-old tradition of scribes who read and wrote hieroglyphs.

So with the new Christian religion, we have the death of hieroglyphs. For 1,400 years no one would be able to read them. Recovering a language was a long, slow process that began by figuring out sounds that the hieroglyphs meant. The meaning of those sounds would come later.

Right now, we are learning the sounds associated with the hieroglyphs. Let me give you a surprise quiz. I've written a few names of famous people in hieroglyphs. Let's see if you've learned your alphabet and can read them.

Sound it out. Remember, don't go by the spelling of the name. We are transliterating. All we care about is the sound.

The first name of this person is the first three hieroglyphs. It is a bit difficult because we're missing vowels, but still, we can sound it out. The first hieroglyph is the *dj* sound. Then the mouth *r* and then the second *dj* sound. *Dj-r-dj* "George." I left out the O because Middle Egyptian doesn't have one. I could have put in an arm hieroglyph for the E. I thought it sounded closer without it, so I left it out also. It's a matter of taste. Notice how I grouped the mouth under the serpent. That's how the Egyptians would have done it because it looks nice.

Our second name is easier. We start with the quail chick, which is either *u* or *w*. Then the vulture *a*. This is followed by our pool *sh* and a reed *i*. Now we have the water sign *n* on top of the jar-stand *g* because they are both short hieroglyphs, one's on top of the other. Next the bread *t* and the quail chick *u* followed by another water sign *n*. "Washington." George Washington. I used a quail chick *u* for the *o* sound at the end of Washington because I think it approximates the sound pretty well.

Let's try another.

This one isn't too difficult if you know your alphabet. It's just one name. The foot is the *b* sound. The vulture is an *a*, the double reed, a *y*. So far we have "Bay" The loaf is a *t*. The viper is an *f*, the arm an *eh* sound, and last the water sign is an *n*. So let's say it aloud and see if we can hear something familiar. *Baytehfn*. Yep, it's Beethoven. I used the viper *f* because we don't have a *v*. It was a close as we could get to a *v*.

How about this one?

I bet you'll get quickly. Again, just one name this time. What do you think? Yes, Madonna. The owl is the *m*, the vulture the *a*, the hand the *d*. The name is spelled with two *n*'s, but we only hear one, so we only need one water sign. Finally, we end with an *a* vulture for the final a.

OK, not bad. Now let's add some vocabulary words to the few we already know. Each day we'll learn another ten or so and before you know it, you'll be scribes. To keep track of the new vocabulary words, I suggest you keep a notebook just for your vocabulary words. This will be your own personal dictionary. Our exercise book has a dictionary, but it is very good practice to make you own. It really helps learning the words.

Reserve a page for each letter of the hieroglyphic alphabet. You won't need a page for O or L because the Egyptians didn't have them. As we add new hieroglyphic words, add it on the appropriate page.

We already have a word that begins with owl, our word for "in." So that goes on the owl or M page. Let's start with our owl word.

The owl is pronounced *m,* and we usually say *em* when it is by itself, rather than *mmm.* As we have seen, it means "in," but it has several other meanings. It can also mean "from" and "out of" So it's an important word. It's a one-letter word, written with just the owl, but when it was pronounced as the word for "in," in ancient Egypt it may have been "am," "um," "im" or something else. We just don't know for sure because they didn't like the vowels.

Sometimes ancient Egyptian scribes substituted another hieroglyph for the owl. It is a statue base, on which a sculpture could rest.

⊂⃞

If you see it, just think owl, it's an M.

We have the other words from our mystery sentence, "The sun is shining in the sky."

So we can add to our vocabulary list, "shine," "sun," and "sky."

If we make a slight change to the word for "sun," we can have the name of the sun-god, Re.

Just replace the sun determinative with the god determinative and that's Re, the sun-god. I bet you've heard it pronounced "Ra." That's fine too. Remember, we aren't sure about the vowels.

The god determinative is a seated man wearing a long garment, so his knees are covered by it. The long, curved beard tells us he's a god.

Let me show you how to draw him because he's important. We will see this hieroglyph a lot.

Start with the head, come down to the back. Then across. And now we need a curve up and down for the knees. Then up to the head again. Add his headdress, and finally the beard. Now you've got a god.

The fact that the Egyptians used different words for the sun and for the sun-god, Re, shows us something important about the ancient Egyptian religion. They didn't worship the fiery globe in the sky. The sun was associated with a god, but was not the god itself. This is a much more sophisticated position than just worshipping inanimate objects.

Now let's add some more simple words.

If you put a reed leaf in front of the owl, it has a slightly different meaning from "in."

This variant means "herein." Because we have a reed before the owl. Put this word on the I page of your homemade dictionary.

The water hieroglyph is pronounced *n* and means "to" but only with regard to persons. As in, "I gave it *to* Alice."

If we want to go to a place or do something to a thing we use the mouth sign.

⌒

It's pronounced *r* for R, and it means "to" with regards to places, as in, "I went to the city. Remember, because the ancient Egyptians didn't write the vowels, we say *r*. It could have been *ir*, or *ar ru*, etc. Same with our owl for "in," "from," etc. It could have been *am, im, mu,* etc.

Now. I'll give you your next word vocabulary, and you tell me how it was pronounced.

⌒
〰

That's right, ten, *te n*. We put in the short *e* just to make it easier to say. That's the word for "this." It is the feminine form. Easy to remember because almost all feminine words have a *t* at the end. I know, I know, *ten* doesn't have a *t* at the end, it has it at the beginning. It's just an oddity. The word "this" comes after of the word it modifies, like most adjectives in ancient Egyptian. So "this sky" would look like this,

⌂⌒
〰

We know that "sky" is feminine because it ends in a *t*. The sky determinative doesn't have a phonetic value here. So we would say *pet ten*.

Now the masculine form of "this" is the rectangular reed mat and a water sign pronounced *pen*.

▯
〰

Notice how it is written. Because they are both short hieroglyphs, one is on top of the other, just like *ten*. So the two demonstrative adjectives for "this" go after the nouns. This is usual; almost all adjectives follow their nouns.

Let's look at a pair of adjectives that is the exception to the rule.

Now, pronounce it for me. Yep, *key*. The basket is the *k*, and the double reed leaf the *y*. We put in the short *e* to get *key*. That's how it is pronounced. It means "another." This is the masculine form, and unlike most other adjectives, it goes before the noun.

The feminine form is *ket*.

Which makes sense. It's feminine, and it ends in a *t*.

So, how would you write "another sky?"

First, you think about our word for "sky."

It's feminine; it ends in *t*, so we need the feminine form of "another" which is *ket*.

Now we have to remember that "another" goes before the noun. So "another sky" would be *ket pet*.

Let's just add two more words to our vocabulary.

How would you pronounce this? Yes, *bew*. The foot is the *b* and the chick the *u* or *w*. The word means "place." Not the verb, "to place" but the noun, meaning a location.

One last word for today. I know this is a lot.

How is it pronounced? *khet*. That's right. And it means "thing."

Now for next time, practice writing these words as you enter them in your dictionary. Creating your own dictionary will improve your handwriting and also help you to learn the words. When you enter the words in your dictionary, also indicate how they sounded. Transliteration is important because it helps us remember the vocabulary words. If we didn't attempt to reconstruct how the words sounded, all we would have is visual memory, how the words look. The transliteration adds a second dimension to how we can remember our words.

There are several ways we can indicate pronunciation of our words. Linguists use the International Phonetic Alphabet, which is basically our Latin letters with a few extra symbols. For our course, we won't use the that. We can approximate the sounds with our alphabet, but even here we have choices.

For example, let's look at our word for "sky."

We know the vowels were not written, and at the end of this word is a determinative that was not pronounced, so we are left with *pt*. One option is to leave it just like that. So, in our dictionary, after the written word we could put in parentheses (*pt*) to indicate what we know about how it. But I think there is a better option. As I mentioned before, there is a convention when vocalizing the words to insert a short *e* between consonants when we don't know the missing vowels. This makes it easier to say it. So, *pt* becomes *pet*, easier to say and I think, easier to remember. So let's go with that option. So in our dictionaries, on the P page, our entry for "sky" would look something like this,

▱ (*pet*) sky

We have "pet," the sound and then the definition. In the cases where we have an idea from the Coptic of what the missing vowels were, we'll use that. We will always go with the best bet.

One last thing. With a word like *khet,* "thing,"

⊜
◠

because we transliterate it with a *k*, we can put it on the K page of our dictionary.

I have one last minor additional homework assignment for you. Translate the phrase "to another place."

I'll see you next time.

Napoleon in Egypt

I n the last lecture, we talked about how the ability to read hieroglyphs was
lost. In this lecture, we'll see how it was rediscovered during Napoleon's
invasion of Egypt. In 1798, France's governing body, the Directory,
suggested Napoleon attack England. He demurred, instead invading Egypt
for two reasons: If France could control Egypt, it would cripple England's
trade route with India; and Napoleon wanted to follow in the footsteps of his
hero, Alexander the Great. This lecture focuses on that invasion, and then
on some new vocabulary words.

Napoleon in 1798

- In 1798, a 28-year-old General Bonaparte returned to Paris,
  victorious from his Italian campaign. The Directory didn't want an
  unemployed hero hanging around, so they suggested he invade
  England, France's enemy. Bonaparte suggested an alternative: an
  invasion of Egypt.

- When he prepared for his Egyptian campaign, Napoleon recruited
  France's top scientists, known as savants. They would describe
  every aspect of Egypt, from botany to zoology. He brought more
  than 150 of the best minds of the time, including the mathematician
  Joseph Fourier, the geologist Déodat de Dolomieu, and the
  naturalist Étienne Geoffroy Saint-Hilaire.

- This was an all-star cast. They also brought their students.
  Jean-Baptiste Jollois and Édouard Devilliers were only 21 and
  18, respectively, when they went along. They teamed up for the
  expedition and went up and down the Nile together, recording
  its monuments.

The Battle of the Pyramids

- The Battle of the Pyramids was the army's first test in Egypt. They were fighting the Mamelukes. Ostensibly, Egypt was controlled by Constantinople, but the Ottoman Empire was crumbling and the Mamelukes had a free hand in running Egypt.

- *Mameluke* is Arabic for "bought man." Centuries earlier, the sultan of Egypt bought hundreds of young boys from the Circassian mountains to be trained as his military elite. They were educated, well fed, and clothed. When they became adults, they revolted, killed the sultan, and took control of Egypt. They were fierce warriors.

- As the Mamelukes massed to fight the French, Bonaparte's men formed squares, with cavalry on the inside and rifles along the edges. Artillery was positioned at the corners. The men were instructed not to fire until the Mamelukes were upon them.

- As the Mamelukes charged, the French held fire till the horsemen were practically on top of them, then they blew them away. The battle was over in less than two hours. The Mamelukes were no match for a disciplined European army. They charged Bonaparte's squares several times, but to no avail. Bonaparte was now in control of Egypt, but not for long.

The Battle of the Nile

- The Battle of the Nile doomed the Egyptian campaign. The French vice admiral François-Paul Brueys anchored the French fighting ships at Aboukir Bay, very close to shore. He was convinced no one could sail between his ships and the shore. All his guns faced seaward so that if the English found the fleet, all the firepower would be aimed at them.

- On August 1, 1798, England's rear admiral, Horatio Nelson, found the anchored fleet and went straight into battle. He sailed between the anchored French fleet and the shore, which Brueys thought was impossible. With all their cannons fixed seaward, the French were vulnerable. The English blasted away, sinking almost the entire fleet.

- The battle was a total victory for Nelson. With their fighting ships gone, the French were stranded with no way of getting supplies or reinforcements.

After the Battle

- Undaunted, Bonaparte set up the Institut d'Égypte, a society devoted to the study of Egypt. But he was also fighting a losing war. Bonaparte marched his men to Acre, which is in Israel today, but was then in Sidon, part of the Ottoman Empire. He needed to head off an invasion of Turkish soldiers. Djezzar Pasha, a ruthless man with a reputation for cruelty, controlled the fort at Acre.

- Acre was on the water and the British were supplying Djezzar from the sea. Bonaparte didn't have the cannons needed to bombard the fort, so he ordered his men to storm the fort using tall ladders. Assault after assault failed with the loss of many men. Acre was Bonaparte's his first loss on land, and things were going to get worse.

- Napoleon's army was decimated by the plague, had no supplies, and was cut off from France. One year after he landed, Bonaparte deserted his men and sailed for France.

Discoveries after Desertion

- While the army Bonaparte left behind was fighting a losing war, they shored up an old fort at Rosetta, where they discovered a large inscribed stone built into the wall near the foundation. It seemed to have the same message in three different scripts: one hieroglyphic, one unknown, and the third Greek. Since the savants could translate the Greek, they hoped it would be the key to deciphering hieroglyphs.

- The Rosetta Stone was not the only contribution the Egyptian campaign made to decipherment. When the savants finally returned to France, they published the *Description de l'Égypte*, one of the largest publications in the history of the world. It included numerous volumes of engravings that recorded the antiquities of Egypt.

- Some of the savants went beyond mere recording and made important archaeological discoveries. The young friends, Jollois and Devilliers, copied the Dendera Zodiac and caused a sensation in Paris when they returned. When scholars saw how the constellations were depicted on the zodiac, they were astonished. It suggested that the Egyptian civilization and the world itself were much older than was previously believed.

- They also discovered the tomb of Amenhotep III in the Valley of the Kings. They, of course, couldn't decipher the hieroglyphs, so they didn't know whose tomb they had found, but it was still a great adventure.

Ushabtis

- As they explored the tomb by the light of their candles, they came upon a group of small statues. They brought them out of the tomb, did their drawings, and later published them in the *Description de l'Égypte*. Today, Egyptologists call these statues *ushabtis.*

- Ushabti figures were intended as servants for the next life. On tomb walls of the nobles, we often see painted scenes of the next world. The deceased are at banquets, hunting in the marshes, and sometimes working in the fields, but always in their finest linens. The statues these two young men discovered were intended to do this work.

Ushabtis were made of various materials, depending on what a person could afford. The least expensive were terra cotta.

- The word *ushabti* is derived from the ancient Egyptian word for "answer": *usheb*, or 𓊩𓏤𓏲 × 𓀁.

- The man has his hand to the mouth because the word has something to do with speaking. It's unclear why what looks like an *x* is there. The little statues were called *ushabtis* because when your name was called in the next world to work on the irrigation ditches, the little statue would come to life and answer for you: "Here I am!"

- Napoleon's savants made all kinds of of contributions to the new science of Egyptology. In addition to recording scenes, the savants published drawings of hieroglyphs, books of the dead, and inscriptions on tombs. But the most important discovery was the Rosetta Stone, the topic of the next lecture.

Man and Woman

- Let's add some more vocabulary words and translate some real sentences. The hieroglyphs for the words "man" and "woman" are very important.

- The word for "man" is *z*: 𓀀

- Often the word is just written with an ideogram stroke: 𓀀𓏤. Sometimes the stroke is omitted, leaving just the man hieroglyph.

- The word for "woman" can also be written several ways. One is phonetically, with the woman determinative, pronounced *zet*. Here's the woman hieroglyph: 𓏏 𓁐

- If you want to say "people," you write the man and woman hieroglyph together: 𓀀𓁐. This would have been pronounced something like *retchu* when spoken. Note the three strokes. That's how you indicate a plural.

Verbs

- Now let's learn some verbs so that our man and woman can do things. This will let us translate real sentences. Below are some hieroglyphs, their pronunciation, and their meaning.

- ⟨glyph⟩ is pronounced *iew* or *yew*. It means "to be." The good news is it doesn't have to be conjugated.

- ⟨glyph⟩ is prounounced *djed*. It means "to speak" or "say."

- ⟨glyph⟩ is pronounced *ger*. It means "to be silent."

- ⟨glyph⟩ is pronounced *rekh*. The determinative at the end is a papyrus roll. It has been rolled, tied with a string, and sealed with clay to ensure confidentiality. This is the verb "to know." The idea is that knowledge can be written.

- ⟨glyph⟩ is pronounced *khem*. The position of the arms practically says, "I don't know," which is this verb's meaning.

Nouns and a Conjunction

- Now for a couple of nouns. First up is a proper noun, a name: ⟨glyph⟩. This is the name of a god, Ptah. He's a god of creation who is usually shown wearing a distinctive cap. His feet are together, like a mummy's.

- ⟨glyph⟩ is pronounced *ren*; it means "name."

- Now for a conjunction. The ancient Egyptians didn't have a direct parallel for our word *and*, but they had this word: ⟨glyph⟩. It is pronounced something like *heneh*. It means "together with."

- So if we wanted to say "the man together with the woman" we would have this: ⟨glyph⟩. It would have been pronounced something like *z heneh zet.*

Translating Sentences

- We'll do some translation next. Here's our first sentence: 🕊️📿🔆.

- What's our first word? The verb "say" or "speak." The next is "man," followed by the verb "to be silent." The last word is "woman." This sentence is a sexist maxim: "When man speaks, woman is silent."

- In spite of this proverb, women in ancient Egypt had more power and rights than anywhere else in the world. They even had women who ruled as kings (not queens), such as Hatshepsut.

- Here's our next sentence: 🕊️📿🔆. The verb is first, and it's "is." Then comes "Ptah." Then "in." Next is "place," *bew*, and then "this," *pen*. In English, "this" comes first, but not in hieroglyphs. Our translation would be, "Ptah is in this place." It would have been pronounced something like: *Yew Ptah em bew pen.*

Dictionary Entries

- Now that we are starting to accumulate some real vocabulary words, let's review how we will set up our dictionary. Let's begin by seeing how we would enter the two forms, masculine and feminine, for "another" in our dictionaries.

- First we go to our page we have set aside for words that begin with K. The top of the page will look like this: ⌒—K. Then we enter our word, ⌒. Then, in parentheses, we put our transliteration to remind us how it sounded, making ⌒ (*ket*). Then we can note it is feminine and add the meaning: ⌐ (*ket*) f. another

- The process is the same for the masculine form:
  ⌒𝄫 (*key*) m.   another

- For "Ptah" we would go to our page set aside for words beginning with *p* and write this: ⌐𝄇 (*Ptah*) Ptah

Lecture 3's Homework Answer

The previous lecture asked you to translate "to another place." First we need the word for *place*. That would be *bew:* 𓃀𓏤. *Bew* is masculine, so we need *key*, the masculine form of *another:* 𓂋𓏭𓏭. This goes in front of the noun: 𓂋𓏭𓏭𓃀𓏤.

The last word to translate is *to*. We have two *to*'s, one for people (𓈖) and one for things and places (𓂋). A place is a thing, so we know to use 𓂋, the mouth *r*. So our phrase "to another place" is 𓂋𓏭𓏭𓃀𓏤, or *r key bew*.

Note that the mouth *r* is right above the basket *k*. This is for aesthetics. Normally the Egyptians didn't merge words this way, but with a single-sign word, it was sometimes acceptable.

Lecture 4's Homework

Translate these sentences from English into ancient Egyptian.

1. The woman does not know this man.

2. Re and Ptah are together in this place.

3. The man does not know another thing.

4. The woman knows this name.

Napoleon in Egypt

Welcome back. Last time we talked about how the ability to read hieroglyphs was lost. Today, we'll see how it was rediscovered during Napoleon's invasion of Egypt.

The year is 1798, and a 28-year-old General Bonaparte has just returned to Paris, victorious from the Italian Campaign. He's undefeated and a hero, and the Directory—the governing body of France—doesn't want an unemployed hero hanging around. So they suggest that he invade England—France's enemy. Bonaparte looks at France's fleet and wants no part of this venture, but he suggests an alternative—invade Egypt. There were two reasons for this—one political, one psychological.

First, the political. England's economy depended to a great extent on trade with India. Egypt was England's land route to the Red Sea, which provides quicker access to India. If France could control Egypt, then England's vital trade would be cut—thus weakening the enemy's economy. This all makes political sense.

Bonaparte's other reason for invading Egypt was psychological. He wanted to follow in the footsteps of his hero, Alexander the Great. Bonaparte even said that the careers of all great men begin in the East. So it's off to Egypt.

Many people dislike Napoleon, but almost everyone agrees he was a genius. He was well-educated and fearless, and he wrote the Code Napoléon that still serves as the basis for French law. He was a member of the French Academy of Science in mathematics and was a supporter of the arts and sciences. And he even wrote fiction.

When he prepared for the Egyptian Campaign, Napoleon recruited France's top savants—scientists who would describe every aspect of Egypt from botany to zoology. He brought more than 150 savants—the best minds of the time.

There was Joseph Fourier, the famous mathematician behind the Fourier transformation—a function used today in digital electronics and signal processing.

Dolomieu, the geologist, after whom the Dolomite Mountains in Italy are named.

Étienne Geoffroy Saint-Hilaire, the brilliant young naturalist who would later bring the first giraffe to France.

There was Pierre-Joseph Redouté—the great naturalist painter.

This was an all-star cast, and they also brought their students. Jean-Baptiste Jollois and Édouard Devilliers were only 21 and 18 years old, respectively, when they went along. They teamed up for the expedition and went up and down the Nile together recording the monuments. Devilliers took his schoolbooks with him. He was examined in Cairo by his professor and was certified as an engineer.

When Bonaparte landed in Egypt, he introduced the Arabic printing press to Egypt. Believe it or not, Egypt had never printed a book in Arabic. Bonaparte looted his Arabic typeface from the Vatican. He wanted to use his presses for propaganda to convince the Egyptian population he was there to liberate them from the Mamelukes, a fierce warrior class ruling the country. The first Arabic document ever printed in Egypt proclaimed Bonaparte's noble intentions. It didn't work. Nobody believed him.

Still, this was an amazing intellectual adventure, but there was also a war to be fought.

The Battle of the Pyramids was the army's first test in Egypt. They were fighting the Mamelukes. Ostensibly, Egypt was controlled by The Sublime

Port, Constantinople. But the Ottoman Empire was crumbling, and the Mamelukes had a free hand in running Egypt.

Mameluke is Arabic for "bought man." Centuries earlier, the Sultan of Egypt bought hundreds of young boys from the Circassian Mountains to be trained as his military elite. They were educated, well fed and clothed. And when they became adults, they revolted and killed the sultan. They took control of Egypt. They lived in opulent palaces, dressed in colorful silks, but were fierce warriors.

The Mamelukes were horsemen, and each went into battle with a lance, a sword, and two pistols. Each horseman was followed by two servants on foot. After the pistols had been fired, they threw them over their shoulders to the servants, who would then reload as their masters continued fighting with swords and lances. Once reloaded, the Mamelukes would ride back to their servants and retrieve the pistols. The Mamelukes had never been defeated in battle.

Bonaparte's troops were disciplined, and they, too, were undefeated. The Mamelukes were fierce horsemen, but they fought as individuals. As the Mamelukes charged, the French held their fire until the horsemen were practically on top of them, then they blew them away. The battle was over in less than two hours. The Mamelukes were no match for a disciplined European army. Bonaparte was now in control of Egypt, but not for long.

The Battle of the Nile will doom the Egyptian campaign. Vice Admiral François-Paul Brueys has anchored the ships of the line, the fighting ships at Aboukir Bay, very close to shore. So close that he's convinced no one could sail between his ships and the shore. So he's positioned all his guns seaward so that if the English find the fleet, all the firepower will be aimed at them.

On August 1, 1798, England's Rear Admiral Horatio Nelson finds the anchored fleet and goes straight into battle. He does something totally unexpected. He sails between the anchored French fleet and the shore, which Brueys thought was impossible. With all their cannon fixed seaward, the French are sitting ducks, and the English blast away—sinking almost the entire fleet.

When the French flagship, *L'Orient*, catches fire and explodes—it housed the French supply of gunpowder—it's the loudest manmade noise ever heard on earth. It's so shocking, fighting stopped for 10 minutes.

In the end, the battle is a complete victory for Nelson. With their fighting ships gone, the French are stranded with no way of getting supplies or reinforcements. You see, when you send your supply ships across the ocean, they need fighting ships, ships of the line, to protect them. Otherwise, they can just be seized.

Nelson correctly assessed the situation by saying basically, "Bonaparte is in a jam, and he won't get out of it." And Nelson just sailed away. He wasn't going to fight any land battle.

When Bonaparte heard his fleet had been sunk in Alexandria, he only mentioned that his sailors were covered in glory; he never mentioned the defeat. Undaunted, Bonaparte set up the Institut d'Egypte—a society devoted to the study of Egypt. It was the birth of Egyptology. The savants, architects, and engineers would record Egyptian temples, collect antiquities, and study flora and fauna. In a way, it was the world's first ethnographic study by a scientific team. The savants occupied palaces that were vacated by the fleeing Mamelukes and settled in for their scholarly work.

But a losing war was also being fought. Bonaparte was forced to march his men to Acre, which is in Israel today, but was then in Sidon—part of the Ottoman Empire. He needed to head off an invasion of Turkish soldiers. The fort at Acre was controlled by Djezzar Pasha, a ruthless man with a reputation for cruelty. *Djezzar* means "butcher" in Arabic.

Normally, Bonaparte could surround the fort and starve those inside into submission, but Acre was on the water, and the British were supplying Djezzar from the sea. Bonaparte didn't have the needed cannons to bombard the fort, so he ordered his men to storm the fort using tall ladders. Assault after assault failed, and the loss of many men ensued. Acre was

Bonaparte's first loss on land, and things were going to get worse. The army began to suffer great losses on another front. They were decimated by the plague. They had no supplies and were cut off from France. One year after he landed, Bonaparte deserted him men and sailed for France.

Bonaparte didn't even let his army know he was leaving till he was on board his ship heading for France. He left a letter for General Jean-Baptiste Kléber—his next in command—telling him to continue the victories, collect the taxes, and send the revenue back to Paris. Kléber was outraged. Like everyone else, he knew the Egyptian campaign was a lost cause. He immediately began to discuss with the British terms for an honorable withdrawal of French troops from Egypt. But it was not to be. Kléber was assassinated by a religious fanatic, and the discussions ended.

Kléber was respected by everyone; his successor, Abdullah Menou, was not. Menou had converted to Islam so he could marry a bathkeeper's daughter and was viewed as a fool by the army he commanded. The war dragged on for another two years.

While the army Bonaparte left behind was fighting a losing war, they shored up an old fort at Rosetta, where they discovered a large inscribed stone built into the wall near the foundation. It seemed to have the same message in three different scripts—one hieroglyphic, one unknown, and the third, Greek. Since the savants could translate the Greek, they hoped it would be the key to deciphering hieroglyphs.

In the next lecture, we'll look closely at the Rosetta Stone, but let me emphasize here that the Rosetta Stone was not the only contribution the Egyptian campaign made to the decipherment. When the savants finally returned to France, they published the *Description de l'Égypte*, one of the largest and most sumptuous publications in the history of the world. Five massive volumes of engravings recorded the antiquities of Egypt. They produced the first detailed map of the Valley of the Kings. For the first time, the ancient temples and tombs were accurately drawn by Napoleon's architects and engineers.

Sometimes, their drawings are the only record we have of the monuments. One remarkable case is the city that the Roman Emperor Hadrian built in Egypt. While Hadrian was visiting Egypt, his young lover, Antinous, drowned in the Nile. Hadrian built an entire city, Antinopolis, as a memorial. It was fabulous, complete with wide streets, temples, triumphal arches— everything you'd expect in a Roman city. The savants realized the city's importance and recorded it in detail. It's a good thing they did. In the 1830s, the entire city was dismantled, and the blocks ground into cement to build a sugar refinery. Today, all we have are the savants' drawings.

There were times when they didn't even know the importance of what they were recording. This is a drawing of great historical event, though the savants didn't know it when they copied it. It's from the now ruined temple of Armant in Upper Egypt. This temple was built by Cleopatra VII to commemorate the birth of Caesarion, her son by Julius Caesar.

We are looking at Cleopatra giving birth to Caesarion. She's kneeling— women in Egypt gave birth sitting down on a birthing stool. The wall is damaged, and the artist has indicated that damage. But you can still see the newborn Caesarion's feet emerging. It is remarkable that we have a historical record of this event, and it's all thanks to Napoleon Bonaparte.

Some of the savants went beyond mere recording and made important archaeological discoveries. The young friends—Jollois, Devilliers—copied the Dendera Zodiac and caused a sensation in Paris when they returned. When scholars saw how the constellations were depicted on the zodiac, they were astonished. It suggested that the Egyptian civilization and the world were much older than was previously believed.

Remember, hieroglyphs hadn't been deciphered yet, so no one knew how far back in time Egypt stretched. Many still believed the civilization started in Greece. Even worse, Bishop Ussher, using the begats in the Bible, calculated that the world was created 4,004 years ago. And many still believed him. The Dendera Zodiac changed all that. So the work of Jollois and Devilliers was very important to how scholars viewed the age of the world. They guys were young, but they accomplished fantastic things.

They also discovered the tomb of Amenhotep III in the Valley of the Kings. They, of course, couldn't decipher the hieroglyphs, so they didn't know whose tomb they'd found. But, it was still a great adventure. As they explored the tomb by the light of their candles, they came upon a group of small statues. They brought them out of the tomb, did their drawings, and later published them in the *Description de l'Égypte.* Today, Egyptologists call these statues ushabtis.

Ushabti figures were intended as servants for the next life. The Egyptians believed that the next life would be a continuation of this life, only air-conditioned. Often, tomb walls of the nobles show painted scenes of the next world. The deceased are at banquets, hunting in the marshes, and sometimes working in the fields, but they're always in their finest linens. The statues these two young men discovered were intended to do this work.

As we discussed at the very beginning of this course, the Egyptians were used to working together on public works projects. In the Old Kingdom, there were pyramids to be built. But throughout Egypt's long history, there were always irrigation ditches to be dug. So once a year there was the corvée, a roll call for every able-bodied man to come and work for the benefit of the country. The Egyptians believed there would probably be roll call in the next world too, so to avoid doing the work themselves, they took magical servants with them.

The word "ushabti" is derived from the ancient Egyptian word for "answer," *usheb.*

The man has his hand to his mouth in the word because the word has something to do with speaking. I have no idea what looks like an x is doing there.

The little statues were called ushabtis because when your name was called in the next world to work on the irrigation ditches, the little statue would come to life and answer for you, "Here I am!"

These statues were made of various materials, depending on what you could afford. The least expensive were terra cotta, clay, sometimes only two inches long—mass-produced from molds. Another material commonly used was faience, a kind of ceramic, fired in a kiln. These also varied in quality. Here's a small ushabti for a poor man.

The finer examples showed the deceased shaped like a wrapped mummy holding farm implements. Here's an ushabti of a nobleman. See, his legs are wrapped like a mummy. Peeking out of the wrappings of his hands, which hold farm implements. If we turn him over, you can see his little seed pack on his back. And all along the front is a magical spell to bring him to life in the next world. Usually, it's something simple like: "Oh ushabti, if I am called upon to do work in the next world, answer, 'Here I am.' Plough the fields, fill the canals with water, and carry the sand of the East to the West."

Jollois and Devillier had found some of the earliest royal ushabtis. Napoleon's savants were making all kinds of contributions to the new science of Egyptology.

In addition to recording scenes, the savants published drawings of hieroglyphs, books of the dead, and inscriptions on tombs. Every time the savants saw a new hieroglyph, they added it to a table they were compiling to help in the decipherment.

They did the same with cartouches. These would later provide material with which the decipherment of hieroglyphs could move forward.

The *Description de l'Égypte* also included two volumes of natural history engravings in which the savants showed Europe the birds, minerals, and plants of Egypt. But that's not all. There were even two volumes showing modern Egypt—Egypt as it was around 1800 when the French were there.

Along with the engravings were nine volumes of text, articles by the savants describing the fruits of their labors. It would take 22 years to publish the *Description*, but it contributed significantly to the beginning of Egyptology and the quest to resurrect a lost language.

But the most important discovery was the Rosetta Stone. You can see it today, not in the Louvre, but in the British Museum. Remember, Napoleon lost.

Next time, we'll see what the Rosetta Stone says, but now it's time to put on your scribes robes, get you reed brushes and ink—we are going to do some hieroglyphs. I would like to add another 10 or so words to our vocabulary, so we begin reading sentences that are more complex.

Last time I asked you to translate "to another place." Let's go step by step.

First, we need the word for "place." That's easy. It's *bew*.

Now comes the decisions. It's "another place," so we have to decide if we use the masculine or feminine. What is *bew*? Masculine or feminine? Well, it doesn't end in a loaf *t*. So it must be masculine. Good. So now we know to use *key*, the masculine form of "another."

Our next question is: Does "another" go in front of the noun or after? Yep, in front, so it's *key bew*.

OK. The last word to translate is the "to." We have two "to's," one for people, the *n* water sign, and one for places, which is the mouth *r*. A place is a thing. So we know to use the mouth *r*. So our phrase "to another place" is *r key bew*.

Note that the mouth *r* is right above the basket *k*. This is for aesthetics, so it looks nice. Normally, the Egyptians didn't merge words this way, but if you have a single-sign word, it was sometimes OK.

Now, let's add some more vocabulary words and translate some real sentences.

First, let me show you the hieroglyphs for "man" and "woman" and also how to draw them. They're very important.

The word for "man" is z.

Often the word is just written with an idiom stroke.

Sometimes the stroke is omitted, and you have the "man" hieroglyph. There's a lot of flexibility when writing hieroglyphs. You have to remember this. Let me show you how to draw the "man" hieroglyph.

Note, I alter this one a bit from the way Gardiner presents it in his book. My way is to start with the head and shoulders. Now, for the most important part—draw what I call the sock. It looks like a sock, yes? Next, we add the knee, then the foot sticking out, and finally, the arms.

The word for "woman" can also be written several ways. One is phonetically, with the woman determinative.

It's pronounced *zet*. To draw the woman, start at the head and go straight down. Now, add the front of the body. Then do the knees drawn up beneath her dress. That's how you draw a woman.

If you want to say "people," you write the man and the woman hieroglyph together.

That's people. But, it would have been pronounced something like *retchu* when spoken. Note the three strokes. That's how you indicate a plural in ancient Egyptian.

Now that we can write "man" and "woman," let's learn some verbs, so they can do things. And we can translate real sentences.

I'll show you the hieroglyph for a word, and you pronounce it.

Yes, something like *iew* or *yew*. This is the verb "to be." The good news is, it doesn't have to be conjugated. Egyptian isn't like French or Spanish, where you have to worry about "je suis," "tu es," "nous sommes" or "yo estoy," "nosotros estamos." It stays "reed," "leaf," "quail chick," no matter who is or who are. Same for other verbs. They don't change.

Here's another.

Pronounced? Yes, *djed*. It means "to speak" or "say." Good.

Now a related verb. Pronounce this one and then guess what it means from the determinative—a man with his hand to his mouth.

You have the pronunciation, *ger.* That's right. But what does it mean? Hint—it's related to the last verb. It's the verb "to be silent."

Now, for another pair of related verbs.

You'll know how to pronounce it. Yes, *rekh*. But, I bet you're wondering what the determinative is at the end. Well, it's a papyrus roll. It's been rolled up the papyrus, tied with a string, and that little semicircle is a clay seal to ensure confidentiality. If anyone opened it, you would know because the seal would be broken. This is the verb "to know." I think the idea is that knowledge can be written.

Now for the related verb.

Pronounce it. Yes, *khem*. Look at the determinative. Our previous verb meant "to know." What does this one mean: "Not to know" or "to be ignorant of?" I love the determinative. The position of the arms practically says, "I don't know."

OK, that's it for verbs. Now for a few nouns. First a proper noun, a name.

Pronounce it and you'll have the name of a god. Yes, it's *Ptah. Ptah. Ptah.* A god of creation, who is usually shown wearing a distinctive cap, and his feet are together like a mummy's. He was the primary god of the ancient city of Memphis in the north. We'll talk more about him later.

Next, try this noun.

Pronounce it. Yes, *ren*. It means "name."

One last word for today, a conjunction. The ancient Egyptians didn't have a direct parallel for our word "and," but they had this word.

How is it pronounced? Yes, something like *heneh*. It means "together with."

So if we wanted to say "the man together with the woman," we would have this:

And it would've been pronounced something like *z heneh zet.*

Now let's translate some real ancient Egyptian sentences. Here's one:

Let's first break it into words that we recognize. Then, we'll go after the meaning of the sentence. What's our first word?

Yes, it's the verb, "say" or "speak." What's next?

Yes, "man." OK, next? Another verb, "to be silent." Remember, the man with his hand to the mouth? It's not a symbol for "man." It's a determinative.

And our last word? That's right, "woman."

Now, we can go after the overall meaning. Your clue is that it's a sexist maxim. Yes, "When man speaks, woman is silent." It would've sounded something like *djed z ger zet.*

In spite of this proverb, let me emphasize that women in ancient Egypt had more power and rights than anywhere else in the world. They even had women who ruled as kings—not queens. Because women were important, I bet you can name some Egyptian queens. Name one.

Cleopatra's perhaps the most famous. Name another. Good, Nefertiti. Keep going, one more—Hatshepsut, the woman who ruled as king. Now, name an ancient Greek queen. A deathly silence falls over the room. The reason it's more difficult is that the Greek queens weren't important. They didn't go down in history, unlike in Egypt.

OK. Let's translate another Egyptian sentence.

𓇋𓏤𓊪𓏏𓎛𓅓𓃀𓏤𓈖

Take it a word at a time. Yes, the verb is first, and it's "is." Then "Ptah." Then "in." Next is "place," *bew,* and then "this." In English, "this" comes first, but not in hieroglyphs. So our translation would be, "Ptah is in this place." It would have been pronounced something like *yew Ptah em bew pen.* Good!

Now that we're starting to accumulate some real vocabulary words let's review how we'll set up our dictionary. Let's begin by seeing how we would enter the two forms, masculine and feminine, for "another" in our dictionaries.

First, we need to go to our page we have set aside for words that begin with K. The top of the page will look like this:

◠ K

Then we'd enter our word.

◠
◠

Then, in parentheses, put our transliteration to remind us how it sounded.

◠
◠ (ket)

Then we can note it's feminine.

◠
◠ (ket) F.

And finally, the meaning:

◠
◠ (ket) F. - another

Same for the masculine form:

▭𓏏𓏏 (key) M. - another

For "Ptah," we'd go to our page set aside for words beginning with a P and write this:

𓊪𓏏𓎛 (Ptah) Ptah

OK, that's our lesson for today. Now, for homework. Let me give you a few sentences and phrases to translate from English into ancient Egyptian. First, "The woman does not know this man." Next, "Re and Ptah are together in this place." Try, "The man does not know another thing." And last, "The woman knows this name."

That should keep you out of trouble for a while. I'll see you next time.

Early Attempts to Decipher the Rosetta Stone

In this lecture, we will discuss early efforts to decipher the Rosetta Stone, which contained two languages: Greek and Egyptian. The French discovered the Rosetta Stone, but it was an Englishman who started the ball rolling: Thomas Young, perhaps the greatest scientist of his time. A polymath, he is best remembered for the wave theory of light, but he also made contributions to physiology and Egyptology. We'll cover his efforts to decode the stone, and then move on to some new dictionary entries.

The Rosetta Stone's Contents

- From the very beginning, there was no mystery about what the Rosetta Stone said. Many of the savants in Egypt with Bonaparte could read the Greek section. It was basically a thank-you note written in 196 B.C. from the priests of Egypt to King Ptolemy V, the Greek ruler of Egypt.

- Ptolemy had granted some favors to the priests, especially reducing their taxes, so they erected the stela to thank him. After listing the specific benefits granted to priests, they also thanked him for general kindness to the people: releasing prisoners, restoring sacred buildings, and so on.

- Stelae were the bulletin boards of ancient Egypt. If you wanted something known, you carved it on a round-topped stone and erected it in front of the temple, where everyone would see it. The Rosetta Stone was one of these.

- Students used to learn that the Rosetta Stone contained three languages. This is wrong. It contains only Greek and Egyptian.

The Rosetta Stone

However, the Egyptian was written in two different scripts, a bit like cursive versus printed English.

- The hieroglyphic script at the top is the most damaged, and a great deal of it is missing. Herodotus dubbed the second script Demotic (from the Greek word for "popular"). It is an extremely cursive form of hieroglyphs.

- The Greek script at the bottom is the most complete. It is important for several reasons. First, it gave a readable version of the text. Second, at the end it says that the stela contained the same message in all three scripts, providing a strategy for decipherment. Third, it provided the name King Ptolemy, which would prove to be the most important of all clues.

Thomas Young

- The English scientist Thomas Young began deciphering the Rosetta Stone during his summer vacations. But Young was working under the mistaken belief that hieroglyphs were primarily ideographic, that they were picture writing. He was not the only one laboring under this error—the Big Mistake.

- His great insight, however, was that the name Ptolemy, which he saw in the Greek text, must also appear in the Demotic and hieroglyphic texts as well. He realized that the hieroglyphs and Demotic characters for the name couldn't be ideographic.

- There is no picture of what a Ptolemy was, so at least for names, there must have been an alphabet. Others before Young had suggested that the ovals called *cartouches* by Bonaparte's men held the names of the kings. Young agreed and began to work on the cartouche:

- He figured that the hieroglyphs inside the cartouche must correspond to letters spelling out Ptolemy. The rectangle must be a *P*, the semicircle a *t*, the loop an *o*, the lion an *l*, the statue base an *m*, the reed leaves a *y*, and the folded cloth an *s*, forming "Ptolmis." The Greek version of the name is actually "Ptolemaios," which is pretty close. Young figured out this approximation. He now had seven letters of the alphabet.

- The beginning of decipherment was extremely difficult. The process took 20 years. Young published his findings in the 1819 supplement to the *Encyclopaedia Britannica*. He presented his partial alphabet and also made some correct (and incorrect) guesses for groups of words, but he never took it much further. The problem was that he never gave up his conviction that hieroglyphs were ideograms, an idea that had been firmly entrenched for centuries.

Kircher's Attempt

- In the 5th century, a mysterious Egyptian named Horapollo wrote *Hieroglyphica*, the earliest work on hieroglyphs. In his book, Horapollo explains how hieroglyphs work. But he clearly doesn't have a full grasp of how hieroglyphs work. For example, he is correct when he says that the duck hieroglyph, 🦆, represents the word "son," a male offspring, but the explanation he offers is wrong.

- The reason he gives is that the duck fights so fiercely for its offspring that it is associated with children. Horapollo believed, incorrectly, that hieroglyphs are basically picture writing.

- But the duck actually phonetically represents the syllable *sa*; it's what we call a *biliteral*, a hieroglyph that represents two sounds. There are even hieroglyphs that represent three sounds, called *triliterals.*

- The word *sa* in ancient Egyptian meant "son." Therefore, the duck has phonetic value, not ideographic. This book by Horapollo presenting the Big Mistake threw off everyone who wanted to decipher hieroglyphs. But it is not all his fault.

- From the 3rd century on, many students of the occult believed there was a corpus of secret texts written by Hermes Trismegistus, or "Thrice Great Hermes." Written in mystical hieroglyphs, these texts were intended to be kept secret, revealed only to the initiated. This belief in the essential secret nature of hieroglyphs permeated the study of ancient Egyptian texts right up till the Renaissance.

- No one imagined hieroglyphs were used to record history, or workmen's wages. They were sacred texts of Hermes Trismegistus. The only problem was that Hermes never existed. The belief in Hermes also lasted into the Renaissance and greatly influenced Athanasius Kircher's attempt at decipherment.

- A Jesuit, Kircher was, by many accounts, a genius in several disciplines. He built automata, studied volcanoes and botany, was a master of a dozen languages, and was considered by some to be the greatest mind the 17th century. Others considered him a fraud.

- For much of his life, he lived in Rome and worked under the protection of the pope. This was an era when obelisks that the Roman emperors had brought from Egypt were being rediscovered beneath the streets of Rome and re-erected. Kircher turned his extensive learning to the task of translating the hieroglyphs on Rome's obelisks.

- The word "obelisk" is not Egyptian; it's from the Greek *obeliskus*, which refers to a meat skewer. This was the ancient Egyptian word in hieroglyphs:

- It was pronounced *tekhen*. The last hieroglyph is the determinative; it's an obelisk standing on its base. Notice the compact, pleasing arrangements of the hieroglyphs, rather than this one:

- Kircher believed the hieroglyphs were picture writing and contained wisdom of the ancients. He was guessing when he claimed they had religious significance. He translated most of the obelisks in Rome, but it was pure fantasy. They merely contained the names and titles of the pharaohs who erected them in Egypt.

More Verbs

- Let's learn some more words so we can say more complex things, starting with some new verbs.

- is *khed*, which means "to fare downstream."

- is pronounced something like *ha*. The word means "to go down" or "to descend."

- is a similar word, pronounced *hab*. It means "to send."

- is an unusual one. The ear hieroglyph is a triliteral, representing three sounds, one after the other: /s/, /dj/, and /m/. It's pronounced *sedjem* and the word means "to hear." When you add this word to your dictionary, add it on the S page since it begins with an /s/ sound.

- is pronounced *depet*. This is the kind of boat people used.

- ⟨glyph⟩ is pronounced *wia*, and it is a sacred boat—one in which a god might ride across the sky.

- ⟨glyph⟩ is unusual. It seems to have two determinatives: a face in profile and a papyrus roll. It may have been pronounced *reshwet*. The word means "joy" or "gladness." It's like the profile is there because you see joy on the face. The papyrus roll, which usually determines abstract things, may be there because joy is an internal state. The ancient scribes never left us an explanation.

- ⟨glyph⟩ is pronounced *sekher* and means "plan" or "counsel." Again, this is an abstract concept—not something you can touch.

- ⟨glyph⟩ means "town." What we are looking at is a crossroads, and where two roads cross, you have a town. It was pronounced *niwit*. This one would be added to the N page of the dictionary since it begins with the sound /n/.

- Be sure to add these words to your personal dictionary in alphabetical order.

Lecture 4's Homework Answers

1. The first sentence to translate was "The woman does not know this man." Start with the verb, *khem*, "to not know." Next we put "woman," followed by "man" with the masculine version of "this." In the end, we get: ⟨glyph⟩, pronounced something like *khem zet z pen*.

2. The second sentence was "Re and Ptah are together in this place." This is ⟨glyph⟩, pronounced *Yew Re heneh Ptah em bew pen*.

3. The next sentence was "The man does not know another thing." We start with the verb, ⟨glyph⟩. Next is the subject, "man," which gives us

𓆓𓏤𓃀𓈖𓏏. "Another" comes next, but we have to determine if "thing" is masculine or feminine so we can decide which "another" to use. *Khet*, 𓆓𓏤, is feminine, ending in a /t/, so we know we must use the feminine form of "another," *ket*. That is 𓎡𓏏. This adjective comes in front of the noun, so the whole sentence is: *Khem z ket khet*. In hieroglyphs, that is 𓆓𓏤𓃀𓈖𓏏 𓎡𓏏.

4. Our last sentence was, "The woman knows this man." Start with the verb, *rekh*, "to know": 𓂋𓐍. Next we add the subject, "woman," making 𓂋𓐍𓁐. Last we need "this man." "Man" is obviously masculine so for the "this" we need *pen*. It goes after the noun: 𓂋𓐍𓁐𓀀𓈖.

Lecture 5's Homework

Here are four sentences to translate into hieroglyphs.

1. "Ptah goes down in another boat." Note: Be careful. This is just "go down," not "fare downstream."

2. "[When] this man fares downstream, the city is in joy." Note: There is no word for "when" in Middle Egyptian, so you can't translate it. It is understood.

3. "This woman listens to Ptah."

4. "A man is there in the city."

Early Attempts to Decipher the Rosetta Stone

Welcome back. Today, we'll discuss the first attempt to decipher the Rosetta Stone.

From the very beginning, there was no mystery about what the Rosetta Stone said. Many of the savants in Egypt with Bonaparte could read the Greek section. It was basically a thank you note written in 196 B.C. from the priests of Egypt to King Ptolemy V, the Greek ruler of Egypt. Ptolemy had granted some favors to the priests, especially reducing their taxes, so they erected the stela to thank him. After listing the specific benefits granted to priests, they also thank him for general kindness to the people—releasing prisoners, restoring sacred buildings, and things like that.

Stelae, which is the plural of stela, were the bulletin boards of ancient Egypt. If you wanted something known, you carved it on a round-top stone and erected it in front of the temple where everyone would see it. The Rosetta Stone was one of these.

The hieroglyphic script at the top is the most damaged, and a great deal of it's missing. Originally the stela was round-topped and probably had a winged sun at the top and a procession of the gods with the Pharaoh Ptolemy V.

The second script was called Demotic by Herodotus—from the Greek for "people" because it was what the people used for business, letters, and things like that. It's an extremely cursive form of hieroglyphs, used extensively during the Late and Ptolemaic Periods.

The Greek script, at the bottom, is the most complete and is important for several reasons. First, it gave a readable version of the text. Second, at the end, it says that the stela contained the same message in sacred characters—hieroglyphs, native characters—Demotic, and Greek characters. This was a critical bit of information. It made clear that the three scripts all said the same thing and thus provided a strategy for decipherment. Third, it provided the name Ptolemy, which would prove to be the most important of all clues.

The French discovered the Rosetta Stone, but it was an Englishman who started the ball rolling. Thomas Young was perhaps the greatest scientist of his time. A polymath, he's best remembered for the wave theory of light, but he also made contributions to physiology and, as we shall see, Egyptology. Schooled in Greek, Latin, and other languages, he began working on deciphering the Rosetta Stone during his summer vacations. But, Young was working under the mistaken belief that hieroglyphs were primarily ideographic—that they were picture writing. As we'll see, he was not the only one laboring under what I call the Big Mistake.

His great insight, however, was that the name Ptolemy, which he saw in the Greek text, must also appear in the Demotic and hieroglyphic texts as well. He realized that the hieroglyphs and Demotic characters for the name couldn't be ideographic. It couldn't be a picture because There's no picture of what a Ptolemy looked like. So at least, for names, there must be an alphabet. Others before Young had suggested that the ovals—called cartouches by Bonaparte's men because they looked like cartridge shells—held the names of the kings. Young agreed and began to work on the cartouche.

He figured that the hieroglyphs inside the cartouche must correspond to letters of the alphabet spelling out Ptolemy. The rectangle must be a *p*, the semicircle a *t*, the loop an *o*, the lion an *l*, the statue base an *m*, the reed leaf maybe a *y*—the reed leaves, and the folded cloth an *s*—Ptolmis. The Greek version of the name is actually Ptolemaios, But it's pretty close. Young figured out this approximation. He now had seven letters of the alphabet. Decipherment wasn't easy.

To give you an idea of what this pioneering work was like, let me put you in Thomas Young's shoes for a couple of minutes. I want you to look at a temple wall and see what you can figure out. Remember, at this stage, Thomas Young knew less about hieroglyphs and Egyptian civilization than you do.

Before we get to the hieroglyphs, let's look at the big picture. We can see two people making offerings to the gods. The man holds an incense burner. Incense was called "what the gods like to smell." He wears the double crown—the tall white crown of Upper Egypt and the short red crown of Lower Egypt. So he's probably a king. There are two cartouches in front of him, so that's more evidence that he's the king.

Behind him, we see a queen. We can see her cartouches too. She's wearing an elaborate headdress consisting of horns and a solar disk, often worn by the goddesses Isis and Hathor. In her right hand, she holds a *sistrum*, a musical instrument, a bit like a rattle, that was used in rituals.

In her other hand, she holds a keyhole-shaped object called a *menat*. Priestesses of Hathor often wore heavy decorative pectorals around their necks. This would've created a strain on the neck, so they wore *menats*— counterweights made of metal that hung down the back. It took the weight off the neck. So we have a king and a queen making offerings to the gods. But, who are the king and queen? That's the kind of question Thomas Young was wrestling with. Let's look at the cartouches. Ladies first.

Let's begin with the one in front. First hieroglyph—it's small—just above the lion's back. It's the hill sign, a *q*. You'll remember, a lion was an *l* in Ptolemaic times, so we have Q-L. But from our earlier discussions, you know the *q* was also a *k*, so you've probably already figured out— it's Cleopatra.

We can see the lasso *o* that was used in Ptolemaic times. There's the rectangle *p*. We have a vulture *a*. We have a hand beneath the vulture and beneath that is our mouth *r*, and finally another vulture—Cleopatra. You were right.

On either side of the last vulture are an egg and a loaf *t*. Both indicate a female name. Young would figure that out later.

You probably noticed that the cartouche has been defaced. The animals have been chiseled out. It's strange, and I don't know why this was done. In later times, the Christians chiseled out the faces of the gods and kings and queens, so they would lose their powers. That, by the way, is where we get our term "defaced." But, just defacing the animals is very unusual.

OK, we have Cleopatra, but which one? There were seven Cleopatras. Let's look at her other cartouche. This one reads from right to left. So we start with a P-T-O-L. You've got it already, Ptolemy. This just reaffirms that our queen is a Ptolemy. There's an *m*—the statue base *m*—under the lion, then the double reed leaf, which is a *y*, then a folded cloth *s* for the Greek ending *Ptolmis*.

Now, all the other hieroglyphs that follow would tell us which Cleopatra she is if we could decipher them. But like Thomas Young, we can't, so we don't know. But we can, however, spot a name we know, at the bottom right of the cartouche. Do see it? Ptah. So this queen has Ptah in her title.

Just to the left of the Ptah is the name Isis. It's the throne, an egg, and *t* hieroglyphs. We'll talk all about the names of the gods in a later lecture, but you can see how difficult it is to figure things out. That's what Thomas Young was up against. Now, you can have more sympathy for the difficulty of his task.

But, can we figure out something about the king? The cartouche in front of him is easy for us—Ptolemy, but that's all it says. It doesn't even give a clue to which Ptolemy, and there were more than a dozen. The second cartouche will reveal his identity if we can read it. Let's take Thomas Young's approach, let's sound it out a letter at a time.

First letter? Yes, basket *k*. Next letter? Yes, the double reed. Remember this is a right to left reading text. So we have K-Y. Next, is the folded cloth, giving us K-Y-S. Now the lion's tricky. We know it was used for the *l* in Cleopatra and in Ptolemy. However, it sometimes also doubled as an *r*, and that's what it's doing here. This gave all the decipherers problems for a while, but they figured it out eventually. But again, it wasn't easy. OK, we have K-Y-S-R and then a bolt z below—KYSRZ.

Where does the name end? How long do we have to keep going? That's another problem we have to deal with. Well, the next group of four hieroglyphs is our answer. Young saw this phrase—these four hieroglyphs—over and over again at the end of different names. It means "living forever," but Young didn't know this. But, he did deduce that it couldn't be part of the name—it must be something like a title or an epithet.

So we know where the name ends. The entire name is KYSRZ. Who's that? We have to keep saying it aloud, trying to hear a name. We know the queen is a Cleopatra. Whose name, during that period of Egyptian history, sounded like *KYSRZ*? KYSRZ. Caesar. Yes, it's the Roman Caesar. But, it isn't Julius Caesar.

Cleopatra named their son Caesar after his father. And that's who we see here, Cleopatra and her son, Caesar, shown as King of Egypt. Later, he'd be known as Caesarion—Little Caesar. So we are looking at Cleopatra VII, the last Ptolemy to rule Egypt. But, you can see how difficult it is at the beginning of decipherment. It wasn't just, "Oh, the Rosetta Stone was found, and that did it." It took 20 years Young was a pioneer and a very smart guy.

Young published his findings in the 1819 supplement to the *Encyclopaedia Britannica*—20 after the Rosetta Stone was discovered. He presented his partial alphabet and also made some correct guesses—and some incorrect ones too—or groups of words, but he never took it much further. The problem was that he never gave up his conviction that hieroglyphs were ideograms, an idea that had been firmly entrenched for centuries.

You see, in the 5th century, a mysterious Egyptian named Horapollo wrote *Hieroglyphica*, the earliest work on hieroglyphs. We know little about him. Some scholars even think his book was written as late as the 11th century, but his name is a great combination of Egyptian and Greek. "Hor," the first part, is the ancient Egyptian name for *Horus*, the falcon god. The Greeks added the *us* ending. Apollo is, of course, the Greek god of music. So my bet is that he was an Egyptian who spoke Greek.

In his book, he explains how hieroglyphs work. Even though he's an Egyptian living only a century after the last hieroglyphic inscription was written, he clearly doesn't have a full grasp of how hieroglyphs work. For example, he's correct when he says that the duck hieroglyph

represents the word "son," a male offspring, but the explanation he offers is dead wrong.

The reason he gives is that the duck fights so fiercely for its offspring that it's associated with children. Horapollo believes, incorrectly, that hieroglyphs are basically picture writing. That the duck represents a duck and one of the properties of the duck—fighting fiercely for its young—determines the meaning.

Actually, the duck phonetically represents the syllable *sa*. It's what we call a biliteral, a hieroglyph that represents two sounds—he /s/ and the /a/. We'll learn about biliterals soon. There are even hieroglyphs that represent three sounds, one after the other. We'll see one later today.

But now back to our word, *sa*. The word *sa* in ancient Egyptian meant "son." So the duck has phonetic value, not ideographic. It's not a picture. This book by Horapollo presenting the Big Mistake threw off everyone who wanted to decipher hieroglyphs. But it's not all his fault.

From the 3rd century on, many students of the occult believed that there was a corpus of secret texts written by Hermes Trismegistos—Thrice Great Hermes. Written in mystical hieroglyphs, these texts were intended to be kept secret, revealed only to the initiated. This belief in the essential secret nature of hieroglyphs permeated the study of ancient Egyptian texts right up to the Renaissance.

No one imagined hieroglyphs were used to record history or workmen's wages. They were sacred texts of Hermes Trismegistos. The only problem was—Hermes never existed. The belief in Hermes also lasted into the Renaissance and greatly influenced Athanasius Kircher's attempt to decipher.

Kircher has been called The Last Man Who Knew Everything. A Jesuit, he was by many accounts a genius in several disciplines. He built automata, studied volcanoes and botany, was a master of a dozen languages, and was considered by some to be the greatest mind the 17th century. Others considered him a fraud.

For much of his life, he lived in Rome and worked under the protection of the pope. This was an era when obelisks that Roman emperors had bought from Egypt were being rediscovered beneath the streets of Rome and re-erected. Kircher turned his extensive learning to the task of translating the hieroglyphs on Rome's obelisks.

The word "obelisk" is not Egyptian; it's Greek. When the Greeks first entered Egypt and saw these tall pointy things, they reminded them of meat skewers—as in shish kebab. That's what *obeliskus* means—"a meat skewer." This was the ancient Egyptian word in hieroglyphs:

How was it pronounced? That's right, *tekhen*. The last hieroglyph is the determinative; it's an obelisk on its base. Notice the arrangements of the hieroglyphs. It's compact and pleasing. It could've been written as individual hieroglyphs in a row like this:

But that's not as elegant as grouping the loaf and the placenta together—above the water sign.

Obelisks almost always came in pairs—placed in front of temples to proclaim who built the temple. They never had anything mysterious or significant inscribed on them.

Working in the Hermetic tradition. However, Kircher believed the hieroglyphs were picture writing and contained wisdom of the ancients. He was guessing when he claimed that they had religious significance. He translated most of the obelisks in Rome, but it was pure fantasy. They merely contained the names and titles of the pharaohs who erected them in Egypt.

Everyone trying to translate hieroglyphs was still making the Big Mistake. But we don't have to. So get on your scribe's robes; it's time for hieroglyphs and real translations.

Last time I gave you a few sentences to translate from English to hieroglyphs. Let's see how you did.

The first sentence was: "The woman does not know this man." Start with the verb, *khem,* "to not know."

Next, we put "woman." No need for the article "the"—there's no such thing in ancient Egyptian.

Remember, we don't always need the stroke for the word "woman." It's written both with and without it.

Now, we add the "this man." "Man" is clearly masculine, so we use the masculine form of "this," *pen.* Remember, that "this" follows the noun.

And that's it. "The woman does not know this man." This would have been pronounced something like *khem zet z pen.*

Our next sentence was "Re and Ptah are together in this place." Start with the verb, "to be," *yew.*

That will give us the "are" part of the sentence.

Now we add the subjects—the gods Re and Ptah, and we join them with our word for "together with," *heneh*:

So now we have our verb and subjects. Let's add "in," which is the owl.

Last, we have to say "this place." Well, "place" is *bew*.

Since it doesn't end in a *t*, it's masculine. We know we must use the masculine form of "this," which is *pen*.

And we remember that "this" follows the noun—so the whole sentence reads *yew Re heneh Ptah em bew pen*. Good.

The next sentence was: "The man does not know another thing." Well, we all know we start with the verb.

Next, the subject, "man." We know there are no articles in ancient Egyptian—no "the's" or "a's," so we just write "man."

"Another" comes next, but we have to determine if "thing" is masculine or feminine, so we can decide which "another" to use. Well, *khet*

is feminine—it ends in a *t*, so we know we must use the feminine form of "another," *ket*.

This adjective, "another," comes in front of the noun. We have to remember that. So the whole sentence is *Khem z ket khet.* Good.

Our last sentence was "The woman knows this man."

Start with the verb, *rekh,* "to know":

Next the subject, "woman."

Last we need "this man." It's obviously masculine, so for the "this" we need *pen*, and it goes after the noun. And now we've got it.

Well done. Let's learn some more words, so we can say more complex things. We want to get past, "See spot run," sentences.

Let's start with a few more verbs. I'll give you the hieroglyphs, and you tell me how they're pronounced. It's good practice. Here's one:

How's it pronounced? That's right, *khed*. The boat doesn't have a phonetic value. It's a determinative and helps us determine the meaning of the word. So we know it has something to do with boats. The word means "to fare downstream."

Next word.

How's it pronounced? Something like *ha*. Again, the feet are a determinative, not pronounced, but telling us the word has something to do with walking. The word means "to go down" or "descend."

Let me show you a similar word, not to be confused with *ha*.

How would you pronounce it? Yes, *hab*.

It means "to send." So that I don't confuse similar words, I try to make up mnemonic devices to remember them. So for *hab*, I try to think of sending my friend Hobbs somewhere. Whatever works for you.

Let's learn another verb. Here it is.

This is an unusual one. Look at it. You won't be able to tell me how it's pronounced because it's tricky. The ear hieroglyph, that's our first hieroglyph—an ear—is a triliteral, representing three sounds one after the other—/s/, /dj/, and /m/. It's as if we wrote the folded cloth, serpent, and owl, one after the other.

It's pronounced *sedjem* and the word means "to hear." The owl is probably just a phonetic complement, a bonus to remind you how it is pronounced. To pronounce it, we put in the short *e* vowels, but we're not sure we're right.

Remember, we have learned the alphabet, hieroglyphs representing just one sound. But there are other hieroglyphs that represent two sounds, called biliterals and some that represent three sounds. The ear hieroglyph is one of the triliterals.

When you add this word to your dictionary, add it on the S page since it begins with an /s/ sound.

Now, let's add another word for boat.

Pronounced *depet*, this is the kind of boat people used. But, let me show you another kind of boat. Here it is.

How's it pronounced? *Wia*—it's a sacred boat. One in which a god might ride across the sky.

We're just beginning our study of Middle Egyptian and already we have three words with a boat hieroglyph. Boats were very important in ancient Egypt. Besides walking, if you wanted to cover a long distance, a boat was your only option. So when the Egyptians imagined the journey to the next world, it was in a sacred boat.

In temples, a statue of the god was kept in a sealed room called the "Holy of Holies." At festival times the statue was placed inside a gilded wood shrine and carried out to the temple courtyard for the people to see. That shrine was shaped like a boat, a *wia*, a sacred boat.

Carved on the walls of Karnak and Luxor temple are scenes of shaven-headed priests carrying the boat shrine.

Now let me give you a strange-looking word.

It's unusual. It seems to have two determinatives, a face in profile and a papyrus roll. Let's pronounce it first and then figure out what's going on. How would you pronounce it? *Reshwet.* Good. That's right. Reshwet. That's how it probably sounded.

The word means "joy" or "gladness." I think the profile is there because you see "joy" or "gladness" on the face. The papyrus roll, which usually determines abstract things, may be there because "joy" or "gladness" is an internal state. That's just a guess. Pure surmise. The ancient scribes never left us an explanation.

Let's look at another word with a papyrus roll determinative.

It's pronounced *sekher* and means "plan" or "council." Again, an abstract concept, but not something you can touch.

Here's our last word.

Can you tell me how the top hieroglyph is being used? Is it a phonetic hieroglyph? A determinative? Or an ideogram? The stroke tells us it's an ideogram. It's a picture of what it means. Now the problem is, what's it a picture of?

The word means "town." What we are looking at is a crossroads, and where two roads cross, you have a town. We also know it's feminine because we have the loaf *t*. From other contexts, I can tell you it was pronounced *niwit. Niwit.* This is one that would be added to our dictionary in our N page because it begins with the sound *n*.

OK, that's enough words for today. I don't want to overload you. Be sure to add them to your personal dictionary in alphabetical order.

But you're not getting off without homework. Let me give you four sentences to translate into hieroglyphs.

First, "Ptah goes down in another boat." Be careful. This is just "go down," not "fare downstream."

Next, "(When) this man fares downstream, the city is in joy." Let me tell you, there's no word for "when" in Middle Egyptian, so you don't translate it. It's understood.

Next, "This woman listens to Ptah."

And last, "A man is there in the city."

Next time, we'll see more progress towards decipherment, and we'll also see how you did on the new sentences.

I'll see you then.

William Bankes and the Keys to Decipherment

This lecture discusses two crucial steps along the road to the decipherment of hieroglyphs. Both involve a rather unusual antiquarian named William Bankes, who made some huge contributions to decipherment. In this lecture, we'll cover some of Bankes's discoveries, and then discuss some misconceptions classicists held about the beginnings of civilization. After that, we will continue building our vocabulary. We'll also cover the previous lecture's homework assignment and close with a new one.

William Bankes's Grand Tour

- In 1810, William Bankes took a seat in the House of Commons, but politics was not to his liking. He was far more interested in art and architecture. He could read Latin and Greek, was an accomplished artist and draftsman, and was extremely interested in the new discoveries being made in Egypt and the Middle East.

- Bankes was a gay man, and this was a serious matter in homophobic 19th-century London. The previous year, 21 young men had been hanged for merely having "indecent thoughts," so William decided to leave London and go on the Grand Tour—a tradition among wealthy Englishmen. He wasn't eager to return.

- In Bankes's time, during the Grand Tour, one was expected to go to Italy to see the ruins of Rome, to study the paintings and sculpture in Florence, and to experience the atmosphere and architecture of Venice. Then it would be off to Greece, to see where Western civilization was born. The more adventurous and wealthy could continue on to Turkey and Egypt, and William Bankes was both adventurous and wealthy.

- Bankes's Grand Tour would last from 1815–1819, a full four years. He visited Egypt twice, first in 1815–1816, and then he returned to Egypt in 1818 for a second look.

Philae

- When Bankes reached Philae, the beautiful temple built on an island in the Nile, he fell in love with the place. Bankes decided he had to have something from Philae for his estate back in England.

- There was a 20-foot-tall inscribed obelisk still resting on its original pedestal. Bankes made arrangements with Giovanni Belzoni, a 6'7" Italian strongman who was making his living by excavating, finding large sculptures, and selling them back in Europe. Belzoni agreed to ship both the pedestal and obelisk to England for him.

- After the obelisk was lowered from its pedestal, Belzoni was loading it onto a boat when it slipped into the water. Only lots of rope and many men pulling saved it. There were difficulties, too, with the pedestal, which was left behind on the banks of the Nile for two years before it made its way to England.

- When everything finally arrived and Bankes returned from his Grand Tour, he erected the obelisk on its pedestal on his estate, where it can be seen today. Modern tourists in Egypt only see a poor quality concrete replica of the obelisk, and most walk by it without knowing what it is or the part that its original played in the decipherment of hieroglyphs.

- The base of the original obelisk has a Greek inscription while the obelisk itself is in hieroglyphs; like the Rosetta Stone, it's bilingual, in Greek and Egyptian. Bankes could read the Greek, which bore the names of Ptolemy and Cleopatra.

- "Ptolemy" had already been deciphered, so Bankes correctly deduced the other cartouche must be "Cleopatra." He sent his copy of the inscription to Thomas Young, who by looking at the hieroglyphs, , was able to confirm his earlier findings and also add some letters to the alphabet.

- That cartouche starts with the hill *q*, which is close to the /k/ sound. Since Cleopatra starts with a /k/ sound, Young added that hieroglyph to his alphabet as a /k/ sound. He was correct.

- The next letter, a lion, must be an *l*, and this confirmed that letter in Ptolemy's name. The reed leaf and the rope loop he had already seen in Ptolemy's name, so he confirmed these. The vulture *a* does not appear in Ptolemy, though, so Young had a new letter to add to his alphabet.

- Now the hand hieroglyph, the /d/ sound, gave him a bit of a puzzle, but he figured it out. Its position corresponds to the *t* in Cleopatra's name. But Ptolemy also had a *t* in his name; it was the loaf hieroglyph: ⌐.

- Young figured the two hieroglyphs had pretty much the same sound, and he was right with respect to the Greek pronunciation of Cleopatra: *Kleopadra*. Later he would see in other cartouches of Cleopatra's name that it was often spelled with a loaf *t*.

- The mouth *r* doesn't appear in Ptolemy's name, so Young had a new arrow in his quiver *r*. Imagine how excited he must have been as he added more and more letters to his alphabet.

- Young even realized that the last two hieroglyphs, the egg and the loaf *t*, had no phonetic value but were determinatives for female queens, goddesses, and princesses. Real progress was being made.

The Temple of Abydos

- Bankes's second big contribution was at the temple of Abydos. Today the temple is visited by millions of tourists each year, but when Bankes found it, it was filled in with sand. We must also remember that hieroglyphs hadn't been translated yet, so no one knew who had built it.

- According to Egyptian mythology, Osiris, the god of the dead, was buried at Abydos. Egyptians wanted to make a pilgrimage to Abydos to place an offering at Osiris's grave, so they, too, would be resurrected.

Seti I, the father of Ramses II, built the temple of Abydos. In the hall of the ancients, you can see Seti with young Ramses, reading the names of all the kings.

- Bankes had the sand that choked the rooms inside the temple cleared and made an incredible discovery: a hall of the ancients. When pharaohs built a temple, they often listed all the pharaohs before them, to show what a long lineage they had. This hall of the ancients had the longest list of pharaohs ever discovered, and in near-perfect condition.

- When Bankes discovered this list, he understood that it was important, and made a very accurate copy of it to bring back to England for Young. This provided many more names for Young, so even more letters of the alphabet could be deduced.

Civilization's Beginning

- At first, everyone in Europe was convinced that Greece was the source of civilization. Once the hieroglyphs were deciphered and the Egyptian records could be read, the question had to be raised: Could Egypt be the source of civilization?

- There was tremendous resistance to this idea. Astonishingly, late into the 19th century, classicists were still claiming that Greece was where it all started. Yet Herodotus said Greece learned how to build in stone from the Egyptians.

- Herodotus acknowledged that Greek gods were derived from the much older Egyptian pantheon. He recounted how he was shocked by how far back Egyptians could trace their ancestors.

- The classicists were ignoring everything the ancient Greeks said about Egypt. Why the resistance? It seems they couldn't accept the idea that an African civilization could have been so advanced thousands of years before Europe had writing. It was racism.

- Today, Western civilization's debt to Egypt is well known and acknowledged, but it has been a rocky road. In 1954, a book titled *Stolen Legacy* by George James attempted to point out our debt to Egypt, but it was tragically flawed and scholars attacked it.

- In 1987, a far more serious book on the subject appeared: *Black Athena* by Martin Bernal. Here was a real Cambridge scholar who was pointing out the 19th-century racism that refused to credit Egypt with her accomplishments.

- But Bernal's expertise was Chinese political history, and because he was writing on a subject outside his field of expertise, he made errors and overstated his case. This book, too, was widely criticized, but it is worth reading.

New Vocabulary Words

- In this lecture, we'll learn vocabulary necessary for talking about the earth and a couple types of people. We'll also encounter some ideograms.

- ⬛ is pronounced *heru*. The determinative at the end tells us it has something to do with the sun, or time. The word means "day."

- ⬛ is pronounced *gereh* and means "night." The determinative is a bolt of lightning coming out of the sky.

- ⬛ sounds something like *yeah*. The determinative is the phases of the moon, and the word means "moon."

- The next word, ⬛, has two determinatives. It is pronounced *nedjes*. The first determinative, the small bird, usually determines things that are small or bad. With the man hieroglyph at the end, we know it is a person. The word means "commoner," who, in a social sense, is a small person. The word also means "poor man," so it wasn't so good to be a commoner.

- Now for a couple of ideograms.

- ⬛ is pronounced *sesh*. It is obviously a man of some kind from the last ideogram in the word. The key is the other ideogram, which represents writing implements. The rectangle that looks like a traffic light is a scribe's palette. The two circles are the red and black inks. A man with writing implements is a scribe. That's the word: "scribe."

- ⌂ is pronounced *akhet*. The ideogram is a sun rising or setting in a notch in a mountain. It means "horizon" and is feminine.

- ⌂ might be pronounced something like *she*. The little sign next to the ideogram stroke is probably an irrigation channel that feeds a lake or pool. And that's what the word means, "lake" or "pool."

- ⌂ was pronounced *ta*, and means "land." The thin oval is a spit of land, and the three dots means it comes in chunks, like clumps of dirt. The other sign is probably an irrigation canal. We know it's masculine because it doesn't have a loaf *t*.

Lecture 5's Homework Answers

1. "Ptah goes down in another boat" was the first sentence. We start with *ha*, "to go down," because it's the verb and verbs come first. Next comes Ptah, the subject, followed by "in," which is the owl. For "another," we use the feminine *ket*, and then we add "boat." The end result is ⌂, pronounced *Ha Ptah m ket depet*.

2. Next we had "[When] this man fares downstream, the city is in joy." The "when" is understood, not written, so we start with a verb, *khed, "to fare downstream."* It's this one: ⌂. Notice the position of the boat determinative.

    ○ Now we need "this man." We use the masculine *pen*, and it follows the noun. ⌂

    ○ For the second half of the sentence, the verb is "is." In hieroglyphs, that's *yew*, the reed leaf and the quail chick. ⌂

- ○ Next we have "city," the subject (pronounced *niwit*).

- ○ Now we need "in joy." Well, the owl *m* is the "in," and "joy" is our strange word *reshwet* with the double determinative. In the end, we get [hieroglyphs] as our second sentence. That is pronounced something like: *Khed z pen yew niwit em reshwet.*

1. "This woman listens to Ptah." Start with the verb, *sedjem*, then add "this woman," creating [hieroglyphs]. We use the water hieroglyph for "to," then just add Ptah, giving us [hieroglyphs].

2. "A man is there in the city." We start with our verb, "is," then add "man," then our reed leaf and owl: [hieroglyphs]. We don't have the word "the" in ancient Egyptian, so we just add city, *niwit*, and we're done. We end up with [hieroglyphs], which is pronounced *Yew z im niwit.*

Lecture 6's Homework

For homework, translate these three sentences.

1. "The moon rises in the sky."

2. "The scribe is silent day and night."

3. "This poor man knows a plan."

William Bankes and the Keys to Decipherment

Welcome back. Today, I'd like to talk about two crucial steps along the road to the decipherment of hieroglyphs. Both involve a rather unusual antiquarian named William Bankes.

Bankes came from a wealthy English family. He was well educated, attending Trinity College, Cambridge, where he became close friends with Lord Byron. William's father was a career politician, and William was expected to follow in his footsteps. And he did. In 1810, he took a seat in the House of Commons, but politics wasn't to his liking. He was far more interested in art and architecture. He could read Latin and Greek, was an accomplished artist and draftsman and was extremely interested in the new discoveries being made in Egypt and the Middle East.

He was also gay, and this was a serious matter in homophobic London in the early-19th century. The previous year, 21 young men had been hanged for merely having indecent thoughts, so William decided to leave London and go on the Grand Tour. And he wasn't eager to return. The year was 1815.

In William Bankes' time, it was part of a wealthy Englishman's education to make the Grand Tour. One was expected to go to Italy to see the ruins of Rome, to study the paintings and sculpture in Florence, and to experience the atmosphere and architecture of Venice. Then it would be off to Greece, to see where Western civilization was born. The more adventurous and wealthy could continue on to Turkey and Egypt, and William Bankes was both adventurous and wealthy.

In the early part of the 19th century, there was no organized tourism in Egypt—it was pure adventure. In Cairo, one hired a dragoman—an interpreter and guide—a small ship and crew, and sailed up the Nile.

The pace for the first half of the trip was determined by the winds. This was the journey was south because you were going against the current and were at the mercy of the wind. If there were no wind, sometimes the crews would walk along the banks of the river pulling the ship at a painfully slow pace. So when you were traveling south, if you had the wind, you went with it. Often when you arrived at Luxor, with all its fabulous temples, if you had the wind—you sailed on by. You could stop on the way back when you had the current with you and didn't need the wind.

Bankes' Grand Tour would last from 1815–1819, a full four years. He visited Egypt twice, first, 1815–1816, before going on to the Holy Land. And then he returned to Egypt in 1818 for a second look.

The highlight of the first trip was visiting the then extremely remote temple of Abu Simbel in Nubia. It had only recently been discovered by a Westerner, John Lewis Burckhardt, a Swiss scholar and adventurer who traveled the Middle East dressed as an Arab. Several years earlier Burckhardt had discovered the huge rock-cut temple but was unable to enter it because the entrance was buried in tons of sand. He told Bankes about it, and Bankes was determined to see it.

The trip to Abu Simbel was difficult and involved changing boats at the first cataract and then continuing on via boat and camels to the uncharted temple. William was amazed by the temple and knowing that he was perhaps the first Englishman to see it—inspired him even more.

He desperately wanted to enter, but the mounds of sand covering the entrance were too large to move with his small crew.

Bankes was more than just an adventurer, however. He was a serious student of antiquity. He made sketches and vowed to return, and he did. The return is where he makes a major contribution to decipherment, but I'll save that story for next time. For now, let me outline his two other important contributions to cracking the code.

When Bankes reached Philae, the beautiful temple built on an island in the Nile, he fell in love with the place. Philae was built over a period of three centuries during the Greco-Roman Period, when Egypt was ruled by Greeks and then the Romans. Each Ptolemy or Roman emperor added his part to Philae. So it wasn't planned as a unit, it just growed. What's remarkable, given the way it was built—piece-by-piece—is its overall beauty. It is definitely special and has been called the "Jewel of the Nile.

For every traveler going up the Nile in the 19th century, Philae was a must see. The monument bears the marks of these travelers, who often inscribed their arrival on the temple's walls.

A kiosk, built by the Emperor Trajan, is covered with these early travelers' graffiti.

Even military expeditions, returning from the Sudan, felt the place was sacred and left memorials to their dead carved on the ancient walls.

Banks visited Philae well before most of these travelers and probably had the place to himself when he stopped there on his Grand Tour. And he, too, knew it was a special place. But the Philae that Bankes visited is not the Philae that tourists visit today. When a dam was built at Aswan at the beginning of the last century, Philae was periodically flooded by the higher Nile waters held back behind the dam. Later in the century, when the dam was raised even higher, Philae was going to be completely flooded. So UNESCO organized a rescue operation. Philae was dismantled block by block and moved a half a mile away to a higher island, where it was reassembled. So when, we, modern tourists see it, it's not where Bankes saw it. And there's another important difference.

Banks decided he had to have something from Philae for his estate back in England. There was a 20-foot-tall inscribed obelisk still resting on its original pedestal, and Bankes made arrangements with Giovanni Belzoni, an Italian strongman who was making his living by excavating, finding sculptures, and selling them back in Europe. Belzoni agreed to ship both the pedestal and the obelisk to England for him.

When Banks returned from his Grand Tour, he erected the obelisk on its pedestal on his estate, where it can be seen today. So modern tourists in Egypt only see a poor quality concrete replica of the obelisk, and most just walk by it without knowing what it is or the part that its original played in the decipherment of hieroglyphs.

The important thing is that the base of the original obelisk has a Greek inscription while the obelisk is in hieroglyphs. Like the Rosetta Stone, it's bilingual—Greek and Egyptian. Bankes could read the Greek, which bore the names of Ptolemy and Cleopatra. Ptolemy had already been deciphered, so Bankes correctly deduced the other cartouche must be Cleopatra. He sent his copy of the inscription to Thomas Young, who was looking at the hieroglyphs was able to confirm his earlier findings and also add some new letters of the alphabet.

Let's look closely at the cartouche. It starts with the hill *q*, which is close to the /k/ sound. And since Cleopatra starts with a /k/ sound, Young added that hieroglyph to his alphabet as a /k/ sound. He was right; the Greeks were using the hill as a *k*. Remember, Cleopatra is spelled with a kappa in Greek.

The next letter, a lion, must be an *l*, and this confirmed that letter in Ptolemy's name was that. So Young was both adding new letters and confirming letters he had already surmised from Ptolemy's name.

The reed leaf and the rope—he had already new from Ptolemy's name. Also, he confirmed these. The vulture, the *a*, doesn't appear in Ptolemy. So Young had a new letter to add to his alphabet, concluding it had to be an *a*.

Now, the hand hieroglyph, the /d/ sound, gave him a bit of a puzzle, but he figured it out. Its position corresponds to the *t* in Cleopatra's name. But

Ptolemy also had a *t* in his name, and it wasn't the hand—it was the loaf hieroglyph.

◠

Young figured the two hieroglyphs had pretty much the same sound, and he was right with respect to the Greek pronunciation of Cleopatra—Kleopadra. Later, he would see it in other cartouches of Cleopatra's name and was often spelled with a loaf *t*.

The mouth *r* doesn't appear in Ptolemy's name, so Young had a new arrow in his quiver, the letter *r*. Imagine how elated he must have been as he added more and more letters to his alphabet. He owed William Bankes big time.

Young even realized that the last two hieroglyphs—the egg and the loaf *t*—had no phonetic value there, but were determinatives for female queens, goddesses, and even princesses. Real progress was being made.

So the bilingual obelisk and its pedestal were very important in extending the Egyptian alphabet. Still, they couldn't translate yet. Thomas Young was merely filling in the sounds. But this wasn't Bankes' only contribution to decipherment. Remember, I said he made three. His second was at the Temple of Abydos.

Today, the Temple of Abydos is visited by millions of tourists each year, but when Bankes found it, it was filled in with sand. We must also remember that hieroglyphs hadn't been translated yet, so no one knew who had built Abu Simbel or Abydos Temple. It was all a mystery.

Abydos is a very special temple, for several reasons. First, it's dedicated primarily to Osiris, but also six other gods. According to Egyptian mythology, Osiris, the God of the Dead, was buried at Abydos, so every Egyptian wanted to make a pilgrimage to Abydos to place an offering at Osiris's grave—so they, too, would be resurrected.

Bankes had the sand that choked the rooms inside the temple cleared and made an incredible discovery. He discovered a Hall of the Ancients. When pharaohs built a temple, they often listed all the pharaohs before them to show what a long lineage they had. This is the Hall of the Ancients, with the longest list of pharaohs ever discovered and in near perfect condition.

Abydos was built by Seti I, the father of Ramses II—Ramses the Great. And in the Hall of the Ancients, you can see Seti with young Ramses, reading the names of all the kings.

Young Ramses, with his side-lock of youth, is holding a papyrus scroll. They're performing a religious ritual that will ensure that their ancestors have what they need in the next world. They're reading a prayer called the *Hotep-di-nesu* in ancient Egyptian—and by the end of this course, you'll be able to read it, just as young Ramses did. By reading this prayer, Seti and Ramses are making sure that the deceased kings will have food and drink, cattle, geese, fine oils—everything that their ancestors would need in the next world. There's an ancient Egyptian saying that "To say the name of the dead is to make him live again." So just by reading the names of their ancestors, the king, and the prince were giving them life.

When Bankes discovered this kings list, he understood it was important and made a very accurate copy of it to bring back to England for Thomas Young. This provided many more names for Young, so even more letters of the alphabet could be deduced.

At this point in time, Frenchman Jean-François Champollion enters the picture, intending to beat the Englishman to the decipherment of hieroglyphs. Champollion was only 9 years old when the Rosetta Stone was discovered, but even then he was a recognized prodigy of languages. By the time he was 11, he knew Latin and Greek and soon went on to add Hebrew and Arabic to the list of languages he mastered.

Joseph Fourier, one of Napoleon's savants in Egypt, heard about this young genius and invited him to his home. He showed Champollion the artifacts he had brought back from Egypt and explained that no one could yet read the hieroglyphs. Champollion vowed—he would become the first.

Now, 10 years later, Champollion and Young were in a race to decipher hieroglyphs, but neither could translate yet. Once again, Bankes would provide the key. But that's for our next lecture. For now, it is enough to credit Bankes with copying the kings list at Abydos and also for bringing back the bilingual pedestal and obelisk with Cleopatra's name.

It's hard for us today to appreciate just how important the contributions of men like Bankes, Young, and Champollion were to our view of civilization. What they did goes far beyond Egyptology and the decipherment of hieroglyphs. It affects our whole worldview. When Bankes was clearing the sand from Abydos temple, back in London, no one really knew how old Egypt was. Remember, the Dendera Zodiac caused a tremendous controversy because it suggested Egypt was more than 2,000 years old. Everyone in Europe was convinced that Greece was the source of civilization.

Once the hieroglyphs were deciphered, and the Egyptian records could be read, the question had to be raised, "Could Egypt be the source of civilization?" There was tremendous resistance to this idea. Late into the 19th century, classicists were still claiming that Greece was where it all started. I find this incredible. It goes against all the evidence, and I don't just mean the Egyptian records.

Of all people, classicists had access to what the Greeks had said about Egypt. Herodotus said Greece learned how to build in stone from the Egyptians. He was honored to acknowledge that Greek gods were derived from the much older Egyptian pantheon. He recounted how he was shocked by how far back Egyptians could trace their ancestors. There's even a Greek account of how Athens sent a delegation to Egypt for their advice about how to make the Olympic Games fair for the foreigners who competed. Greeks were bowing to Egyptian wisdom.

Everything the ancient Greeks said about Egypt was being ignored by the classicists. After all, what do they know? They're Greeks. It's nuts. Why the resistance?

I think they couldn't accept the idea that an African civilization could've been so advanced thousands of years before Europe had writing. It was racism. Think about what they would be forced to admit. Because the Egyptian language could now be read—thanks to Bankes, Young, Champollion et al—it was becoming clear that Egypt produced masterpieces of art thousands of years before Europe had Christianity. Worse, it was a good bet that monotheism, a concept basic to Western civilization, was first voiced in Egypt. The early contributions of the decipherers went far beyond Egyptology. They shook up the whole Eurocentric view of civilization.

Today, Western civilization's debt to Egypt is well known and acknowledged, but it was a long rocky road. In 1954, a book titled *Stolen Legacy* by George James attempted to point out our debt to Egypt, but it was tragically flawed and scholars attacked it. The claims were overstated, and the scholarship was nearly nonexistent. It's hard to imagine what Egyptian text the author could have been thinking of when he said, "The Greeks were not the authors of Greek philosophy, but the Black people of North Africa, the Egyptians." Pure nonsense. There were no Egyptian philosophical texts. That's one thing we didn't get from Egypt.

In 1987, a far more serious book on the subject appeared, *Black Athena* by Martin Bernal. Here was a real Cambridge scholar who was pointing out the 19th-century racism that refused to credit Egypt with her accomplishments. So far, so good. But the road is still rocky. You see, Bernal's expertise was Chinese political philosophy and because he was writing on a subject outside his filed of expertise—he made errors and overstated his case. This book, too, was widely criticized by my Egyptologist colleagues, but I still think it is worth reading. Look it up, and I think you'll enjoy it.

Perhaps part of the reason for the extremely strong criticisms it received is its title. *Black Athena* correctly suggests Greek religion owed a debt to Egypt, but it raises the question of whether are Egyptians are a black civilization, whatever that may mean. Interestingly, Bernal never discusses this in the book, so why the incendiary title? Years ago I asked him, and he said, "It was my publisher's idea." It may have sold more books and certainly got a lot of press, but I don't think it helped the case.

Still, I think much of the early decipherers have changed our worldview. It's more than just reviving a language.

OK, now it's time for scribe's robes, pens, and ink. We're going to do some hieroglyphs.

Last time, I gave you four sentences to translate. Let's see how you did.

Our first sentence was: "Ptah goes down in another boat." OK, what's our first word?

Yes, *ha,* "to go down" because it's a verb and the verb comes first.

𓉐𓅐𓂻

Next? Yes, *Ptah*, the subject. Good.

𓉐𓅐𓂻𓏭𓏤

"In" is next, and that's our owl *m*.

𓉐𓅐𓂻𓏭𓅐

Now, for "another," we must decide whether to use the masculine or the feminine form. What's "boat"? Clearly, it's feminine because it ends in a *t*. So we use *ket*, the feminine form of "another." And that goes before the noun, so we can add it now to our sentence.

𓅐𓂻𓏭𓅐𓏏

Now, we just add "boat," and we have it.

𓅐𓂻𓏭𓅐𓏏𓊛

"Ptah goes down in another boat." *Ha Ptah em ket depet.* Good.

Next, we had: "(When) this man fares downstream, the city is in joy."

Remember, the "when" is understood, not written, so we start with a verb again. Yes, *khed*, "to fare downstream."

Notice the position of the boat determinative; it's not on the bottom of the line. It's in the middle. Often if a low horizontal hieroglyph, like the boat, was by itself, the scribe might write it in the middle of the line because it looks better than at the bottom. We'll see it both ways. I want you to remember to always be flexible.

OK, we have "to fare downstream." Now we need "this man." Again, we have to decide, masculine "this" or feminine. No problem here with "man," clearly masculine. So we use *pen*, and since it follows a noun—we add it after the "man." Good.

Now, we have a compound sentence, one with two verbs and two subjects. For the second half, the verb is "is"—in hieroglyphs *yew*, the reed leaf, and the quail chick.

This verb could sometimes be omitted. The ancient Egyptians often left off the verb when it was at *yew*. Either way is correct. I just want you to remember again—be flexible.

Next, we have "city," the subject—pronounced *niwit*.

So now we need "in joy." Well, the owl *m* is the "in."

And "joy" is our strange word with a double determinative. Remember? *Reshwet*.

So that's our second sentence: "When this man fares downstream, the city is in joy." It may have sounded something like *Khed z pen yew niwit em reshwet*. It's a long sentence, but you did it. Good.

Next, we have to translate. "This woman listens to Ptah."

Well, we know we start with our verb, which is *sedjem*.

Then we add "this woman."

Note, that I've omitted the bolt *z* and the *t* in "woman." Often it's written in this simple form. We know "this" is feminine and follows the noun, so we add *zet ten*.

Now, we need the "to," and here we have a decision to make—which "to" do we use? There's the mouth hieroglyph the *r* "to" for things—like "to the boat." Well, Ptah is not a thing, he's a person—actually a god—but you know what I mean. So we use the water hieroglyph for "to."

Last, we just add *Ptah,* and we have it. Well done.

Now, for our last sentence, "A man is there in the city." We start with our verb, "is."

Next, we add "man."

For "there in" we can use our reed leaf and owl from our earlier vocabulary lesson.

We don't have a word for "the" in ancient Egyptian, so we just add city, *niwit*. And we're done.

Yew z m niwit. Good!

Now, let me add just a few more vocabulary words, and then you'll be ready for some really interesting sentences.

As usual, I'll give you the word, and you tell me how it's pronounced.

Pronounce it. Yes, *heru*. The determinative at the end tells us it has something to do with the sun or time. The word means "day."

Here's another.

Pronounced? *Gereh*, yes. Remember, the twisted flax hieroglyph is an *h*. The word means "night." The determinative is a bolt of lightning coming out of the sky. We have "day," and we have "night," so let's do another related word.

Pronounced? Sound it out. Yeah, something like *yeah*. The determinative is the phases of the moon, and the word means "moon."

Our next word has two determinatives.

First, pronounce it, then we'll figure out what it means. Yes, *nedjes. Nedjes.*
The first determinative, the small bird, usually determines things that are
small or bad. With the man hieroglyph at the end, we know it's a person.
The word means "commoner." Who, in a social sense, is a small person.
The word also means "poor man," so it wasn't so good to be a commoner.

]

Now for a couple of ideograms.

You can't tell me how it sounds because it's an ideogram; it doesn't have
any of our letters of the alphabet. I'll tell you how it's pronounced—*sesh.*
Can you figure out what it means? It's obviously a man of some kind from
the last determinative in the word.

The key is the other ideogram. It's writing implements. The rectangle that
looks like a traffic light is a scribe's palette. The two circles are the red and
black inks. It's solid, like Chinese ink. In the middle may be a little pot of
water. You dip your brush—that's what's on the right side—in the water,
touch the ink, and then you write. So a man with writing implements is a
scribe. That's our word for "scribe."

This is a real scribe's palette. It wasn't just a tool for writing. When you
walked by holding your scribe's palette, you showed the world you were
somebody! Being a scribe was the way you moved up in Egyptian society.
First, you learned to write; then you got a job—perhaps as a lowly temple
scribe—keeping track of temple inventory. Then if you were bright, you
might be noticed, move up to a higher position—perhaps even a royal
scribe associated with the pharaoh.

There's even an ancient Egyptian wisdom text called, "Be A Scribe." It exhorts the young student to be a scribe. In the military, you're always marching, and your feet hurt. Construction workers are always injured. Tanners smell terrible, but the scribe wears white linen and always has a good meal. So, be a scribe. We'll look at the text carefully in a later lecture. It's wonderful.

Let me show you another ideogram.

Again, you can't tell me how it was pronounced because there are no alphabetic signs, but I'll tell you—*akhet*. The ideogram is a sun, rising or setting, in a notch in the mountain. The word means "horizon." Ideograms of words that are feminine have the loaf *t* at the end, so we know it's feminine.

For many ideograms, we know how they were pronounced from Coptic, which is the late form of Egyptian language. You'll hear a lot more about that in our next installment of the story of the decipherment of hieroglyphs.

Two more words that are ideograms, and then we'll leave our vocabulary for today.

You might be able to figure out how this one was pronounced. The rectangle is one of the alphabetic signs, remember? Yes, it's /sh/. So the word might be pronounced something like *she*. The little sign next to the ideogram stroke is probably an irrigation channel. It feeds a lake or pool. And that's what our word means, "lake" or "pool."

Here's our last word.

It was pronounced *ta*, and it means "land." The thin oval is a spit of land, and the three dots means it comes in chunks—like clumps of dirt. The other sign is probably an irrigation canal. We know it's masculine because it doesn't have a loaf *t*.

So, for homework, let's translate three sentences.

First, "The moon rises in the sky."

Next, "The scribe is silent day and night."

And last, "This poor man knows a plan."

Next time, we'll check our homework, complete the story of the decipherment of hieroglyphs, and we will also learn biliterals—hieroglyphs that represent two sounds. I'll see you then.

Jean-François Champollion Cracks the Code

When the Rosetta Stone was discovered, everyone thought the code would be cracked quickly, but it wasn't. It took more than 20 years before someone would finally be able to read the ancient Egyptian inscription. Everyone had been making the Big Mistake, assuming that the language was primarily ideographic. Even as Thomas Young and the French historian Jean-François Champollion were figuring out the alphabet, they both made that mistake. Today we will see how Champollion made the big breakthrough and became the first man in 2,000 years to read hieroglyphs.

The Competition

- Champollion and Young competed to be the first to decipher hieroglyphs. But this was more than just a matter of academics. France and England were at war. William Bankes, an Englishman, gave Young, another Englishman, the inscription on his obelisk and the king's list from Abydos. Young shared information with Champollion.

- Champollion, however, denied that Young was the first to figure out an alphabet. In 1822 Champollion published his *Lettre à M. Dacier*, which proclaimed that he had cracked the code and could read hieroglyphs.

- Around the time that Champollion was wrongly claiming he could translate ancient Egyptian, his friend, Jean-Nicolas Huyot, visited him. Huyot was a member of the team that Bankes had hired to copy inscriptions in Egypt and was there on Bankes's second visit to Abu Simbel.

- Huyot showed Champollion his drawings of Abu Simbel. Inside one of the cartouches he had copied were four hieroglyphs: ⊙𝕞𝕝𝕝. This was where Champollion's knowledge of Coptic became crucial.

- He saw the circle and figured it was the sun, but he also knows that the Coptic word for sun is *ra*. Now he was left with three hieroglyphs to decipher. From his alphabet he also knew that the last two hieroglyphs were *s*. So, he had Ra__ss. Champollion also knew from classical sources that there was a King Ramses, so he guessed that the unknown sign was an *m*. He was very close. The unknown sign is really an *ms* biliteral, but still, he has the name correct: Ramses.

- Huyot had his drawings from other sites as well, and he showed Champollion another cartouche: (🐦 𝕞𝕝𝕝).

- It was known that the ibis represented the god Toth. With the other hieroglyphs he came up with Tothmosis, another king's name known from the classical writers. But this wasn't the breakthrough.

- The breakthrough was when Champollion realized that *mss* is very much like the Coptic word for birth, *mise*. Now the names of Ramses and Tothmosis didn't just have phonetic value. They meant something: "Ra is born" and "Toth is born." The phonemes spell out words with meanings; hieroglyphs weren't just ideographic. The Big Mistake was over.

- Champollion rushed over to his brother's house, announced his achievement, and fainted. He was so overcome and exhausted that he remained in bed for five days. When he finally got out of bed and resumes work, Champollion started reading out loud all the words he had on the Rosetta Stone and listened for Coptic matches.

- Soon he had dozens and dozens of words; he really could translate hieroglyphs. It was all due to Bankes's taking draftsmen with him to the temple and tombs of Egypt to copy inscriptions.

- Champollion published his findings in 1824 in his *Précis du système hiéroglyphique des anciens Égyptiens* and never credited Young, who was always a gentleman in the race to decipher. Even Champollion's teacher and mentor, Silvestre de Sacy, warned Young early on that Champollion would try to claim all the credit.

- When Young published his findings in 1823, he did so under the title *An Account of Some Recent Discoveries in Hieroglyphical Literature and Egyptian Antiquities: Including the Author's Original Alphabet, as Extended by Mr. Champollion.*

- In any case, thanks to Young and Champollion, we could learn the ancient Egyptian language.

Biliterals

- Biliterals are signs that represent two sounds, one after the other. Biliterals are difficult to remember because there are so many of them.

- To make them easier to remember, we organize them into groups that end with the same sound. In this lecture, you'll learn biliterals that end in the sound /a/. Don't try to memorize them. You will learn them when you see them in words and also by writing them.

Birds

- is the *ba* biliteral. His most distinctive feature is the leash around his neck, but he also has a long beak. In the entry after next, you will see a similar bird, a pin-tailed duck. You can write the *ba* bird the same way and then just add the leash and long bill.

- is the *pa* bird; he represents /p/ and /a/ together. To draw him, start with the head. Then extend the body. Next, add more body and a tail, then a wing. Finish with the second wing and feet.

- is the *sa* bird, a pin-tailed duck. He's also the word for "son." This hieroglyph frequently appears because one of the pharaoh's names was always preceded by *Sa Re*, meaning "Son of the sun god Re." In hieroglyphs, that's 🦆, with the sun determinative for the god Re.

- 🦆 is the *tcha* bird. His distinctive feature is that he looks like he is coming in for a landing on the water. He's actually a duckling. To draw him, start with the head and lower body. Next, complete the little wings and body. Finally, give him some feet. Note that while this may look like a triliteral at first, the *tch* is only one sound, made by expelling air once through your teeth while the tip of your tongue is touching the roof of your mouth.

Other Biliterals

- ⚘ is *kha*, a lotus plant. When it stands alone, it is the hieroglyph for 1,000. The 6,000 captives on the Narmer Palette had six papyrus plants to indicate 6,000. The papyrus plant later evolved into the lotus plant.

- ⚒ is *dja* and is a bow fire drill. Using a bow, you rapidly turn the obelisk-shaped piece of wood in a smaller block of wood. The friction generates enough heat to start a fire.

- ⚊ is pronounced *eha* and is a wooden column. It's also used vertically.

- ⚘ is pronounced *ha* and is plants.

Body and Soul

- ⊔ looks like a modern field-goal sign. It is pronounced *ka* and is the word for "soul." There were several aspects to the soul, and the *ka* was something like a double for the body. The wealthy Egyptians even had *ka*-statues so that if something happened to their actual body, the statue could take the place of the body.

- But just having your *ka* in the next world wasn't enough for immortality. You, as a person, were composed of several elements. A crucial part was your *ba*. This was your personality. Often papyri showed the deceased as having the body of a bird and the head of a person. That's the *ba*. Sometimes it is spelled out with the *ba*-bird biliteral.

More Biliterals

*   ⟋ is the *ma* biliteral, and it is a sickle. There were several ways of writing the word for "truth," and most involved the *ma* biliteral. A common one was ⟋⟋. The long thin rectangle is the base on which a statue stood, and is another way of writing an *m*. It's equivalent to an owl. The arm is usually an *eh* sound, but the word for "truth" is usually transliterated as *maat*. We can see the loaf *t* at the end.

Ka-statue of King Hor

*   ⟋⟋ is of plants growing in a field, and is pronounced *sha*.

*   ⟋ is pronounced *ta*, and we think the hieroglyph depicts a potter's kiln, but we're not sure about this one.

*   ⟋ is a rope with a loop, and is pronounced *wa*. By Greek times it was used as the letter *o*.

Learning Biliteral Words

*   ⟋⟋⟋ is a good biliteral-using word to start with. The sickle is pronounced *ma* and has a phonetic complement, a silent vulture. But there are two vultures. That means the word is pronounced

maa. The eye determinative shows us that it has something to do with seeing. Indeed, it is the verb "to see."

- To help you learn the biliterals, make a chart of them. For now, we only have the *a*-family, so take a sheet of paper and write A on the top with a vulture next to it since that's /a/.

- Below that, draw the biliterals in alphabetical order with their sounds written next to them. The only exception to the alphabetical order is that it might be a good idea to write the four birds in the *a*-family together. They will be easier to remember that way.

- Our new word, *maa*, "to see," will go on the M-page, along with our owl and other words beginning with /m/. Our word "to remember," *sekha*, will go on the S-page. This will help us to learn how to write the biliterals and also to remember their sounds.

More Biliteral Words

- has the *ba* bird, with no phonetic complements, followed by the basket *k*. This word is *bak*. The man determinative tells us it is a person. The word means "manservant."

- is the word "maidservant," pronounced *baket*.

- means "vizier" and can also be written . In the first version, we have the *tcha* biliteral and a *t*, so it looks like *tchat*. But it is also sometimes written with a double reed, as in the latter version. That has a /y/ sound, so we usually say *tchaty*. In ancient Egypt, the vizier was the second-highest official in Egypt after the pharaoh.

- is pronounced *kha*. The word means "office" or "hall."

- is pronounced *dja*. Given the boat determinative, it obviously has something to do with boats. It's the verb to "ferry across," or just "cross."

- ⟨hieroglyphs⟩ is pronounced *wat*. The vulture is once again a silent phonetic complement. The word means "road." Often this word is simply written as an ideogram: ⟨hieroglyph⟩.

- ⟨hieroglyphs⟩ is pronounced *niwit* and means "city."

- ⟨hieroglyphs⟩ is pronounced *sa* and means "son." It's an idiom because we don't know why there's a stroke.

- ⟨hieroglyphs⟩ is the word for "daughter" and is pronounced *sat*.

- ⟨hieroglyphs⟩ is pronounced *eha* and means "donkey." The phallus is there to show us it's a donkey instead of a sterile mule.

- ⟨hieroglyphs⟩ is pronounced *seshta*. It's the word for "secret."

Lecture 6's Homework Answers

1. "The moon rises in the sky" translates to ⟨hieroglyphs⟩, pronounced *Weben yeah em pet*. To get there, just start with the verb (⟨hieroglyphs⟩ or *weben*), then add the symbol for the moon, then the owl for "in," and the word for "sky," *pet*.

2. To translate "The scribe is silent day and night," we start with the verb, *ger*. ⟨hieroglyphs⟩. The subject is "scribe," or *sesh*. Adding that gives us ⟨hieroglyphs⟩. Then we need "day" and "night," but there is no conjunction in Middle Egyptian, so we just add the two nouns, giving us ⟨hieroglyphs⟩. That's pronounced *Ger sesh haru gereh*.

3. "This poor man knows a plan." We start with the verb, *rekh*, then add the subject ("poor man"), *nedjes*. That gives us ⟨hieroglyphs⟩, to which we add "this," the masculine *pen*. And "plan" is *sekher*. Our end product is ⟨hieroglyphs⟩, or *Rekh nedjes pen sekher*.

1. Translate, "The maidservant knows the secret."

2. Translate, "The vizier is in the office."

3. Translate, "The donkey is in the road."

4. Translate, "The daughter ferries across in the boat."

Jean-François Champollion Cracks the Code

Welcome back. The road to the decipherment of hieroglyphs was not a short one. When the Rosetta Stone was discovered, everyone thought the code would be cracked quickly, but it wasn't. It took more than 20 years till someone could finally read an ancient Egyptian inscription. Everyone had been making the "Big Mistake"—assuming that the language was primarily ideographic, picture writing. Even as Thomas Young and Jean-François Champollion were figuring out the alphabet, they both made that mistake. Today we'll see how Champollion made the big breakthrough and became the first man in 2,000 years to read hieroglyphs.

As you'll remember, Champollion and Young were competing to be the first to decipher hieroglyphs. But this was more than a matter of academics. France and England were at war. William Bankes, an Englishman, gave Young, another Englishman, the inscription on his obelisk, and also the Kings List from Abydos. Young, a gentleman, shared the information with Champollion. Champollion, however, was far more selfish and even denied that Young was the first to figure out an alphabet.

In 1822 Champollion published his *Lettre à M. Dacier*, which proclaimed that he had cracked the code and could read hieroglyphs—Dacier was the Secretary of the Academy of Inscriptions and Literature. In it, Champollion claimed to be able to translate. The truth is, he couldn't. He had taken the alphabet further than Young, figured out the names of more kings, but like Young, he still believed that hieroglyphs are ideographic, and he really didn't understand how the language works. In his *Lettre*, he didn't acknowledge Young's contribution to the endeavor, and he never would.

Around the time that Champollion was wrongly claiming he could translate ancient Egyptian, his friend, Jean Nicolas Huyot visited him. This will be crucial. Huyot was a member of the team that Bankes hired to copy inscriptions in Egypt. When Bankes returned to Abu Simbel for the second time in 1819, he intended to hire enough men to clear the sand and enter the temple. He was disappointed to discover that Belzoni had beaten him to that honor, but there was still plenty of glory left for Bankes.

Unlike Belzoni, Bankes was a scholar at heart, interested in information more than treasure, so Bankes brought with him a team of artists and architects to help copy the inscriptions in the temple. Remember, this is before tourism; there were no restaurants, not even villages nearby. Bankes brought a provisions ship with chickens, goats, and all the food they would need. There was no light inside the deep rock-cut temple, so they gathered palm fronds and attached dozens of candles to them so they could copy the inscriptions. Bankes and his team spent weeks copying the inscriptions and scenes of Ramses at the Battle of Kadesh that covered the walls of Abu Simbel. But they didn't know it was Ramses. No one could translate hieroglyphs yet, but that would soon change.

Huyot showed Champollion his drawings of Abu Simbel. Inside one of the cartouches he had copied are four important hieroglyphs.

Now this is where Champollion's knowledge of Coptic becomes crucial. He sees the circle and figures out it's the sun, but he also knows that the Coptic word for sun is *ra*. Now he is left with three hieroglyphs to decipher. From his alphabet, he also knows that the last two hieroglyphs are *s*. So, he has *Ra__ss*. Champollion also knows from classical sources that there was a king Ramses, so he guesses that the unknown sign is an *m*. He's very close. The unknown sign is really a *ms* biliteral, but still, he has the name correct, Ramses.

Huyot has his drawings from other sites as well, and he shows Champollion another cartouche.

(𓅓𓏤𓏠𓊪𓊪)

It was known that the ibis represented the god Toth, and with the other hieroglyphs he comes up with Tothmosis, another king's name known from the classical writers. But this isn't the breakthrough yet.

So far he just has another name figured out. The breakthrough is when Champollion realizes that *mss* is very much like the Coptic word for birth, *mise*. Now the names of Ramses and Tothmosis don't just have phonetic value, they mean something—"Ra is born," "Toth is born." The phonemes spell out words with meanings—hieroglyphs aren't just ideographic. The "Big Mistake" is over.

Champollion rushes over to his brother's house and announces, "I've done it!" and faints. He is so overcome and exhausted that he remains in bed for five days. When he finally gets out of bed and resumes work, Champollion starts reading out loud all the words he has on the Rosetta Stone and listens for Coptic matches. Soon he has dozens and dozens of words; now he really can translate hieroglyphs. It's all due to Bankes' taking draftsmen with him to the temple and tombs of Egypt to copy inscriptions that can be now read.

Champollion published his findings in 1824 in his *Précis du système hiéroglyphique des anciens Égyptiens* and never credited Young, who was always a gentleman in the race to decipher. Even Champollion's teacher and mentor, Silvestre de Sacy, warned Young early on that Champollion would try to claim all the credit. So when Young published his findings in 1823, he did so under the title *An Account of Some Recent Discoveries in Hieroglyphical Literature and Egyptian Antiquities. Including the Author's Original Alphabet, as Extended by Mr. Champollion.*

With Champollion's breakthrough, the world now knew that Ramses the Great built the temple of Abu Simbel and that not all hieroglyphic inscriptions were religious, mystical texts. Sometimes hieroglyphs were telling about a battle; sometimes they were a mere boast of a long dead pharaoh of having built a temple. And Athanasius Kircher's fantasy translations of the obelisks of Rome were revealed to be just that, pure fantasy.

Still, not everyone was convinced that Champollion had really cracked the code. For nearly 10 years there were still some scholars who were holdouts and refused to accept Champollion's system of translation. In the end, though, everyone had to agree. The evidence was just too great.

Thanks to Young and Champollion, we can learn the ancient Egyptian language. So get your scribal pens and ink ready. We still have some hieroglyph work to do.

We should begin by translating the homework sentences. First was, "The moon rises in the sky." Well, we know we start with the verb. We had this verb in our very first hieroglyphic sentence: *weben re m pet.* "The sun is shining (rising) in the sky." So, we start with *weben.*

Next, we need the moon. That's *yeah.*

Our word for "in" is the owl. So we add that.

Now all we need is the word for "sky," *pet.*

"The moon rises in the sky." *Weben yeah m pet.* And that's our first sentence.

My guess is that this is now becoming easy for you. If you've been doing your homework, you remember most of the vocabulary words and don't have to look everything up. You know the verb comes first, and you know how to group the signs. I'm going slowly because I don't want anyone to get lost.

Let's do the next sentence: "The scribe is silent day and night." First the verb.

Ger, "to be silent," with the hand to the mouth determinative.

Add the subject, the "scribe." That's sesh.

Next, we need "day," which is haru.

There's no conjunction "and" in Middle Egyptian so we just add "night." Our word heneh, "together with," really won't do it. We don't want to say, "The scribe is silent day together with the night." That doesn't work, so we just put "day" and "night" together.

"The scribe is silent day and night." Ger sesh haru gereh. And that's it. Sometimes they would add the owl m before "day and night" so it would read "by day and by night." Remember there are no formal written rules of grammar yet.

Last homework sentence. "This poor man knows a plan." Verb first. Rekh, "to know."

Next our subject, the "poor man." *Nedjes* is "poor man."

𓏏𓌷𓀀𓀀𓀀

Now we add "this." *Pen* because it's masculine.

𓏏𓌷𓀀𓀀𓀀𓏤

Plan is *sekher*.

𓏏𓌷𓀀𓀀𓀀𓏤𓂻𓏏𓏤

And we've got it. "This poor man knows a plan." *Rekh nedjes pen sekher.*

Now I'd like to show you some biliterals, signs that represent two sounds, one after the other. When we talked about Champollion's breakthrough, his "Aha!" moment, we saw that the hieroglyph 𓌳—that looks like the McDonalds sign—was crucial. The sign represents animal skins drying on a rack, but it represents the sounds *m* and *s*, one after the other. Today I'd like to show you some more biliterals.

Biliterals are a little difficult to remember because there are so many of them. To make them easier, we organize them into groups that end with the same sound. Today we'll learn the *a*-family—biliterals that end in the sound *a*. So we'll see hieroglyphs that represent the sounds, *ba*, *ka*, *sa*, *ta*, *tcha*, and so on. Don't try to memorize them. You'll learn them when you see them in words and also by writing them.

There are four different birds in the *a*-family. Let's do them together in alphabetical order.

This is the *ba* biliteral. His most distinctive feature is what I call the leash around his neck, but he also has a long beak. In a minute I'll show you another, similar bird, a pin-tailed duck. I'm going to suggest that you write the *ba* bird the same way as the pin-tailed duck and then just add the leash and the long bill.

Let's first look at the *pa* hieroglyph. I'm taking them in alphabetical order.

I call him the *pa* bird because he represents the sounds *p* and *a* together. It's as if you wrote the rectangle *p* and the vulture *a* together. It's an important hieroglyph because it's used so often. Let me show you how to draw it. He's a flying duck. Start with the head. Then extend the body. Next, more body and a tail. Now a wing. Last, the second wing and feet. That's the *pa* bird. You have this one in our exercise book, along with the other difficult hieroglyphs to draw, so don't worry if you don't get it right now.

Here's the *sa* bird. He's a very important bird. As I said, he's a pin-tailed duck. Used a lot. He's also the word for "son." Remember when we talked about Horapollo's book on hieroglyphs and how he said that the duck represents the word "son" because they fight so fiercely for their offspring? He was right about the meaning but wrong about the reason.

The duck represents the sound *sa*, which was the ancient Egyptian word for "son." You will see this hieroglyph often because one of the pharaoh's names was always preceded by *Sa Re*. "Son of the sun god Re."

Notice that they just use the sun determinative for Re, the god. Everyone knew what it meant, so there was no need to write it out with the god determinative.

Let me show you how to draw the *sa* bird. Start with the head and body. Next add feet. Last, complete the top of the body and give him a wing and tail. He's the one that I said is similar enough to the *ba* bird that you can do some cosmetic changes and get away with it. Just add a leash and long bill for the *sa* hieroglyph and then you'll have the *ba* hieroglyph—it works.

Here's the *tcha* bird and his distinctive feature is that he looks like he's coming in for a landing on the water. He's actually a duckling. He too is important, but we'll see him often. Start with the head and lower body. Next, complete the little wings and body. Finally, give him some feet.

You may be thinking that the *tcha* bird looks like a triliteral. After all, if we wrote out the sound we would write *tcha,* and that looks like three sounds: *t*, *ch*, and an *a*. No, it is really only two sounds. The *tch* is only one sound; it may be spelled *tch,* but it's one sound. It's made by expelling air once through your teeth while the tip of your tongue is touching the roof of your mouth. Try it. *Tch.* In English, we need three letters to represent the one sound, but it is still just one sound. It's similar to our alphabetic pool hieroglyph for *sh*. We need two letters to represent it, the *s* and the *h,* but it's one sound—*sh*.

As we learn words that use these bird biliterals, you'll see just how wrong everyone was when they thought hieroglyphs were only ideographic. None of these bird hieroglyphs represent the concept of a bird. They are purely phonetic. This will be reinforced when we see biliterals are used in words. But let's complete the *a*-family.

Pronounced *kha*, this is a lotus plant. When it stands alone, it's often the hieroglyph for 1,000. Do you remember the 6,000 captives on the Narmer Palette, where there were six papyrus plants to indicate the 6,000? Well, this later evolved into the lotus plant.

Let me show you the *kha* biliteral in action, so you can see how biliterals are used in words; that's how you learn them.

This word was pronounced *sekha*. The *s* in front of the biliteral is our usual folded cloth *s*. Once you remember the next hieroglyph is the *kha* biliteral you realize that the *a*, the vulture after it is a phonetic complement. It helps you remember the biliteral's pronunciation. The hand to the mouth, that's a determinative that suggests the word has something to do with speech or thinking, and it does. The word means "to remember." So we would pronounce this word *sekha*.

Here's a curious-looking hieroglyph:

It's pronounced *dja* and is a bow fire drill. Using a bow, you rapidly turn the obelisk-shaped piece of wood in a smaller block of wood. The friction generates enough heat to start a fire.

This biliteral is pronounced *eha*. It's a wooden column. It's also used vertically; you'll see it upright.

Let's do another one.

It's pronounced *ha,* and it's obviously plants, but here we're only concerned about the sound, *ha*.

This one I call the field goal sign because it looks like the indication referees give in football games when a field goal is successfully completed. It is pronounced *ka*, and it's the word for "soul."

There were several aspects to a person, and the *ka* was a kind of double for the body. The wealthy Egyptians even had *ka*-statues in case something actually happened to their body, the statue could take the place of the body.

We'll talk a lot about this later when you learn to translate the prayers recited by *ka*-priests.

There is a fabulous wood statue of King Hor of the Middle Kingdom. It's in the Egyptian Museum in Cairo, and people always wonder what the arms are doing on his head. Well, now we know. It's a label for the gods, proclaiming that this is the *ka*-statue of King Hor.

But just having your *ka* in the next world wasn't enough for immortality. You, as a person, were composed of several elements, and you needed them all. A crucial part of you was your *ba*. This was your personality, what made you you. Often papyri showed the deceased as having the body of a bird and the head of a person. That's the *ba*. Sometimes it's spelled out with the *ba*-bird biliteral.

Let's try another biliteral.

This is the *ma* biliteral, and it's a sickle. It too is an important hieroglyph because it's part of the word for "true," and "truth" There were several ways of writing the word for "truth," and most involved the *ma* biliteral. Let me show you one common one.

The sickle is, of course, the *ma* biliteral. The long thin rectangle is the base on which a statue stood, and it's another way of writing an *m*, we remember that. It's equivalent to the owl. So that's a phonetic complement. The arm is usually an *eh* sound, but the word for truth is usually transliterated as *maat*. You can see the loaf *t* at the end. We'll soon see the sickle in another word, and it will become more and more familiar to you. Don't worry.

This hieroglyph is of plants growing in a field and is pronounced *sha*.

This one, pronounced *ta*, and we think the hieroglyph depicts a potter's kiln, but I'm not sure about this one.

Just one more biliteral, hang in there.

This one is a rope with a loop and is pronounced *wa*. From the names "Ptolemy" and "Cleopatra" you will remember that by Greek times it was used as the letter *o*.

There are a couple of others in the *a*-family of biliterals, but they're rarely used. We come across them when we're translating, we can learn them then.

Now for some words that use the biliterals. This is the way you'll learn them.

This is a good one to start with. It'll reinforce how biliterals are used in words. First, how would you pronounce it? Well, here's how you should be thinking. "I haven't seen that eye hieroglyph yet, I bet it's a determinative." —it is, even though it comes in the middle of the word, which is unusual. So we don't pronounce it. It'll just help indicate the meaning of the word.

Next important point to remember: biliterals often have phonetic complements—an alphabetic hieroglyph that helps you remember the biliteral's sound, but it's not pronounced, as in the word for "remember" that we just saw. We have that here. The sickle is pronounced *ma* and has a phonetic complement, a silent vulture. But there are two vultures. That means the word is pronounced *maa*. The sickle and the first vulture is *ma*, but when we add the second vulture, we get *maa*. The eye determinative shows us that it has something to do with seeing. Indeed, it's the verb, "to see."

To help you learn the biliterals, I suggest you make a chart of them. For now, we only have the a-family, so take a sheet of paper and write A on the top with a vulture next to it since that's the a sound. Then below, draw the biliterals in alphabetical order with their sounds written next to them. The only exception to the alphabetical order is that it might be a good to start with the first four birds in the a-family. They will be easier to remember that way—put the birds together. So you'll have ba, pa, sa, and tcha birds up top on the chart. Then complete the rest the of chart with the a-family in alphabetical order.

Also to help remember them, you'll be adding the vocabulary words that contain the biliterals to your dictionaries. All this will help them sink in. Don't feel overwhelmed—you'll get it.

Our new word, maa, "to see," will go on the M-page, along with our owl and other words beginning with the sound m. Our word "to remember," sekha, will go on the S-Page. This will help us to learn how to write the biliterals and also to remember their sounds.

Let's try another word with a biliteral.

Let's pronounce it. We have the ba bird, with no phonetic complements, followed by the basket k. So it is just bak, that's right. The man determinative tells us it is a person. The word means "manservant." We'll add this to our b-page in the dictionary.

What do you think the word for "maidservant" would be? Same as "manservant," but with the feminine t and female determinative.

It's pronounced baket. This word sometimes appears in royal names. For example, one of Akhenaten's daughters was named Baketaten—"servant of the Aten."

Pronounce this one.

We have the *tcha* biliteral and a *t*, so it looks like *tchat*. But it is also sometimes written with a double reed which has a *Y* sound, so we usually say *tchaty* for this word.

So even though it looks as if it's feminine, it isn't because it really ends in a double reed. The word means "vizier." In ancient Egypt, the vizier was like the prime minister. He was the second-highest official in Egypt after the pharaoh. Sometimes there were two viziers, one for Upper Egypt, and one for Lower Egypt.

How about this one?

This word's pronounced *kha*. The vulture is the silent phonetic complement. The determinative is a building with columns. The word means "office" or "hall."

This one is pronounced *dja*. Given the boat determinative, it obviously has something to do with boats. It's the verb to "ferry across," or just "cross."

And this word is pronounced *wat*. The vulture is once again a silent phonetic complement. The determinative is a road, perhaps with canals on the side, and the word means "road." Often this word is simply written as an ideogram; it's much simpler this way.

The *t* is under the ideogram to show that the word is feminine. It's like our word for "city," *niwit*. Remember?

Here's one we have talked about.

It's pronounces *sa* and means "son." It's an idiom because we don't know why there's a stroke, so we call it an ideogram.

Bet you can figure out the word for daughter. Yes, *sat*.

She doesn't have the stroke, perhaps because she needs the feminine *t* and they want the composition of the hieroglyphs to be pleasing, so the *t* is placed almost on the duck's back.

Here's an unusual one, and it's interesting. It has two determinatives. So our pronunciation all we have to do is sound out the wood column biliteral, *eha*. The donkey determinative tells us it means "donkey." Now, can you tell me why there's a phallus there? I think the clue is the difference between a donkey and a mule. Any farmers out there? A mule is the product of a male donkey and a female horse. Mules are always sterile. So the phallus shows us it's a donkey, which is non-sterile.

Another cool thing about this word. The ancient Egyptians loved onomatopoetic words—words that sound like what they are. For example, their word for "cat" was *miaw,* and their word for "donkey" was *eha*. I think it's onomatopoetic.

One last vocabulary word for today.

Let's pronounce it. *Seshta*. That's our potter's kiln *ta* with two phonetic complements, the *t* and the *a*. The papyrus scroll tells us it's something abstract, not seen. It's the word for "secret."

That's quite a bit to absorb for today. Let me give you a two-pronged homework assignment to help you remember all this. Don't worry, it'll come.

First, write a line of each of the biliterals we have learned today. Practice your hieroglyphic handwriting it will help you remember the sounds. You can follow the steps in our exercise book for the sequences of how to draw them. It's just what I showed you today. Also, start your biliteral list, with the signs you've learned today.

Finally, let me give you a few phrases or sentences to translate from English to hieroglyphs for next time. Again, it'll give you a chance to practice drawing our new biliterals.

First: "The maidservant knows the secret." Next: "The vizier is in the office." Third: "The donkey is in the road." And last: "The daughter ferries across in the boat."

That's it for now. I'll see you next time.

Suffix Pronouns and the Hieroglyphs of Ptah

This lecture marks a turning point in our course. We have completed the story of the decipherment of hieroglyphs. It is important to understand how the code was cracked, but from now on, we won't begin the lectures with background material and end with hieroglyphs. From here on, we'll start with hieroglyphs, and then at the end of the lecture we will apply what we have learned to art, civilization, religion, and so on.

Vocabulary

- We'll start this lecture by adding a few vocabulary words to our dictionary so we can translate more real texts.

- ⌒◻𓂋𓈙𓀁 has two determinatives, so the only thing we have to worry about are the first two alphabetic hieroglyphs, *r* and *sh*. It is pronounced *resh*, similar to *reshwet*, which is ⌒◻𓇋𓏏𓀁 and means "joy" or "gladness." The variant *resh* means "to rejoice" or "be glad." The double determinative shows that it involves emotions, which one can see on the face or express by speech.

- 𓆑◻𓀀 is an idiom. The horned viper hieroglyph is silent; the word is pronounced *it* and means "father."

- 𓆑◻𓊹𓈗 is pronounced *iteru*; the three water signs at the end form the determinative that shows it has something to do with water. It's the word for "river."

- 𓃟𓏏𓆚 is pronounced something like *mezeh*. Its determinative gives it away. It's the word for "crocodile."

- ⟨r⟩ has the ideogram stroke sign, so this is a picture of the concept. We know the *r* hieroglyph is a mouth, so the word means "mouth." It also means "utterance" or "spell," as in a magical spell. As you would expect, it is pronounced *r*.

- ⟨her⟩ is another ideogram; it means "face." It also means "sight." It is also the word for "upon," and can mean "concerning" and "with respect to." This one is pronounced *her* and is important because it has many uses.

Pronouns

- Now we're going to start a new grammar unit: pronouns, which stand in for a noun or noun phrase. In this lecture, we're going to focus on suffix pronouns, which are added at the ends of words. Unlike in English, the suffix pronouns are going to be the same for possession and in the nominative.

- ⟨hieroglyphs⟩ is a sentence with two pronouns. The man sign is the word for both "I" and "my." It is our first suffix pronoun.

- Now let's translate the sentence. The verb comes first, as it should, and *yew* is the word for "is." Next we have our suffix pronoun, the man sign attached to the verb, so we know it is not going to be possessive. This gives us "I am."

- The owl has several meanings, and we have to pick the right one. Let's look at the end of the sentence. The house hieroglyph is being used as an ideogram. The man hieroglyph attached to it is the possessive, since it is attached to a noun, so we have "my house."

- It looks as if the best meaning for the owl is "in," which gives us "I am in my house."

- The feminine version of the same statement uses the woman hieroglyph: ⟨hieroglyphs⟩. It's pronounced something like *Yew.i m per.i.*

- Because suffixes are technically part of the word they are attached to, we don't separate them in transliterations. We conjoin them to the word by means of a dot or period.

- "You" or "your" (masculine) is simply the basket *k*: ⌐.

- "You" or "your" (feminine) is the tethering ring *tch*: ⌐.

- If you wanted to say, "You speak," to a man, you would write ⌐ and the transliteration would be *Djed.k*. If you were talking to a woman, it would be ⌐, transliterated as *Djed.tch*.

- "He," "his," "it," or "its" is a horned viper: ⌐.

- "She," "her," or "it" is a folded cloth: ⌐.

Plural Suffix Pronouns

- The above section covers the singular suffix pronouns. Now let's look at the plural suffix pronouns.

- "We," "us," or "our" is the water sign with three strokes for plural: ⌐, pronounced *n*. Three strokes are used for plurals of all sorts. "We hear" would be ⌐, pronounced *Sedjem.n*.

- We don't have to worry about masculine or feminine in the plural. It is what we call *common*. One suffix pronoun fits all.

- For "you" or "your" plural we have the tethering ring, water sign, and three plural strokes beneath them, pronounced *tchen*: ⌐.

- Our last plural is for "they," "them," or "their." That's a folded cloth, water sign, and three strokes, pronounced *sn*: ⌐. "Their scribe" would be ⌐, pronounced *sesh.sen*.

- ⌐ is pronounced *tu*. This is the impersonal pronoun. It means "one," as in "One should always be kind."

Translating Sentences

- That's it for suffix pronouns. Now we need lots of practice translating so we learn them.

- ⬡𓊪𓁐𓏢𓏲𓈖 is pronounced *Resh sesh yew.n em per.f.* The first word is *resh*, "rejoice," and ends with the man with his hand to his mouth. The next word is *sesh* "scribe," which ends at the man determinative. Next is a very familiar verb, "to be," pronounced *yew.* Then we have a suffix pronoun pronounced *n* and meaning "we."

- Then we have an owl ("in" or "from"), a house, and a viper (pronounced *f* and meaning "his.") The full English translation is, "The scribe rejoices [when] we are in his house." *When* is bracketed because that's probably the meaning and the Egyptians didn't have the word *when*. It was understood.

Shabaka and Ptah

- Now for an excursion into ancient Egyptian religion, focusing on Ptah. Ptah is one of the gods intimately connected to writing and words. Ptah was viewed as a creator god. In one myth, Ptah is presented as the god who creates the world with words.

- We have only one copy of the text of this myth. It dates from the 25th dynasty, which extended from about 760 to 656 B.C. This was when the Nubians marched north and conquered Egypt. For years the Nubians had been under Egyptian rule, but now Egypt had been invaded several times by foreign powers and was weak, and the Nubians saw their chance.

- The Nubians didn't like the idea that Egypt controlled Nubia, but they also admired Egyptian civilization. So when the Nubian kings conquered Egypt, they didn't plunder.

- They built their own temples to honor Amun, Egypt's most powerful god during this period, and even copied old religious texts to preserve them. One of these ancient texts, relating to the god Ptah, is called the Shabaka Stone, after the Nubian king who had it copied.

- Today it is in the British Museum. It's shaped like a square and has a hole in the middle. It has an inscription in hieroglyphs all over it, but it is badly worn in the middle. It is sometimes called "The Philosophy of a Memphite Priest."

- The text starts with Shabaka saying, "I found the writings of the ancients damaged, and I restored it better than it was." What exactly does that mean?

- One possibility is that the old text was damaged, it had gaps, and Shabaka filled in the gaps. But the original text was likely on papyrus, so when Shabaka says he made it better, he could also mean that he is taking something that was written on papyrus and is carving it on stone. This was a pious act for Shabaka: He viewed the religious text as his heritage.

Ptah's Creation

- Ptah was the chief god of Memphis, one of Egypt's oldest cities. Egyptian gods usually came in threes: a husband, wife, and child. In Memphis, the triad was Ptah, Sekhmet the lioness, and their son Nefertum.

- The text on the Shabaka Stone describes the world's creation in three steps: First, Ptah thought it, and then he said it on his tongue, and finally, it became real.

- Atum was the traditional creator god of Egypt, who created all the other gods. The Shabaka Stone asserts the primacy of Ptah by saying, "There took shape in the heart [of Ptah], there took shape on the tongue [of Ptah] the form of Atum."

- Later, the text says, "Ptah the very great one gives [life] to the gods and their *ka*s through his heart and tongue."

- Ptah was a very popular god, and Egyptian names often included him. For example, Ptahhotep, 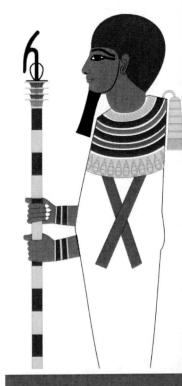 means "Ptah is pleased."

- Ptah is often depicted holding a scepter. In its simple form, the scepter is a *was* scepter. It has the head of a ram, representing the god Amun, and at the bottom is a ram's cloven hoof. *Was* means "power" in ancient Egyptian.

- At the top, the scepter also has a *djed* pillar, representing the backbone of the god Osiris and meaning "stability." There is also an *ankh*, representing "life." You can add this to the A page of your dictionary.

Being a Scribe

- For most people in ancient Egypt, being a scribe was a worthy goal. But many Egyptian boys had to be convinced.

In Egyptian lore, Ptah assisted at the opening of the mouth ceremony during mummification, which ensured the deceased would be able to speak in the next world.

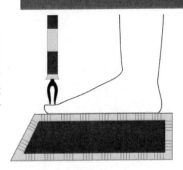

- There is a wonderful papyrus in the British Museum called Papyrus Lansing because Ambrose Lansing owned it and papyri are named after their owners.

- Papyrus Lansing is all about becoming a scribe. Written by the royal scribe, Nebmare-nakht, it is addressed to a student who doesn't realize what a noble calling being a scribe is. It begins with an extolling of the virtues of being a scribe: "You will make friends with those greater than you. You will be advanced by your superiors. ... Love writing, shun dancing. Then you will become a worthy official."

- Nebmare-nakht then goes on to explain why all other professions are inferior: The washerman's limbs become tired; the pot maker gets smeared with oil; the cobbler develops an odor and his hands turn red; and the unskilled laborer is forever burdened, toiling before the scribe.

Lecture 7's Homework Answers

1. "The maidservant knows the secret" translates as *Rekh baket seshta*. That involves us starting with the verb, *rekh* ("to know"), then adding the subject, *baket*, for "maidservant." *Seshta* is the word for "secret." The hieroglyphs come out to ⬡𓏛𓆰𓂝𓏇𓂋𓈖𓆓.

2. "The vizier is in the office" translates as *Yew tchaty m kha*. Our verb is "is," so we start with *yew*, 𓇋𓏲. Next we add the subject, the "vizier," which is pronounced *tchaty* and has our *tcha* biliteral, giving us 𓇋𓏲𓍿𓏭𓍘. We next need "in," and that is our old friend the owl hieroglyph, creating 𓇋𓏲𓍿𓏭𓅓𓆑. Last we need the word for "office," which uses the *kha* biliteral. 𓇋𓏲𓍿𓏭𓆓𓈙𓏤𓉐 is the complete phrase.

3. "The donkey is in the road" requires two biliterals and the verb "is," *yew*. The donkey (*eha*) and the verb (*yew*) make 𓇋𓏲𓂝𓃘. Next, he's "in" the road, so that's our owl. Last we need the "road," which has the *wa* biliteral. The entire word was pronounced *wat*. In the end, we get 𓇋𓏲𓂝𓃘𓅓𓎛𓈐, or *Yew eha m wat*.

4. "The daughter ferries across in the boat" contains the *dja* biliteral (for "ferries across"), a vulture phonetic complement, and a boat determinative: 🪶. The subject, "daughter," uses the *sa* biliteral, but we add the *t* because she's feminine, giving us *sat*. She's in the boat, so we use our owl for "in" and *depet* for "boat. We end up with 🪶 , pronounced *Dja sat m depet*.

Lecture 8's Homework

Translate the following sentences from English to hieroglyphs.

1. "The crocodile is in the river."

2. "The moon rejoices when the sun is in the horizon."

3. "The land rejoices because Ptah is in the city."

Translate the following sentences from hieroglyphs to English.

1.

2.

Suffix Pronouns and the Hieroglyphs of Ptah

Welcome back. Today marks a turning point in our course. We've completed the story of the decipherment of hieroglyphs. It's important to understand how the code was cracked, but from now on, we won't begin the lectures with background material and end with hieroglyphs—we won't do that. From here on, we'll start with hieroglyphs, and then at the end of the lecture we'll apply what we have learned to art, civilization, religion, and other aspects. So let's start with our homework.

I asked you to translate four sentences from English into hieroglyphs. The first was "The maidservant knows the secret." Well, by now we all know we begin with the verb, which is *rekh*, "to know."

Next will be our subject, "maidservant," pronounced *baket*.

Last is our new word for "secret," *seshta*, which contains the *ta* biliteral.

And that's our first sentence: "The maidservant knows the secret." It would have been vocalized as something like *Rekh baket seshta*.

Next, we had "The vizier is in the office." Our verb is "is," so we start with *yew*.

Next, we add the subject, the "vizier," which is pronounced *tchaty* and has our *tcha* biliteral.

We need "in," and that's our old friend the owl hieroglyph.

Last we need the word for "office," which uses the *kha* biliteral.

"The vizier is in the office." *Yew tchaty m kha.* Next, we have "The donkey is in the road." This sentence requires two biliterals, but first the verb, "is," which is *yew*.

It's the donkey who's in the road, so we add our onomatopoetic word *eha*, which uses the *eha* biliteral.

Next, he's "in" the road, so that's our owl.

Last we need the "road," which has the *wa* biliteral, and the entire word was pronounced *wat*.

Yew eha m wat.

Our last sentence is "The daughter ferries across in the boat." "Ferries across," our verb, contains the *dja* biliteral, a vulture phonetic complement, and a boat determinative.

Our subject, "daughter," uses the *sa* biliteral, but we add the *t*—the loaf—because she's feminine, *sat*.

She's "in" the boat, so we use our owl for "in."

Last we just add "boat," which is *depet*.

Dja sat m depet. And that's our sentence, "The daughter ferries across in the boat."

Now let's add a few vocabulary words to our dictionary so we can translate more real texts. Again, I'll write the word, and you tell me how it's pronounced. It's good practice.

This is a version of another word we've already had, so it should be easy. It has two determinatives, so the only thing we have to worry about are the first two alphabetic hieroglyphs, *r* and *sh*. So it's pronounced *resh*. The other similar word we've had before was *reshwet*.

Reshwet means "joy" or "gladness," the noun. Our new variant, *resh*, is the verb "to rejoice" or "be glad." The double determinative shows that it involves emotions, which one can see on the face or express by speech.

Our next word is an idiom, a word that doesn't really follow the rules.

If you figured out that it should be pronounced *itef*, you're thinking correctly, but you happen to be wrong—sorry. The horned viper hieroglyph is silent. That's why I said it's an idiom. The word is pronounced *it*. We know this from Coptic. We can tell it has something to do with a man from the determinative. It means "father."

How is this word pronounced? Yep, it's pronounced *iteru* and the three water signs at the end form the determinative that shows it has something to do with water. It's the word for "river."

In this word, pronounced something like *mezeh*, the determinative gives it away. It's the word for "crocodile."

Let's do a couple more words. They will enable us to read and write more complex sentences.

Here we have the ideogram stroke sign, so we know it's a picture of the concept. We know the *r* hieroglyph is a mouth, so the word means "mouth." It also means an "utterance" or a "spell"—as in a magical spell. As you would expect, it is pronounced *r*.

Here's another ideogram. It means what you'd expect—"face." It also means "sight" and was pronounced *her*. It's also the word for "upon," and it can mean "concerning" or "with respect to." So it's important because it has many uses.

When President Obama visited Egypt, he was inside a tomb and noticed the face hieroglyph on the wall and commented, "It looks like me!" I think it was the big ears.

Once in a while we will see this hieroglyph ⟋⟍substituted for the owl. It's a statue base and also represents the sound *m* just like the owl. We saw this in the word for "truth," *maat*. We should enter this hieroglyph on the *M* page of our dictionary with the same meanings as the owl.

Let me give you, for homework, a few sentences, and phrases with our new vocabulary words to translate into hieroglyphs. "The crocodile is in the river." Try that one. How about, "The moon rejoices when the sun is in the horizon." How about, "The land rejoices because Ptah is in the city." That's a nice one. These sentences will reinforce our new vocabulary words.

OK scribes, get the ink and pens. We're going to start a new grammar lesson: Pronouns.

Remember the old Beatles lyric "I, me, mine; I, me, mine; I, me, mine"? Those are personal pronouns, and we're going to learn those words today. Pronouns take the place of nouns. I can use a name to refer to a person, as in the sentence "Ted is long gone." "Ted" is a proper noun, because it's a name. However, I can also say "He is long gone." In this case, I've replaced the noun with a pronoun, "he."

It's the same with common nouns. I can say, "The house is red." "House" is a noun. I can replace it with a pronoun and say, "It is red," where "it" is the pronoun.

We can also have possessive pronouns that we use to show ownership. I can say, "That's Fido's blanket." Or I can say, "That's his blanket," where "his" is a possessive pronoun.

Today we're going to learn what we call the suffix pronouns. These are added to the ends of words, and that's why we call them suffix pronouns. They can be used at the ends of verbs to show who or what is doing the action—what the grammarians call the nominative case. Or they can be tacked on at the ends of nouns to show possession.

I'm going to show you plenty of examples, so don't worry, it will all be clear at the end of the lecture. But first, let me give you some good news about pronouns in ancient Egypt. The suffix pronouns are the same for possession and in the nominative. This isn't the case in English. For example, I can say "I run," but I can't use the "I" for possession. I can't say "I car." I have to say "My car." I need two different pronouns. In Egyptian, it's the same pronoun for both cases.

Let me show you what I mean. Let's try a sentence with a pronoun, actually two.

Before you try to translate it, let me tell you that the man sign is the word for both "I" and "my." It is our first suffix pronoun and like other suffix pronouns is added to the end of verbs and nouns.

Now let's translate the sentence. The verb comes first, as it should, and *yew* is the word for "is." Next, we have our suffix pronoun, the man attached to the verb, so we know it's not going to be possessive. So we have "I am." Now, what's our owl doing? It has several meanings, and we have to pick the right one. So let's look at the end of the sentence. The "house" hieroglyph is being used as an ideogram. The man hieroglyph attached to it is the possessive since it's attached to a noun, so we have "my house." So it looks as if the best meaning for owl is "in," which gives us "I am in my house."

Now, ladies, I know what you are thinking. "What about me? Do I have to use the man hieroglyph to say 'I' or 'my'?" You don't. Feel free to use the woman hieroglyph. 𓁐 So your version of "I am in my house" would look like this:

𓇋𓃀𓈖𓉐𓏏𓁐

Just replace the two man hieroglyphs with two woman hieroglyphs. It would have sounded something like *Yew.i em per.i*. The suffix pronoun is pronounced *i,* or *i* like that. Actually, the woman hieroglyph was not used in this way till the 19th Dynasty, from 1292 to 1187 B.C., which may show progress for women in ancient Egypt.

Now for the other suffix pronouns. "You" or "your" masculine, is simply the basket *k* 𓎡. "You" or "your" feminine, is the tethering ring *tch* 𓍿.

When we transliterate suffix pronouns, there's a useful convention. Because suffixes are technically part of the word they're attached to, we don't separate them in transliterations. We conjoin them to the word by means of a dot or period. So if I wanted to say "You speak" and I'm talking to a man, I would write. Like this, 𓆓𓂧𓎡 and the transliteration would be *Djed.k*.

If I were talking to a woman, it would be 𓆓𓂧𓍿 *Djed.tch*. The tethering ring makes sense for the feminine because it's a kind of *t* and that's the feminine ending. 𓍿 It's a way to remember it.

"He," "his," "it," or "its" is a horned viper.

𓆑

So "His house" would be,

𓉐𓆑 *Per.f*.

"She," "her," or "it" or "it's" is a folded cloth.

𓏏

So "Her house" would be,

𓉐 𓏏 *Per.s.*

So that's it for the singular suffix pronouns. Now let's look at the plural suffix pronouns. "We," "us," or "our" is the water sign with three strokes for plural.

𓈖
𓏤𓏤𓏤 *n.*

Three strokes are used for plurals of all kinds.

"We hear" would be,

𓄿𓄔𓏤𓏤𓏤 *Sedjem.n.*

We don't have to worry about masculine or feminine in the plural. It's what we call common. One suffix pronoun fits all.

For "you" or "your" in the plural we have the tethering ring, water sign, and three plural strokes beneath them. Pronounced *tchn.*

𓊵
𓏤𓏤𓏤

Our last plural is for "they," "them," or "their." That's a folded cloth, a water sign, and three strokes pronounced *sen.*

𓏏𓈖
𓏤𓏤𓏤

"Their scribe" would be,

𓏺𓀀𓏤𓏤𓏤 *Shesh.sen.*

There's one more pronoun we should know. We'll see it later, but let me show it to you now, so your pronouns will be complete.

How was it pronounced? That's right, *tu*. This is the impersonal pronoun. It means "one," as in the sense of "One should always be kind," or "One should always do one's homework." It's indefinite; it doesn't specify a particular individual.

That's it for suffix pronouns. Now we need lots of practice so we can learn them. They will sink in. I'll give you a hieroglyphic sentence or phrase to translate. But first tell me how it sounds.

Let's see how to vocalize it. Best way to do that is to break it into words and take them one at a time. What's our first word? Where does it end? We know it's probably a verb because verbs come at the beginning of the sentences. Then we recognize an old friend, the word for "rejoice," which is pronounced *resh,* and it ends with the man with his hand to the mouth. That's our first word.

What's our next word? Yes, it's "scribe," which ends at the man determinative and it's pronounced *sesh*. You're getting it. Next is a very familiar verb, "to be," which we know is pronounced *yew*. Next, we have a suffix pronoun, something new that we probably have to look up. Well, it is simply pronounced *n* and means "we" or "our." Since it comes suffixed to a verb, it must be "we." It's not possessive.

Now we have an owl, which is pronounced *m* and is going to mean something like "in" or "from." We'll just have to see from the next few words which is the best sense. Well, the next word is "house"—we see the ideogram stroke, and this is pronounced *per* we know that. This is followed by a lone viper—another suffix pronoun. We remember it's pronounced *f* because it is an alphabetic hieroglyph, but we may have to look it up to see what it means— which suffix pronoun it's. Well, it means "he" or "his"

and since it's attached to a noun, "house," we know it's going to be "his"—
it's possessive.

So the vocalization of the sentence we want to translate would be
something like *Resh sesh yew.n m per.f*. Something like that. Once we've
separated it into words for the vocalization, the transliteration is easy. "The
scribe rejoices (when) we're in his house." I inserted the "when" because
it's probably the meaning and the Egyptians didn't have a word for "when."
It's understood.

I know this is a lot for one day. We have new vocabulary and suffix
pronouns. Don't worry; we're going to go over it and our suffix pronouns will
be very familiar after several lessons.

For suffix pronoun homework, let me just give you two sentences from
hieroglyphs to English. Here's the first.

It's a long one. But you're going to be able to do it. And now a shorter one.

That's it for homework.

Now let's do a little excursion into ancient Egyptian religion. We talked a bit
about the god Ptah before. He was one of the gods intimately connected to
writing and words, so let's examine Ptah's role in Egyptian religion.

Ptah was viewed as a creator god, and that creation is closely connected
with words. So he's particularly relevant to what we're learning. In one
myth, Ptah is presented as the god who creates the world with words. We'll
look at that closely in a minute, but let me tell you how we know about
this myth.

We have only one copy of the text, and it's in the British Museum. It dates from the 25th Dynasty, which extended from about 760 to 656 B.C. and which was a very special period. This is when the Nubians marched north and conquered Egypt. For years the Nubians had been under Egyptian rule, but now Egypt had been invaded several times by foreign powers and was weak, and the Nubians saw their chance. They had a love/hate relationship with Egypt. They didn't like the idea that Egypt controlled Nubia, but they also admired Egyptian civilization. So when the Nubian kings conquered Egypt, they didn't plunder. Just the opposite. They wanted to restore Egypt to its former greatness.

They built their own temples to honor the Amun, Egypt's most powerful god during this period and even copied old religious texts to preserve them. One of these ancient texts relates to the god Ptah and is called the Shabaka Stone, after the Nubian King who had it copied. Today it's in the British Museum, and it doesn't look like much, so everyone walks by it, but it's unique and interesting. It's kind of squarish, and it's got a hole in the middle. And it has an inscription in hieroglyphs all over it, but it's badly worn, especially in the middle.

Originally it was a round-topped stela that Shabaka erected. But in the 19th century, some Egyptian farmers found it and recut it to use as a grindstone. So this stone was being used as a grindstone for decades. That's why there are those radiating lines on the stone, for the grain to slide out. That's why it's so worn. And that's unfortunate because this is a unique text, but there's just enough to make out what it's about.

It's sometimes called The Philosophy of a Memphite Priest. It's almost philosophical. The text begins with a wonderful introduction. Shabaka says, "I found the writings of the ancients damaged, and I restored it better than it was." Now, what exactly does that mean?

One possibility is that the old text was damaged, and it had gaps, and Shabaka filled in the gaps. This is certainly possible. But I have always wondered what was the original text written on? My bet is papyrus, so when Shabaka says he made it better, he could also mean that he's taking something that was written on papyrus and is carving it on stone.

So, when Shabaka is restoring an ancient text, he's probably copying a damaged papyrus. Shabaka viewed this text as his heritage, and he restored it by carving it on stone and erecting it in front of a temple. This is a pious deed, and Shabaka is remembered for it. Very few Egyptian kings are mentioned in the Bible, but the Nubian kings are referred to as "the pious Ethiopian kings." Shabaka's restoration of a religious text is a pious act.

Ptah was the chief god of Memphis, one of Egypt's oldest cities. Egyptian gods usually came in threes—a husband, a wife, and a child. In Memphis, the triad was Ptah; Sekhmet, the lioness; and their son, Nefertum. The text on the Shabaka Stone describes the world's creation in three steps: First, Ptah thought it, and then he said it on his tongue, and then finally, it became real.

The text doesn't exactly say that Ptah "thought it." The Egyptians believed you thought with your heart, they didn't understand the function of the brain. Remember, they threw the brain out when they mummified. So when they talked about thinking, often the heart was mentioned. Our text says:

"There took shape in the heart (of Ptah), there took shape on the tongue (of Ptah) the form of Atum."

Now Atum is the traditional creator god of Egypt, who created all the other gods. The Shabaka Stone is asserting the primacy of Ptah. It's Ptah who creates Atum and thus all the other gods. Later, the text says: "Ptah the very great one gives (life) to the gods and their *kas* through his heart and tongue."

This is not unlike, "In the beginning was the word." Notice that just thinking it wasn't enough. Ptah had to say it—the words were crucial to the creation of the world.

We've been talking about how Ptah created the world, now let's see what he looked like. This is a drawing done by one of Champollion's artists in the 1820s. In addition to creating the world, he has a funerary aspect. First notice that his feet are together, bandaged like a mummy. He assists at the opening of the mouth ceremony during mummification. This ceremony ensured that the deceased would be able to speak and say the magical words in the next world.

Ptah was a very popular god, and often Egyptian names included him. For example, *Ptahhotep* means "Ptah is pleased."

☐𐃔𓏤

The first hieroglyph after *Ptah* is a cone of incense on a reed mat. It's a triliteral, pronounced *htp*, so we say "hotep." The two hieroglyphs under it are the phonetic complements for the *p* and the *t* sounds. The word usually means "to be pleased" so the name *Ptahhotep* means "Ptah is pleased." In the same way, *Amunhotep* means "Amun is pleased." Now back to Ptah's iconography—how he's depicted.

I want to focus on the scepter that he's holding. It's a symbol of power. In its simple form, the scepter is called a *was*-scepter. It's the head of a ram, representing the god Amun and at the bottom is a ram's cloven hoof. *Was* means "power" in ancient Egyptian. It was also the root of the name of the ancient city of Luxor, *Waset*.

𓌀𓏤

So you can see, because it is a town, it has a feminine *t* there, and we have the town determinative helping us figure out what it means. We'll talk more about that in a later lecture on ideograms.

The ancient Egyptians called their city *Waset*, but when the Greeks came into Egypt they marveled at the temples, and they likened it to their Thebes and called it Thebes. Later when the Arabs invaded Egypt and saw all the temples, they thought they were palaces, and called the city Luxor—Arabic for "palace."

Now, back to Memphis and Ptah's scepter. Look at the top. There are three hieroglyphs that give his attributes. There's the *djed*-pillar.

It's a biliteral for the sounds *dj* and *d*—*djed*. It represents the backbone of the god Osiris and is the word for "stability." So Ptah provides stability.

Then we see the *ankh* representing "life." The *ankh* hieroglyph is actually a triliteral for the sounds *eh*—our alphabetic arm *e*—*n, kh*—*ankh*. We add it to our dictionary on our *A* page since it's almost always written that way.

Finally, we have the ram head for power. Amun, the greatest of all gods in Luxor, was often shown as a man with the head of a ram. So his scepter tells us Ptah was power and gives both stability and life.

You can see how even a minimal knowledge of hieroglyphs helps us understand Egyptian art and religion better. We now look at the scepter in a way different from someone who doesn't know hieroglyphs. It's not just an exotic staff; it's saying something. It's good to know hieroglyphs. But apparently, not everyone in ancient Egypt agreed with this. Let me explain.

Certainly, for most people being a scribe was a worthy goal. It was a profession, every mother wanted her son to be a scribe. So you are all junior scribes in training; you realize that just drawing the hieroglyphs is a pleasure, but many Egyptian boys didn't understand this. They had to be convinced.

There's a wonderful papyrus in the British Museum called Papyrus Lansing because it was owned by Ambrose Lansing. But papyri are named after their owners, and Papyrus Lansing is all about becoming a scribe. It's one great sales pitch to "Be a Scribe!" Written by the Royal Scribe, Nebmare-nakht, it's addressed to a student who doesn't realize what a noble calling being a scribe is. It begins with extolling of the virtues of being a scribe.

> You will make friends with those greater than you. You will be advanced by your superiors ... Love writing, shun dancing. Then you will become a worthy official ... Befriend the scroll and palette. It pleases more than wine. Writing for him who knows, it is

better than all other professions. It pleases more than bread and beer, more than clothing and ointment. It is worth more than an inheritance in Egypt, more than a tomb in the west.

Nebmare-nakht then goes on to explain why all other professions are inferior.

The washerman's day is going up and down. All his limbs are weak from whitening his neighbor's clothes every day, from washing linen.

The maker of pots is smeared with soil, like one whose relations have died. His hands, his feet are full of clay; he is like one who lives in the bog.

The cobbler mingles with vats. His odor is penetrating. His hands are red with dye, like one smeared with blood.

Remember the fate of the unskilled laborer. His name is not known. He is forever burdened like a donkey, carrying things in front of the scribe, who is educated.

The papyrus goes on and on, from profession to profession.

You are all willingly signed up for this course, so I don't have to convince you to do your homework, so you won't smell like a tanner, so you won't have your arms tired from washing your neighbor's laundry. I know you'll do your homework. So I'll see you next time.

This lecture begins with practice exercises to assist with learning the suffix pronouns. You'll practice translating from English to hieroglyphs. You have probably discovered that it is more difficult to translate from English to hieroglyphs than the other way around. The reason is that when you have a hieroglyphic sentence in front of us, you don't have to create it. But when you have to create the hieroglyphic sentence, you need to know how to spell the words and how to order them. That's why this type of exercise is so valuable. After the exercises, this lecture adds one very important vocabulary word, and then covers the role of scribes.

Charting

- To help you learn the suffix pronouns, you might want to make a chart of them. You can use the same format you're using for your dictionary. Start with the hieroglyphic word, then add the pronunciation, and then add the meaning. An example is below.

  ⌐   (f)   He, his, him, it, its

Exercise 1: "We send the boat to her city."

- We'll start by translating, "We send the boat to her city."

- Begin with the verb, "to send," which is *hab,* and the suffix pronoun for "we," which is the water sign with three strokes. Those two give us 🚩🦅🔼 for "we send."

- "Boat" is *depet,* giving us 🚩🦅🔼🛶 .The little boat at the end of the word is the determinative. Now we need the "to," and since it is to a place (the city) we use the mouth *r*, creating 𓅂𓀀𓏏𓉐𓈖𓂋 ·

- Next is "city," *niwit*, leading to 𓅂𓀀𓏏𓉐𓈖𓂋𓈖. Finally we add the suffix pronoun "her," which is the folded cloth *s*. It indicates possession here, so we attached it to the noun: 𓅂𓀀𓏏𓉐𓈖𓂋𓈖 .

Exercise 2: "You ferry across the river in our boat."

- Next, we'll translate, "You [feminine, singular] ferry across the river in our boat." Start with the verb *dja*, "to ferry across." The suffix pronoun is the tethering rich *tch*, giving us: 𓀀𓅂𓈖 .

- Next comes the word for "river," *iterw*, and the owl for "in": 𓀀𓅂𓈖𓂝𓏏𓈖𓅂 .

- Next up: "Boat," *depet*, comes first because "our" is a suffix pronoun and must be added to the end of a word. The word order is "boat our." We write the word for "boat," in this case as an ideogram (the boat with a stroke). Then add the suffix pronoun for "our," which is the same word for "we" and is written with the water sign and three strokes.

- The final product: 𓀀𓅂𓈖𓂝𓏏𓈖𓅂𓏏 , pronounced *Dja.tch iterw m depet.n.*

Exercise 3: "They talk to our scribe and she listens."

- To translate, "They talk to our scribe and she listens," begin with the verb, "to say" or "talk," which is *djed*. Next up is the suffix, "they," *sen*. Together, those two elements make 𓆓𓈖𓏤𓏤𓏤 .

- Next is the "to" which is the water sign because it is "to" a person—the scribe, *sesh*. That gives us 𓆓𓈖𓏤𓏤𓏤𓈖𓀀 .

- To the scribe, we attach the "our," which is the water sign and three strokes. Now all we need is "and she listens." The "and" is understood; there is no word for it. For "she listens," we can use the verb *sedjem*, "to hear," and the folded cloth for "she."

- The final product is [hieroglyphs], pronounced *Djed. sen n sesh.n sedjem.s.*

Exercise 4: "He rejoices when his daughter goes down to their house."

- Start with *resh*, "to rejoice." Next comes the viper for "he," giving us [hieroglyphs].

- The "when" is understood, so we go to the next verb, "to go down," which is *ha.*

- Now we have [hieroglyphs].

- "Daughter" comes next, then the suffix pronoun. We add *sat*, "daughter," and attach the suffix pronoun "his" to it. That's the horned viper. At this point, we have [hieroglyphs].

- Coming to the end, we just need "to their house." The "to" is the mouth *r* since it is to a place, the house: [hieroglyphs]. (We could stack the mouth on top of the viper, but since the mouth *r* is usually its own word, we're not doing that here.)

- "House," *per*, comes next, and then "their," which is the folded cloth water sign with three strokes. In the end, we have [hieroglyphs]. That's pronounced *Resh.f ha sat.f r per.sen.*

Exercise 5: "He hears the crocodile from his house upon their road."

- To translate, "He hears the crocodile from his house upon their road," we start with "hears," which is *sedjem*, and "he," which is the viper: [hieroglyphs]. Next we need our crocodile, *mezeh*: [hieroglyphs].

- Up next is "from," the owl: . "His house" is the house followed by the viper: .

- Now it is time to use a word we haven't used much, "upon." It is *her,* the face with the stroke. That gives us .

- "Road" is pronounced *wat.* Adding it gives us .

- It's "their" road, so we will add the folded cloth, water sign, and three strokes for "their." The final product is , pronounced something like *Sedjem.f mezeh m per.f her wat.sen.*

Vocabulary

- In this lecture, our vocabulary addition consists of one word: . It was pronounced *kheper,* and the root is the beetle. It is a trilateral equal to *kh-p-r.*

- Both the hieroglyphic scarab and the actual beetle were very important in ancient Egypt. The scarab hieroglyph was pronounced *kheper* and meant "to exist." But it also meant "beetle" as in the insect.

- The beetle was very special to the Egyptians. The female lays its eggs in a dung ball and then rolls it to a safe place and buries it. Later, little scarabs pop out, like magic. The Egyptians didn't understand the biological process, so to them, this was a remarkable case of procreation. Thus, the beetle became a symbol of existence. They carved little beetles as amulets to be worn to ensure continued existence.

- When Pharaoh Amenhotep III wanted to make announcements to the world, he had large scarabs carved, then wrote his message on the bottom. He famously used a scarab to announce his marriage to Queen Tiye.

Scarabs were so important in ancient Egypt that the god Khepri was depicted with the body of a man and the head of a scarab.

The Greeks on Writing

- Although the social position of the scribe was continuously revered throughout Egyptian history, there was at least one voice in the conversation who did not agree. The Greek philosopher Plato lived between about 428–348 B.C. and was well aware of Egyptian civilization.

- Though he admired much of Egyptian culture, Plato lamented the invention of writing. This belief was shared by his teacher, Socrates. What we know of Socrates comes from a body of works called the dialogues. Socrates often had philosophical discussions with his students (Plato included), and the students wrote down these dialogues for future generations.

- In several of the dialogues, Socrates discusses the invention of writing. He credits the invention to the Egyptian god of writing, Toth, who was often depicted as an ibis-headed man.

- While Socrates credits Toth with the invention, he laments the day writing was conceived. Socrates believes that with writing, man will no longer have knowledge. He will merely have the appearance of knowledge. For Socrates, knowledge is in the mind. Writing is external to the mind, so it can't be knowledge.

The Egyptians on Writing

- As Papyrus Lansing shows, the Egyptians didn't agree with Socrates, and offered materialistic reasons for becoming a scribe. Other papyri give more idealistic reasons to become a scribe. One papyrus in the British Museum, Papyrus Chester Beatty IV, links being a scribe with immortality.

- The papyrus was written during the New Kingdom, a time when Egypt had already collapsed twice: once at the end of the Old Kingdom and once at the end of the Middle Kingdom. Both collapses led to periods of lawlessness, tomb robbing, and general disillusionment with life.

- For the first time, people saw the uncertainty of life. They saw that continuity couldn't be guaranteed, and that even building a stone tomb didn't guarantee your mummy would be preserved so that you could resurrect in the next world.

- Papyrus Chester Beatty IV fully acknowledges all these uncertainties. It suggests that being a scribe is the only sure route to immortality, but it is a different kind of immortality than what was promised by the Egyptian religion. It is the immortality of being an author. Talking about scribes, the author says:

> The reed pen is their child,
> The stone surface their wife…
> Death made them forgotten,
> But books made them remembered.

Papyrus

- Papyrus was a very important medium for writing. Papyrus was viewed as less permanent than stone, but in Egypt's dry climate, papyri have survived for thousands of years quite well.

- Papyrus grew along the banks of the Nile. It could grow to more than 10 feet tall with a diameter of four inches. To create papyrus

Papyrus

sheets, it was harvested and the stalks were cut into sections about 12 inches long.

- These cylinders were then cut into thin strips. Next the strips were placed on a board and overlapped. Then this was beaten with a wood mallet or pressed so the sap comes out and serves as the glue that binds the strips together. The overlapping strips were left in the sun, and when they dried, each sheet would be burnished with a smooth stone to prepare the surface for writing.

- Individual sheets could be glued together to make a papyrus roll as long as desired. Some are more than 100 feet long. Papyrus was used for bureaucratic records, literary productions, international commerce, and religious texts such as the Book of the Dead.

- Papyrus used to grow wild in Egypt on the banks of the Nile, but industrialization has ended that. Today it is farmed to make into sheets so artists can paint ancient scenes to be sold to tourists.

- You can buy sheets of papyrus in most large art supply stores, and you might enjoy trying writing on the real thing.

Lecture 8's Homework Answers
The first part of the homework was English-to-hieroglyphs translations.

1. To translate, "The crocodile is in the river," start with the verb, "is," *yew*, then add the crocodile subject, *mezeh*: 𓇋𓃀𓆊 𓈖. Next comes the owl for "in" and the word for river, *iteru*, giving us: 𓇋𓃀𓆊 𓈖 𓂋𓈖𓈖, pronounced *Yew mezeh m iteru*.

2. "The moon rejoices when the sun is in the horizon" is a compound sentence, one with two verbs and two subjects. Start with the verb, "to rejoice," *resh*, and the subject, "moon," *yeah*: 𓇳𓂝𓏏𓇹. The "when" is understood, so we can skip to the second verb, "is," *yew*, and

the second subject, "sun," *re*: ⟨hieroglyphs⟩. We conclude with the owl hieroglyph for "in" and *akhet* for "horizon": ⟨hieroglyphs⟩, which is pronounced *Resh yeah yew re m akhet.*

3. To translate, "The land rejoices because Ptah is in the city," start with the verb *resh*, "rejoice," and the word for "land," *ta*, creating ⟨hieroglyphs⟩ . There is no word for "because," so it's understood. Next add the verb *yew*, "is," and the second subject, "Ptah," to make ⟨hieroglyphs⟩. Finally we add the owl for "in" and *niwit* for city: ⟨hieroglyphs⟩

The second part of the homework was hieroglyphs-to-English translations.

⟨hieroglyphs⟩

1. ⟨hieroglyphs⟩

- This is a long one. Start with the verb, *maa*, "to see." Next is the word for "man," *z*. So we know a man is seeing something.

- Our next word, *sat*, means "daughter," followed by a viper, so this must be "his daughter"—the viper is a suffix pronoun meaning "he" or "his."

- Next we have an owl, a house, and a viper, which together mean "in his house." Then we see another verb, *yew* for "is" and another viper for "he."

- Next is our owl again, and that's the word "in." Our last word is the long one, *reshwet*, which means "joy." Putting it all together, we have "The man sees his daughter in his house; he is in joy."

- To make the sentence smooth, we can add an understood "when" at the beginning. That gives us, "When the man sees his daughter in his house, he is in joy."

2. ⟨hieroglyphs⟩ starts with the biliteral *dja* and a boat determinative, giving us the word for "to ferry across." Re, the sun god, is being ferried. From the next word, *pet*, we can see that Re is ferrying across the sky.

- Next we have the owl, "in." And that is followed by the word *wia*, which is a sacred boat. Added onto the sacred boat is a suffix pronoun, the horned viper, meaning "his."

- If we put it all together, we have, "Re ferries across the sky in his sacred boat." *Dja Re pet m wia.*

Lecture 9's Homework

Translate these two sentences from hieroglyphs to English.

1. ⟨hieroglyphs⟩

2. ⟨hieroglyphs⟩

The Immortal Scribe

Welcome back. Last time I asked you to translate three sentences from English to hieroglyphs that contain our new vocabulary words. First was "The crocodile is in the river." Well, it's the same old drill. Start with the verb, "is," pronounced *yew*.

Then we add the subject, our "crocodile," *mezeh*.

Now we need our old friend the owl for "in."

Last, we need the word for river, *iteru*.

And that's it. "The crocodile is in the river." *Yew mezeh m iteru.*

Our second sentence was "The moon rejoices when the sun is in the horizon." Poetic isn't it? This is a compound sentence, one with two verbs and two subjects.

Start with the verb, "to rejoice," *resh.*

Next, we add the subject, which is "moon," *yeah.*

The "when" is understood, so we don't include a word for that. What we next need is the second verb, which is "is" because the second half of the sentence is "the sun is in the horizon." So we add *yew*, the reed and quail chick, for "is."

Now we need the word for sun. That's easy it's *re.*

Next, we need the "in," which is our owl.

Last we add "horizon," *akhet,* and we have it: *Resh yeah yew re m akhet.*

"The moon rejoices (when) the sun is in the horizon."

In this sentence we have the word for "horizon" but we haven't seen it for a while. How do we remember it? You can, of course, search your dictionary and you'll find it on the *A* page, so the search won't be too long. But other words that are further down in the dictionary will take longer to find. I suggest that after each lecture, when you're adding your new vocabulary to your dictionaries, read all your words aloud, followed by the meaning. It won't take too long; we really don't have that many vocabulary words, but that will help them stick.

Our last sentence is another one with "rejoice" in it, and it, too, is a compound sentence. "The land rejoices because Ptah is in the city." Again, we start with our verb *resh*, "rejoice."

Add the word for land, *ta*.

It's an ideogram, but no stroke. Remember, be flexible, they wrote it all kinds of ways. There's no word for "because," so it's understood. Now comes the second part of our compound sentence. So we start with the verb *yew*, "is."

Now add the subject, "*Ptah*."

Last we add "in the city." The "in" is the owl, we always remember that.

And we know the word for "city," *niwit.*

And that's it for our English-to-hieroglyphs homework.

Now let's look at the hieroglyph translations. These are the ones involving our new suffix pronouns. I gave you two sentences. Let's start with the first, the long one. It's long, but you can do it.

As usual, we start with a verb. It's *maa*—"to see." Next is the word for "man," *z*. So we know a man is seeing something. Our next word, *sat*, means "daughter." But right after it is a viper, and this is one of our suffix pronouns, meaning "he" or "his." So it must be "his daughter." Next, we have our owl, which will mean "in" because we can see "house" is coming next. Tacked onto "house" *per* is the viper again, so it will be "his house." Now, continuing right along we see another verb, *yew*—"is." So we have a compound sentence, one with two verbs and two subjects. After "is" we have our viper again, so now we know the viper is "he." Next is our owl again, and that's the word "in."

Our last word is the long one, *reshwet*, which means "joy." So putting it all together, we have "The man sees his daughter in his house; he is in joy." In English we don't usually say "in joy" but this is the ancient Egyptian idiom, it's the real thing. To make the sentence smooth, we can add an understood "When" at the very beginning, and that gives us, "When the man sees his daughter in his house, he is in joy." Excellent.

Our next sentence had a mythological overtone.

We have our verb, *dja*, which has the *dja* biliteral that represents the two sounds *dj* and *a*. The vulture is the phonetic complement that reminds us of the *a* sound. The boat's the determinative, telling us the word has something to do with boats. The word means "to ferry across." Now we have to find out who it is that's ferrying across. Well, it's *Re*, the sun god. Note that in this text his name is written with two determinatives, the solar disk, and the god determinative. There are lots of variations. From the next word, *pet*, we can see that Re is ferrying across the sky.

Next, we have the owl "in." And that's followed by the word *wia*, which is a sacred boat. Now, added onto the sacred boat is a suffix pronoun, the horned viper. We are now very familiar with this little fellow, and we know he means "his." So, if we put it all together, we have, "Re ferries across the sky in his sacred boat." It would sound like *Dja Re pet m wia.f*. And that's our homework.

Now I'd like to do some practice exercises with you so that we learn our suffix pronouns. Let's practice translating from English to hieroglyphs, but let me explain why. We have been doing both English-to-hieroglyphs and hieroglyphs-to-English sentences. I'm sure you've discovered that it's more difficult to translate from English to hieroglyphs than the other way around. The reason is that when we have a hieroglyphic sentence in front of us, we don't have to create it, we don't have to think about how the words are spelled, we don't have to remember grammatical rules for ordering the words, etc. All we have to do is recognize the words, and the translation will follow.

When we have to create the hieroglyphic sentence, we need to know how to spell the words, what order they go in. We have to remember that the word for "this" comes after the noun, but the word for "another" comes before it. Because so much more thinking is involved in English-to-hieroglyph translation, this is where the learning really takes place. When you have to look up a word's spelling and then write it, that's when you learn it.

This is why I love doing English to hieroglyphs. I know that we are never going to write a letter to an ancient Egyptian, but if you could write that letter, think how easy it would be to translate the reply. So for today, let's do lots of English-to-hieroglyph sentences using our suffix pronouns. That's how we'll learn them.

To help you learn the suffix pronouns, you might want to make a chart of them. You can use the same format we use for our dictionary. Start with the hieroglyphic word.

Then add the pronunciation.

 (*i*)

And last, add the meaning.

 (*i*) "I, me, my."

Then do the other pronouns. For example, you could do,

⌣ (f)

"He, his, him, it, its" and we can even indicate whether it's masculine or feminine.

Or we could do,

𓏃𓏤𓏤𓏤 (sen) "they, them, their." That's our chart.

Suffix pronouns let us have more variety in our sentences, but we still don't have too many verbs or nouns yet, so there'll be some repetition. But that's OK. The repetition is how we will learn our suffix pronouns. For now, feel free to have your pronoun chart in front of you so you can look them up. After a while, I don't think you'll have to look them up at all. So let's start.

First sentence, "We send the boat to her city." We all know we begin with the verb, "to send" which is *hab*.

𓎛𓃀𓂋

Now for our suffix pronoun. It's "We send," so we need to look up it in our pronoun chart, we find the suffix pronoun for "we." It's towards the bottom of the chart because it's a plural. There it is; it's the water sign with three strokes. So we suffix the water sign and three strokes to "send" and it's "We send."

𓎛𓃀𓂋𓈖𓏤𓏤𓏤

"Boat" is easy, everyone remembers that one. It's funny how some words are easier to remember than others. It's *depet*.

𓎛𓃀𓂋𓈖𓏤𓏤𓏤𓂧𓊛

The little boat at the end of the word is the determinative. Now we need the "to," and since it's to a place—the city—we use the mouth *r*.

𓊪𓄿𓐍𓏏𓉐𓏥𓈖𓏤

Next is "city" and that's another one that everyone remembers, *niwit*.

𓊪𓄿𓐍𓏏𓉐𓏥𓈖𓏤𓊖

Now comes the suffix pronoun, "her." This is where we use our suffix pronoun to indicate possession, so we attach it to the noun. You probably remember that "she" or "her," for the feminine "it" even, for that matter, is the folded cloth *s*. So we add the folded cloth to "city," *niwit*, and we have "her city."

𓊪𓄿𓐍𓏏𓉐𓏥𓈖𓏤𓊖𓋴

So that's it, "We send the boat to her city." Good, you're getting it. OK, let's use some other pronouns. How would we say, "You (feminine, singular) ferry across the river in our boat." We start with the verb *dja* "to ferry across."

Now for the suffix pronoun for "you" (feminine, singular). That's the tethering ring *tch.*

𓆓𓄿𓊛

So you, young lady, are ferrying across. It's not just ferrying across, it's ferrying across the river, so we add our relatively new vocabulary word for "river," *iteru*.

𓆓𓄿𓊛𓇋𓏏𓂋𓈗

"In" is easy, we use it so often, it's the owl.

𓆓𓄿𓊛𓇋𓏏𓂋𓈗𓅓

Now we just need "our boat." "Boat," *depet* comes first because "our" is a suffix pronoun and must be added to the end of a word. So the word order is "boat our." We write the word for "boat." This time, just for practice and fun, let's write it as an ideogram, just the boat with a stroke.

Now we just have to add the suffix pronoun for "our." Again, it's near the bottom of our pronoun chart because it's plural. It is the same word for "we" and is written with the water sign and three strokes.

Dja.tch iteru m depet.n that's how it sounded. So that's "You ferry across the river in our boat." Good. Let's try another sentence.

How about "They talk to our scribe, and she listens." By the way, there were a few female scribes in ancient Egypt, but very few. Again, we begin with the verb, "to say" or "talk," which is *djed*.

Now comes our suffix pronoun, "they" which is plural, so we can look it up at the bottom of our personal pronoun chart and find that it is *sen*—the folded cloth, water sign, and three strokes.

That's "They talk." Next is the "to" which is the water sign because it's "to" a person. It's to "our scribe."

We're now getting pretty good about the word order. We know the suffix pronoun for "our" has to go after the noun, attached to it. So the next word is "scribe," which is, *sesh*.

That's another word that everyone remembers. It's fun to draw. And to it, we attach the "our," which we can look up in the pronoun chart if we need to. It's the same as "we" so it's water sign and three strokes.

Now all we need is "and she listens." The "and" is understood, no written word for it. So we just need "she listens." We can use our old verb *sedjem,* "to hear"—same as listens.

And by now you probably remember that "she" is the folded cloth, so we add that to "listen."

And would have sounded something like *Djed.sen n sesh.n sedjem.s.* And that completes our sentence, "They talk to our scribe and she listens." I think you can see now how, with repetition, the suffix pronouns are not so daunting. They're becoming old friends.

Let's do just a few more suffix pronoun sentences; I don't want to overload you. Let's try "He rejoices when his daughter goes down to their house." It's a long sentence. Yes, we start with the verb *resh* "to rejoice."

Now comes our suffix pronoun, "he" which I bet you remember by now is the viper *f.* So add the viper to *resh.*

"He rejoices." The "when" is understood, so we go to the next verb, "to go down," which is *ha.*

It's "his daughter" who goes down to the house, so we're now quite familiar with the word order. "Daughter" then suffix pronoun. So we add *sat*, "daughter."

𓄿𓏏𓁐 𓈖𓂋 𓅓 𓆑𓏭

And then attach the suffix pronoun "his" to it. That's the horned viper, which by now you probably remember.

𓄿𓏏𓁐 𓈖𓂋 𓅓 𓆑𓏭

Coming to the end, we just need "to their house." The "to" is the mouth *r* since it's to a place, the house.

𓄿𓏏𓁐 𓈖𓂋 𓅓 𓆑𓏭 𓂋

You might be tempted to stack the viper on top of the mouth, and you wouldn't be totally wrong. That was done. However, because we have a suffix pronoun usually the mouth would be considered a separate word, so I haven't stacked them. Now everyone knows "house," *per*, comes first and then "their." So we add the house.

𓄿𓏏𓁐 𓈖𓂋 𓅓 𓆑𓏭 𓂋 𓉐

And to it, we add "their." We might have to look this one up in our suffix pronoun chart, but that's no problem. We can find that "their" is the folded cloth water sign and three strokes.

𓄿𓏏𓁐 𓈖𓂋 𓅓 𓆑𓏭 𓂋 𓉐𓋴𓈖𓏥

Resh.f ha sat.f r per.sen. That's how you write it and say it. "He rejoices when his daughter goes down to their house."

Let's do one more, just to make sure we have our pronouns down pat. "He hears the crocodile from his house upon their road."

OK, we start with "hears," which is *sedjem*, the one with the ear.

We, of course, know that "he" is the viper.

Next, we need our crocodile, *mezeh.*

Now we need "from" and that's our owl, remember owl means a lot of things.

"His house" is easy by now. It's "house his" and "his" is the viper.

Now it's time to use a word we haven't used much, "upon." Remember what it is? It's *her,* the face with the stroke.

How about road? Yes, it's the word with the *wa* biliteral, and it's feminine with a *t,* so it is pronounced *wat.*

It's their road, so we'll add the folded cloth, water sign, and three strokes for "their."

You did it; that's our last suffix pronoun sentence. "He hears the crocodile from his house upon their road." That would be pronounced something like *Sedjem.f mezeh m per.f her wat.sen.* It's a mouthful but it's good.

OK, for your homework assignment, I'll take it easy on you. I am going to give you two sentences to translate from hieroglyphs to English. This should seem like a piece of cake to you by now.

The first one is:

You'll get it just break it up into words. And here's the second:

When you do these sentences, start by breaking them down into words and transliterating. Then the translation will be easy.

Today, for vocabulary, I just want to give you one word, but I would also like to explain the main hieroglyph that is at the root of the word. In its fullest form, the word looks like this,

It was pronounced *kheper,* and the root is the beetle. It's a trilateral hieroglyph equal to the sound *kh-p-r*, all three one after the other, *kh-p-r*. Both the hieroglyphic scarab and the actual beetle were very important in ancient Egypt.

As we've seen, the scarab hieroglyph was pronounced *kheper*; it meant "to exist." But it also meant "beetle"—the bug. Now, the dung beetle was very special to the Egyptians. The female lays its eggs in a dung ball and then rolls it to a safe place and buries it. Later, lots of little scarabs pop out, like magic. The Egyptians didn't understand the biological process of this, so to them, this was a remarkable case of procreation. Thus the beetle became a symbol of existence. That's why they carved little beetles as amulets, to be worn to ensure continued existence. Let me show you an Egyptian scarab. So when you wore a scarab around your neck, you would exist forever. It's a magical amulet.

When the Pharaoh Amenhotep III wanted to make announcements to the world, he had large scarabs and carved on the bottom he wrote his message. These scarabs were about the size of a large paperweight so you'd have plenty of room for the text. Perhaps one of his most famous scarabs was the one announcing his marriage to Queen Tiye. He mentions that "Her parents are Yuya and Tjuya," letting everyone know they're commoners—but you better accept my Queen.

A second commemorative scarab announced that he had built a pleasure lake for Queen Tiye so she could sail her new boat. What's important about this text is that he mentions the name of the boat—The Aten Gleams. This has led some scholars to suggest that Akhenaten, their son who worshiped only the Aten, may have gotten the idea from his mother.

So scarabs were very important in ancient Egypt. There was even a god named Khepri who was depicted with the body of a man and the head of a scarab. We will also see scarabs in the names of many pharaohs. We've done quite a bit of hieroglyphs today, now let's talk about the people who produced them, the scribes.

Last time I told you about Papyrus Lansing, which exhorts the young men of Egypt to become scribes. The papyrus doesn't talk about the joys of forming hieroglyphs with a reed brush, or the pleasure of reading—no, doesn't do that. Rather the budding scribe is given materialistic reasons for choosing the profession: You will meet people of higher status. You will advance your position. You won't smell like a tanner. Your arms won't be tired from manual labor. Be a scribe.

Although the social position of the scribe was continuously revered throughout Egyptian history, there was at least one voice in the conversation who did not agree.

The Greek philosopher Plato lived between about 428–348 B.C. and was well aware of Egyptian civilization. He died just before Alexander the Great entered Egypt and before the Ptolemies began their rule, but like most Greeks, he admired the far older culture of ancient Egypt—but not writing.

Plato actually lamented the invention of writing. This strange belief was shared by his teacher, Socrates.

Socrates, one of the founders of the Greek philosophical method, never wrote anything down, and I don't think this is an accident. What we know today about him comes from a body of works called *The Dialogues*. Socrates often had philosophical discussions with his students—Plato included—and these dialogues were written down by the students for future generations.

In several of the dialogues, Socrates discusses the invention of writing. He credits the invention of writing to the Egyptian god of writing, Toth, who was often depicted as an ibis-headed man. In Chapter 125 of the Book of the Dead, the deceased's heart is weighed against the feather of truth to determine if he will be admitted to the next world. Standing next to the balance scale is Toth, scribe's palette in hand, recording the result.

Socrates was aware of the tradition that Toth invented writing, and while he credits him with the invention, he laments the day writing was conceived. Socrates believes that with writing, man will no longer have knowledge. He will merely have the appearance of knowledge. For Socrates, knowledge is in your mind. Writing is external to the mind, so it can't be knowledge.

Remember, the ancient Greeks were memorists. When you said you knew the *Iliad*, that meant you could recite it. Merely reading it was not knowledge. Socrates was afraid man would lose his memory skills if he relied on Toth's invention of writing. For Socrates, the writing of bureaucratic records, tax lists, that's fine. What's important is knowledge, real knowledge. But the highest knowledge, philosophical truths, couldn't be written.

As we saw from Papyrus Lansing, the Egyptians didn't agree; they offered materialistic reasons for becoming a scribe. But there are other papyri that give more idealistic reasons for becoming a scribe. One papyrus in the British Museum, Papyrus Chester Beatty IV, links being a scribe with immortality. Now there's a reason to be a scribe.

The papyrus was written during the New Kingdom, a time when Egypt had already collapsed twice—once at the End of the Old Kingdom and once at the end of the Middle Kingdom. Both collapses led to periods of lawlessness, tomb robbing, and general disillusionment with life. For the first time, people saw the uncertainty of life, that continuity couldn't be guaranteed, and that even building a stone tomb didn't guarantee your mummy would be preserved so you could be resurrected in the next world.

Papyrus Chester Beatty IV fully acknowledges all those uncertainties and suggests that being a scribe is the only sure route to immortality, but it's a different kind of immortality than what was promised by the Egyptian religion. It's the immortality of being an author. The papyrus says:

> Man decays, his corpse is dust.
> All his kin have perished.
> But a book makes him remembered
> Through the mouth of the reader.
> Better is a book than a well-built house,
> Than tomb-chapels in the west.
> Better than a solid mansion
> Than a stela in a temple.

Talking about scribes, the author says,

> The reed pen is their child,
> The stone surface their wife …
> Death made them forgotten,
> But books made them remembered.

So scribes live on through their writings. This is different from the traditional belief in resurrection of the physical body, but it's still in line with the old Egyptian maxim: "To say the name of the dead is to make him live again." This may be why at the end of a papyrus text, often the scribe who copied it would put his name. That way, whenever anyone read the text, they would read the scribe's name and he would live again.

We have been looking at what papyri have to tell us, but I should also say something about papyrus itself, the medium on which scribes wrote. Papyrus was a very important medium for writing, and many of the sentences we use as exercises in this course were written on papyrus. Papyrus was viewed as less permanent than stone, but in Egypt's dry climate, papyri have survived for thousands of years quite well. Let's take a close look at papyrus and how it was produced.

Papyrus grew along the banks of the Nile. It would grow to more than ten feet tall with a diameter of four inches. To make it into papyrus sheets, it was harvested, the stalks were cut into sections about 12 inches long. These cylinders were then cut into thin strips. Next, the strips were placed on a board and overlapped. Then this was beaten with a wood mallet or pressed so the sap comes out and serves as the glue that binds the strips together. The overlapping strips were then left in the sun, and when they dried, Voila! You had a sheet of papyrus. If you hold it up to the light, you can see the strips. When dry, the sheet would be burnished with a smooth stone to prepare the surface for writing.

Individual sheets could be glued together to make a papyrus roll as long as desired. Some are more than 100 feet long. Papyrus was used for bureaucratic records, literary productions, and also religious texts such as the Book of the Dead. Papyrus facilitated international commerce and eventually became so important that during the Ptolemaic Period it was one of Egypt's largest exports. In later times, it was said that if the papyrus crop failed in Egypt, Rome wouldn't have been able to conduct business.

Papyrus used to grow wild in Egypt on the banks of the Nile, but not anymore. Industrialization has ended that. Today it's farmed to make into sheets so artists can paint ancient scenes to be sold to tourists. You can buy sheets of papyrus in most large art supply stores, and you might enjoy trying to write on the real thing.

But for your homework, you can still do it on ordinary note paper. I'll see you next time.

Hieroglyphs and the Bible

In the previous lecture, you practiced translating English sentences with suffix pronouns into good, hieroglyphic sentences. This lecture covers a few more points you should know about suffix pronouns, then gives you a pair of exercise to round out your work on suffix pronouns. Then the lecture covers the story of the Exodus from the Bible. Perhaps no other story is as closely related to Egypt. Many scholars have wondered if the events of Exodus actually happened. However, with a little knowledge of hieroglyphs, we might be able to shed some light on this question.

Singular, Plural, and Dual

- In the Middle Egyptian language, suffix pronouns can be singular or plural. But Egyptian also has a dual. There are suffix pronouns used only for pairs of people. They are exactly the same as the plurals, except instead of three strokes they have only two strokes. Also, these strokes are drawn at an angle.

- For example, for "we" in the plural, the suffix pronoun is the water sign with three vertical strokes: ⟨ᵐ⟩ ᵢᵢᵢ . But the dual would be the water sign with two slanted strokes: ⟨ᵐ⟩ ₙ .

- The same goes for "you." In the plural, the suffix pronoun is the tethering ring, water sign, and three strokes: ⟨≈ᵢᵢᵢ⟩. For the dual we just have two strokes: ⟨≈ₙ⟩.

- For "they" or "their" in the plural, we would have the folded cloth, water sign, and three strokes: ⟨‖ᵐᵢᵢᵢ⟩. For the dual, we simply change the three strokes to two: ⟨‖ᵐₙ⟩ .

- The duals are pronounced a bit differently than the plurals. They have a /y/ sound at the end. For example, the plural for "they" is pronounced *sen*, but the dual is pronounced *seny.*

- This holds for nouns, too: The word for "obelisk" is pronounced *tekhen*, but if we're talking about a pair of obelisks, it's *tekheny.*

- Suffix pronouns can also be used after prepositions. For example, this could be "to me": 🖼. Here's another example: 🖼. We see our familiar word "together with" (*heneh*) and the folded cloth suffix pronoun for "she" or "her" following it, so we have "together with her."

Exercise 1: "We [dual] send our scribe to him."

- Let's try translating a couple of sentences from English to hieroglyphs to become familiar with our new uses of personal pronouns.

- "We [dual] send our scribe to him" lets us use the two new uses for our personal pronouns: the dual pronoun and a pronoun coming after a preposition.

- We start with our verb, *hab*, "to send." That is 🖼. The little feet determinative suggests walking, as in sending someone out.

- We want to use the dual form of "we," giving us 🖼. That's "we send" when it is two people sending. We are sending "our scribe," so we first need "scribe" then the dual "we." Now we have: 🖼.

- Now for the "to him" part. We need the water sign "to" because "him" is a person. For the "him," we can add the personal pronoun, which is the horned viper. That gives us 🖼, or "We send our scribe to him."

Exercise 2: "They [dual] tell the secret to him [and then] he tells the secret to their father."

- We start with the verb, "to say," or "speak," or "tell," *djed*: [hieroglyphs]. Now we need "they" in the dual, giving us [hieroglyphs].

- Next is "secret," *seshta*, and "to him," the water sign and the viper: [hieroglyphs].

- The "and then" is understood, so next comes our verb "to tell" once more, giving us [hieroglyphs].

- Next up we have "he" and *seshta* again: [hieroglyphs].

- After that, we need the "to," which is the water sign: [hieroglyphs].

- Now we need "father," which has a silent viper and is pronounced *it*. Finally we add the dual "their," giving us: [hieroglyphs] as our final translation.

Bondage

- There are three stages to Exodus: bondage, the Exodus itself, and the Promised Land. This section of the lecture focuses on the bondage segment of Exodus.

- The book of Exodus involves an unnamed pharaoh, but we may be able to figure out who he is. By the time of the events in the book of Exodus, the Israelites (the descendants of Jacob, who was also called Israel) have become numerous, and this bothers the pharaoh.

- The pharoah puts a taskmaster over them and enslaves them. They build store cities in brick—not in stone—for the pharaoh. This is an important detail.

- The pharaoh says to the midwives, "Watch the two stones." The two stones refer to the birthing stools that Egyptian women used to give birth. They gave birth squatting down. The pharaoh tells the midwives to kill the male infants when they are born.

- But even with this directive from pharaoh, the Israelites prosper. The pharaoh asks the midwives why; they reply that the Israelite mothers are giving birth before the midwives arrive.

- One Israelite child's mother was worried her son would be killed, so she put him in a basket and set him adrift on the Nile. The pharaoh's daughter finds the basket, adopts the baby, and names him Moses.

- Traditionally, we are told that she gave him that name because she drew him out of the reeds, and *moshe* in Hebrew means "to draw out." But why would an Egyptian princess speak Hebrew? And would she give him a Hebrew name? It doesn't make sense.

- What does Moses mean in ancient Egyptian? Recall the hieroglyphs 𓄟𓇋𓇋, *mss*, that Champollion figured out meant "birth." It makes more sense that an Egyptian princess would give her newfound baby an Egyptian name meaning "birth."

- Moses grows up in an Egyptian household but has an encounter with the god of the Israelites, Yahweh, who appears to Moses as a burning bush. Yahweh tells Moses to go to the pharaoh and tell him, "Let my people go."

- Moses doesn't think he can do it. So Yahweh tells him to throw down his staff, and it turns into a snake. He next withers Moses' hand, then restores it. Moses is going to have supernatural powers, but he is still hesitant. He is "slow of speech," so Yahweh lets Moses bring his brother, Aaron, to do the talking.

- Moses has an audience with the pharaoh. The pharaoh is never named. He is just called "Pharaoh," which is not an Egyptian word. The word for "king" was *news:* ⸤ hieroglyphs ⸥.

- What does "pharaoh" mean in ancient Egyptian? Well, the two hieroglyphs that make the sound "pharaoh" are ⸤ hieroglyphs ⸥. That consists of *per* (house) and *ah* (great). Therefore, the pharaoh is the guy who lives in the great house. "Pharaoh" is a foreigner's way of saying "king." After the time of Exodus, the word "pharaoh" will enter the Egyptian language to mean "king."

- During his audience with the pharaoh, Aaron throws down his staff and it turns into a snake. But this doesn't impress the pharaoh. His magicians do the same thing with their staves. Still, Aaron's snake swallows those of the pharaoh's magicians, so that is a bit of a victory.

- The Coptic Bible contains the Exodus story, and the Coptic word for "magician" is *seshperonch*. Remember that Coptic is just a different script for writing the ancient Egyptian language, so let's try to think of what hieroglyphic symbols correspond to the sounds in *seshperonch*.

  ○ *Sesh* is our scribe: ⸤ hieroglyphs ⸥.

  ○ *Per* is the house sign: ⸤ hieroglyphs ⸥

  ○ *Onch* is the *ankh* hieroglyph: ⸤ hieroglyphs ⸥.

- When we put them together we get *sesh per ankh*, "scribe of the house of life." Priests in ancient Egypt were educated in a school called the House of Life. Therefore, the magicians were priests. This detail shows that whoever wrote down the Exodus story had an intimate knowledge of ancient Egypt.

The Plagues

- Back to the story: The pharaoh doesn't let the Israelites go. Worse, he tells them they still have to make their bricks, but the straw for the bricks won't be supplied. The Israelites were going to have to gather their own straw and still have the same quota of bricks. Additionally, they were not going to get their three-day religious holiday.

- Next come the plagues: The Nile turns to blood; the Egyptians are tormented with frogs, lice, boils, locusts, darkness, and so on. None of this softens the pharaoh's heart.

- Then comes the 10th plague: the killing of the firstborn, even among the cattle. (The Jewish Passover holiday comes from death passing by their homes, which were marked with lamb's

Darkness plague

blood.) When the pharaoh's firstborn son dies, he relents and lets the Israelites go. Thus bondage ends and the Exodus itself begins.

Exodus and the Promised Land

- Yahweh tells the Israelites to plunder Egypt, and they leave with gold and silver. The Bible says 600,000 men, not including their families. This is a very large number of people and has led some scholars to question the Exodus story.

- Soon after the Israelites depart, the pharaoh has a change of heart and pursues them in chariots. Often it is said that pharaoh's army perishes in the Red Sea, but that's a bad translation of the Hebrew name *Yam Souph,* which means Sea of Reeds. We don't know where this marshy area was, but it parts for the Israelites and then closes to swallow Pharaoh's army.

- Next the Israelites wander in the desert for 40 years, until they reach the Promised Land. The Israelites finally settle. Their wanderings are over.

Hieroglyphic Evidence

- We have seen several places where knowledge of hieroglyphs has added some evidence that the Exodus actually took place, but there is one more bit of hieroglyphic evidence for the story.

- There's a stela in the Egyptian Museum in Cairo that is absolutely unique. It is the only place in the Egyptian record where Israel is mentioned.

- According to the biblical account, Ramses's firstborn son died during the 10th plague. Ramses ruled for 67 years, so many of his sons died before him. His 13th son, Merneptah ("Beloved of Ptah"), succeeded him. The stela in the Egyptian Museum was carved during the fifth year of Merneptah's reign.

- Merneptah brags about all his victories over foreigners. He says: "Canaan has been plundered into every sort of woe. Ashkelon has been overcome. Gezer has been captured. Yano'am is made nonexistent; Israel is laid waste and its seed is not."

- This is the first and only mention of Israel in the Egyptian record. For this reason, many people believe that Merneptah is the pharaoh of the Exodus. But it is important to note that he is not talking about the Exodus. He is talking about battles outside of Egypt.

- The archaeological record is blank on the subject and doesn't support Exodus as an historical event. But with a little knowledge of hieroglyphs, we might be able to form some conclusions about whether Exodus occurred.

- In the Merneptah Stela, if you look at all the countries it mentions, at the end of each of them is the determinative hieroglyph for a foreign land: ⌣⌣⌣. But when Merneptah refers to Israel, we don't have the three hills to designate a foreign country. Instead, the hieroglyphs for people, a man and a woman, are present: 𓀀𓁐.

- In other words, at this point in time, Israel not an established country. Why not? They are still wandering in the desert. So during the time of Merneptah, they have not yet established themselves as a nation.

- If we count backward from year five of Merneptah, when the Israelites were still wandering, we come to the reign of Ramses the Great. The Exodus must have happened during his reign.

Lecture 9's Homework Answers

1. To translate 𓌃𓏏𓈖𓂋𓀀𓁐𓈖, start with the first word, *djed*, which means to "say" or "speak." Then comes the suffix pronoun, which is pronounced *tchen* and means "you" or "your." Since it is attached to the verb it must be "you," making "You say."

- Next is *ren*, the word for "name." We see that the same suffix pronoun is attached to "name," which is a noun, so it must be "your." At this point, we have "You say your name ."

- Now for the water sign. That is "to" as in "to people," and is pronounced simply *en*. The question is: to whom? The answer is "a scribe." We have the word for "scribe," *sesh*. But there is one more word *pen*, which is the masculine form of "this."

- In the end, our sentence means something like "You say your name to this scribe."

2. To translate [hieroglyphs], start with the first word, *hab*, which means "to send." The next word is pronounced *it*—remember the viper *f* in the word "father" is silent. So it is the father who is sending.

- Next we have the pin-tailed duck, the stroke, and the man determinative, followed by the viper. So far, the sentence as a whole means "The father is sending his son."

- We have a mouth sign next, which is the word for "to" in the direction of things or places. The next word we recognize as "town," and it is pronounced *niwit*. So far, we have "The father is sending his son to the town."

- Now we have another verb: The verb *djed* is "to tell" or "to say." We also have the horned viper suffix, so it is a "he" in action, but what is he going to tell or say? The answer is a *sekher*, a plan.

- Next is the water hieroglyph for "to" with regard to people. He's going to tell it to the *sesh*, to the scribe. So, our sentence is: "The father sends his son to the town to tell his plan to the scribe."

Lecture 10's Homework

Translate these two sentences into hieroglyphs.

1. "They [dual] fare down to the city, together with her."

2. "This land is in joy when you [dual] are in the sky." Imagine the sun and moon as the "you" so the dual makes sense.

Hieroglyphs and the Bible

Welcome back. Last time we practiced translating English sentences with suffix pronouns into good, hieroglyphic sentences. Then, since we did so many English-to-hieroglyph sentences, as a reward, I gave you only two hieroglyph-to-English sentences.

Let's start with our first sentence,

The first word is pronounced *djed*, and we know it means to "say" or "speak." Then comes the suffix pronoun. Well, I'm sure you looked it up, and you found that it's pronounced *tchn*, and it means "you" or "your." Since it's attached to the verb, it must be "you"—"you speak." Next is *ren*, the word for "name." We see that the same suffix pronoun is attached to "name," which is a noun, so it must be "your." So we have "You say your name."

Now the water sign. That's "to," as in "to people," and is pronounced simply *n*. Now the question is, to whom? The answer is, a scribe. We have the word for "scribe," *Sesh*. But there's one more word, *pen*, which is the masculine form of "this." So our sentence means something like, "You say, or tell, your name to this scribe." Good. Isn't it a lot easier going from hieroglyphs to English than the other way?

Now for the next sentence—the long one.

We'll have to take this one a word at a time; it's very long. First word is *hab*, "to send." Well, the next word is pronounced *it*—remember the viper *f* in the word "father" is silent. So it's "The father who's sending." Next we have the pin-tailed duck; that's the *sa* biliteral. When it's used to indicate the word "son," it is often followed by the stroke and a man determinative. So that's the word for "son." Tacked onto "son" is the viper, so it must be "his son." The viper is our suffix pronoun for "his." So, "The father is sending his son." Where? Well, we have a mouth sign next, which is the word for "to" in the direction of things or places. So he must be going to a place. Yes, we recognize the next word as "town," and it's pronounced *niwit*. "The father is sending his son to the town."

Now we have another verb, so either we have a compound sentence or two sentences. The verb, *djed* is "to tell" or "say," and we have the horned viper suffix, so it's "he." What is he going to tell or say? A *seckher*, a "plan." And he's going to tell it to—there's the water hieroglyph for "to" with regard to people—he's going to tell it to the *Sesh*, to the "scribe." So, "The father sends his son to town to tell his plan to the scribe." That's our homework; just two sentences.

We haven't covered everything we need to know about suffix pronouns, so let me just add a few more points. First, let me tell you about an unusual feature of the Middle Egyptian language. We've seen that, as in English, suffix pronouns can be either singular or plural. But Egyptian also has a dual. There are suffix pronouns used only for two people—for pairs. They're exactly the same as the plurals, except instead of three strokes, which is for plural, they have only two strokes. Also, these strokes are drawn at an angle.

For example, for "we" in the plural, the suffix pronoun is the water sign with three vertical strokes,

〰
I I I.

Well, for the dual, if there were only two of us, it would be the water sign with two slanted strokes,

〰
\\ .

Same for "you." In the plural, the suffix pronoun is the tethering ring, water sign, and three strokes.

I I I.

For the dual, we just have two strokes,

\\.

Last, for "they" or "their," in the plural, we'd have the folded cloth, water sign, and three strokes,

I I I.

For the dual, we simply change the three strokes to two and put them at an angle,

\\.

The duals are pronounced a bit differently than the plurals. They have a *y* sound at the end. So for example, as we've seen, the plural for "they" is pronounced *sen*,

I I I.

For the dual, we have the two strokes and it's pronounced something like *seny*,

\\.

This *y* ending for duals doesn't just apply to suffix pronouns, it holds for all nouns, too. For example, the word for "obelisk" is pronounced *tekhen*,

Add this one to your dictionary if you haven't already. Well, if we're talking about a "pair of obelisks," then the word would be pronounced *tekheny*, something like that,

So now if you see two strokes at an angle, think dual.

One more thing about suffix pronouns, they can be used after prepositions. For example, this could be "to me",

Here's another example,

We see our familiar word "together with," *heneh*, and the cloth suffix-pronoun for "she" or "her" following it, so we have "together with her."

Let's try translating a couple of sentences from English to hieroglyphs to become familiar with our new uses of personal pronouns. How about "We," in the dual "send our scribe to him." This sentence lets us use two new uses for our personal pronouns—the dual pronoun and a pronoun coming after a preposition.

Let's try it. We start with our verb *hab,* "to send",

That's the easy part. The little determinative suggests walking, as in sending someone out. Now we want to use the dual form of "we." Well, the normal plural "we" is the water sign with three strokes. For the dual, we simply have two strokes instead of three,

That's "we send" when it's two of us sending. "We are sending our scribe," so we first need "scribe,"

𓃀𓅯𓏏𓀁𓈖𓍢𓀀.

There he is. Then we can add "our," but it has to be in the dual since the "we" was dual. So again, we add the water sign with the two strokes,

𓃀𓅯𓏏𓈖𓀁𓀀𓈖𓈖.

Now for the "him" part—"to him." We are going to use our suffix pronoun after the preposition "to." We need the water sign "to" because it is "to him," a person

𓃀𓅯𓏏𓈖𓀁𓀀𓈖𓈖𓈖.

Now for the "him," we can add the personal pronoun, which is the horned viper "him,"

𓃀𓅯𓏏𓈖𓀁𓀀𓈖𓈖𓆑.

And that's it; "We send our scribe to him." Good.

Let's do one more for practice. How about, "They," in the dual, "tell the secret to him," and then "He tells the secret to their father." We start with the verb "to say," or "speak," or "tell," *djed*,

𓆓.

Now we need "they" in the dual. Again, the normal plural for "they" is the folded cloth and water sign with three strokes. For the dual, we merely substitute two strokes for the three,

𓆓𓋴𓈖.

Good. Next is "secret," *seshta*,

𓆓𓋴𓈖𓉐𓂧𓅯.

Now we need "to him," so we use the water sign for "to" and the viper for "him",

𓂝𓏏𓈖𓃀𓅓𓏏𓈖𓃀.

The "and then" is understood, so next comes our verb, "to tell," again,

𓂝𓏏𓈖𓃀𓅓𓏏𓈖𓃀𓂝.

"He" is a pronoun quite familiar to us by now. We all remember that it's the horned viper *f*,

𓂝𓏏𓈖𓃀𓅓𓏏𓈖𓃀𓂝𓆑.

Now we need *seshta* again,

𓂝𓏏𓈖𓃀𓅓𓏏𓈖𓃀𓂝𓈖𓃀𓅱.

Next, we need the "to," which is the water sign,

𓂝𓏏𓈖𓃀𓅓𓏏𓈖𓃀𓂝𓈖𓃀𓅱𓈖.

It's getting easy. Now we need "father," which because of the silent viper in it, everyone seems to remember. It's pronounced *it*,

𓂝𓏏𓈖𓃀𓅓𓏏𓈖𓃀𓂝𓈖𓃀𓅱𓈖𓏏𓀀.

Now we add "their," but in the dual because the sentence began with "they—in the dual—telling the secret." So we use the folded cloth, water sign, and two strokes,

𓂝𓏏𓈖𓃀𓅓𓏏𓈖𓃀𓂝𓈖𓃀𓅱𓈖𓏏𓀀𓈖.

Good. And that's it. "They tell the secret to him, and he tells the secret to their father." He's a tattletale!

I hope suffix pronouns are becoming more familiar. They're very important. Remember, this is only the middle of the course, and look what you can do.

You understand something about Egyptian grammar, you know the verb comes at the beginning, you're comfortable with a small group of verbs and nouns, and you can actually translate some real Egyptian sentences. I'm sure that after another dozen or so lectures, you will be able to translate inscriptions on objects found in Tutankhamen's tomb. That's what we'll do in our last two lectures.

Let me just say a word about the language of the inscriptions in Tutankhamen's tomb, and the New Kingdom in general. As you know, we are learning what is called Middle Egyptian, which is the language spoken during the Middle Kingdom, around 2000 B.C. Like any language, the ancient Egyptian language changed over the centuries.

Think about how much English has changed. Old English, the language in which *Beowulf* is written, is almost unintelligible to the modern reader. Middle English, the language of Chaucer's *Canterbury Tales*, takes quite a bit of effort to understand. The opening sentence, or at least part of the opening sentence, of the prologue is still quite removed from modern English. Let me give you an example.

> *Whan that Aprille with his shoures soote*
> *The droghte of March hath perced to the roote,*
> *And bathed every veyne in swich licour*
> *Of which vertu engendred is the flour.*

That was written in the 14th century. Think how different our spoken language is now. So how can we, learning Middle Egyptian, expect to translate objects in Tutankhamen's tomb that were crafted during the New Kingdom, centuries after Middle Egyptian was spoken? The answer is what linguists and art historians call archaizing—harkening back to the good old days. In the New Kingdom official documents, temple walls, et cetera; they were still using Middle Egyptian as the official language. The Egyptians didn't like change. So Tut's New Kingdom treasures have Middle Kingdom inscriptions on them. So I promise, if you do your homework, you will be able to translate Tut's treasures.

Now, speaking of homework, let me give you just two sentences to translate. First, "They," in the dual, "fare down together with her." That's your first one. Second, "This land is in joy when you" dual, "are in the sky." For this sentence, imagine the sun and moon as the "you" so the dual makes sense. Let's just do those two for homework.

Now, let's do a bit of applied hieroglyphs. It's time to see how a little knowledge of hieroglyphs might help answer some biblical questions. Of all the books in the Bible, Exodus is most closely associated with Egypt; and all the narratives in the Bible, Exodus is mentioned more often than any other, usually in connection with the establishment of Israel as a state.

But there's a mystery about Exodus. As important as it is, there's little archaeological evidence for the events it relates. There's no record of a large number of Israelites in Egypt, no mention of anyone named Moses, and even the word "Israel" is only mentioned once in all the thousands and thousands of hieroglyphic texts. So, many scholars have wondered if the events of Exodus actually happened. Could it be just a story? My belief is that with a little knowledge of hieroglyphs, we might be able to shed some light on this question. There are three stages to the Book of Exodus: Bondage, the Exodus, and The Promised Land. Let's start with Bondage.

We are told in the Bible that there came to the throne a pharaoh who knew not Joseph. If you know your Joseph story, you'll remember that Joseph was sold into slavery in Egypt by his jealous brothers, but rose to become the *vizier* of Egypt. But this was centuries before Exodus, so it's not surprising that the pharaoh didn't know of Joseph. Note, that pharaoh is not named. Nowhere in the Book of Exodus is the pharaoh named, but I think we may be able to figure out who he is.

The Israelites—the descendants of Jacob, who was also called Israel— have become numerous, and this really bothers Pharaoh. This was basically an early immigration problem. So he puts a taskmaster over them and enslaves them. They are building in brick for the pharaoh. This is an important detail. Notice, it's not stone. It's a common misconception that the Israelites built the pyramids. I remember when Menachem Begin, the former prime minister of Israel, stood in front of the pyramids with Egyptian

President Anwar Sadat in 1977—it was a great event. And Begin said, "We built the pyramids." Wrong. The Bible even tells us the Israelites were building the store cities of Ramses and Pithom. Note that one of the cities is named Ramses, so the pharaoh must be named Ramses. But the problem is, which Ramses? There were lots of pharaohs named Ramses.

So the Israelites are laboring in brick to build store cities, but pharaohs aren't happy because they're too numerous. He says to the midwives, "Watch the two stones." The two stones refer to the birthing stools that Egyptians used to give birth. They gave birth squatting—sitting down. This makes some sense since gravity helps the baby descend from the birth canal. And here are the hieroglyphs for birth. You can see the woman is not lying down, she's squatting—. And there's the baby, coming out. So Pharaoh tells the midwives to kill the male infants when they're born. The girls are allowed to live. But even with this directive from pharaoh, the Israelites prosper. Pharaoh asks the midwives, "Why?" And they reply, "Those Israelite women are strong and they give birth before we arrive."

One Israelite child's mother was worried that her son would be killed, so she put him in a basket and set him adrift on the Nile. Pharaoh's daughter finds the basket, adopts the baby, and names him Moses. Now, traditionally scholars tell us that she gave him that name because she drew him out of the reeds, and *moshe* in Hebrew means "to draw out." But why would an Egyptian princess speak Hebrew? And would she give him a Hebrew name? It doesn't make sense.

Well, what does "Moses" mean in ancient Egyptian? Remember the hieroglyphs *mss*,

that Champollion figured out meant "birth"? It makes more sense that an Egyptian princess would give her newfound baby an Egyptian name meaning "birth." Once again, hieroglyphs help answer a biblical question. Why does Moses have the name he does? It also lends a bit of credibility to the Exodus story. The details ring true; just as the midwives being told to watch the bricks rings true.

So, Moses grows up in an Egyptian household but has an encounter with the God of the Israelites, Yahweh, who appears to Moses as a burning bush. Yahweh tells Moses to go to Pharaoh and tell him, "Let my people go"—it's the Charlton Heston moment. Moses doesn't think he can do it. So Yahweh tells him to throw down his staff—his walking stick—and it turns into a snake. He next withers Moses's hand and tells him to put it in his cloak and draw it out, and the hand is restored. Moses is going to have supernatural powers, but he's still hesitant. He's slow of speech—he may stutter—so Yahweh lets Moses bring his brother, Aaron, to do the talking.

Moses has an audience with Pharaoh. As I've said before, Pharaoh is never named; he's just called Pharaoh. Now, "pharaoh" is not an Egyptian word. The word for "king" was *nesu*,

As you can see, there's a silent *t* in there. But pharaoh is what the Israelites call him. So what does "pharaoh" mean in ancient Egyptian? Well, the two hieroglyphs that make up the sound "pharaoh" are *per*, "the house;" and *ah*, the biliteral that means "great",

So the pharaoh is the guy who lives in the great house. Remember, the Israelites are foreigners; they don't speak the language that well. "Pharaoh" is a foreigner's way of saying "king"—the guy who lives in the big house. After the time of Exodus, the word "pharaoh" will enter the Egyptian language to mean "king." This is still another hieroglyphic detail that lends support to Exodus being a record of a historical event.

During his audience with Pharaoh, Aaron throws down his staff, just like Yahweh instructed, and it turns into a snake. But this doesn't impress Pharaoh. His magicians do the same thing with their staves. It must have been the old snake trick that everybody knew. I wondered about this. Many years ago I decided to find out if such a trick were possible. The town of Esna, near Luxor, was famous for its snake charmers, so I went there to see if anyone could reproduce the trick as it's described in the Bible. Sure enough, the first snake charmer we saw took a cobra, stroked it under its neck, and rather quickly it went rigid, like a staff! Then the snake charmer gently tossed it to the ground and it reared up, just like in the Bible. Still, Aaron's snake swallows those of Pharaoh's magicians, so that's a bit of a victory.

In this episode with the magicians, our knowledge of hieroglyphs can once again help us determine if there's any truth to the Exodus story. Here, we're actually going to need a bit of Coptic. You'll remember that Coptic is the last stage of the ancient Egyptian language, written by the Egyptians who converted to Christianity in the early days of the religion. Well, Coptic is still used in the liturgy of the Coptic Church, like Latin was used in the Catholic Church. The Coptic Bible contains the Exodus story, and what's interesting for us is the Coptic word for "magician;" it's *seshperonch—seshperonch*. Now, remember that Coptic is just a different script for writing the ancient Egyptian language, so let's try to think of what hieroglyphic symbols correspond to the sound in *seshperonch*.

Well, *Sesh* is our word for "scribe",

.

Per is the house sign,

.

And *onch* is the *ankh*,

.

When we put them together, we get *Sesh per ankh*, "scribe of the house of life,"

.

Priests in ancient Egypt were educated in a school called the House of Life. So Pharaoh's magicians were priests. This detail shows that whoever wrote down the Exodus story had an intimate knowledge of ancient Egypt.

Anyway, Pharaoh doesn't let the Israelites go. Worse, he tells them they still have to make their bricks, but the straw won't be supplied; they have to gather and chop it themselves. They're not making bricks without straw. This is a common misconception. In the 19th century, there were biblical scholars running throughout Egypt looking for bricks made without straw as evidence of the Exodus. The Israelites were going to have to gather their own straw and still have the same quota of bricks. Not only that, they were not going to get their three-day religious holiday.

So, next come the 10 plagues: the Nile turns to blood, the Egyptians are tormented with frogs, lice, boils, locusts, darkness; all that bad stuff. All intended to convince pharaoh to let the Israelites go. But this doesn't soften pharaoh's heart; he still won't release them. Then comes the 10th plague, the killing of the firstborn, even among the cattle. Yahweh tells Moses to take the blood of a lamb and paint it above the doorsills of the Israelites so the Angel of Death will know to pass over that household and spare the firstborn. That's why Jews celebrate Passover; the Angel of Death passed over their ancestor's households. When Pharaoh's firstborn son dies, he relents and finally lets the Israelites go. Thus ends Bondage, and the Exodus begins.

Yahweh tells the Israelites to plunder Egypt, and they leave with gold and silver. How many leave? The Bible says 600,000 men, not including their families. This is a very large number of people, and this has led many scholars to question the Exodus story. The entire population of Egypt at about this time may have been only a million, so the number is clearly too large to have happened the way it's told in the Bible.

As you'll remember, soon after the Israelites depart, Pharaoh has a change of heart and pursues them in chariots. Often it's said that pharaoh's army perishes in the Red Sea, but that's a bad translation of the Hebrew, *Yam Souph,* which means "Sea of Reeds." We don't know exactly where this marshy area was, but it parts for the Israelites and then closes to swallow

Pharaoh's army. Next the Israelites wander in the desert for 40 years until they reach the Promised Land. The Israelites finally find the land of milk and honey and settle. Their wanderings are over.

We've seen several places where knowledge of hieroglyphs has added some evidence that the Exodus actually took place, but there's one more bit of hieroglyphic evidence for the story, and it's the most interesting of all. As you will remember, a stela was a round-topped stone with an inscription carved on it. This is where we get the idea of a tombstone from, I think. Well, there's a stela in the Egyptian Museum in Cairo that is absolutely unique. It's the only place in the Egyptian record where Israel is mentioned.

Now, according to the biblical account, Ramses's firstborn son died during the 10th plague, along with the other firstborn Egyptians. From Egyptian records we know that Ramses's first-born son was Amun-her-kepshef. A *kepshef* was a curved sword. So his name means "Amun is upon my sword." When Amun-her-kepshef dies, we have to figure out when it happens. We'll see a bit later. Ramses ruled for 67 years, so many of his sons died before him, and it's his 13th son, Merneptah—beloved of Ptah— who succeeds him. Now this stela in the Egyptian Museum was carved during the fifth year of Merneptah's reign.

Merneptah's bragging about all his victories over foreigners. And he says, "Canaan has been plundered into every sort of woe. Ashkelon has been overcome. Gezer has been captured. Yano'am has been made nonexistent. Israel is laid waste and its seed is not." This is the first and only mention of Israel in the Egyptian record. For this reason, many people believe that Merneptah is the pharaoh of the Exodus. But it's important to note that he's not talking about the Exodus. He is talking about battles outside of Egypt. He's listing all the countries beaten up.

So you can see the puzzle about Exodus. It's repeatedly put forward in the Bible as history, in considerable detail. But the archaeological record is kind of blank on the subject and doesn't support Exodus as a historical event. I don't think the debate has to be end here. My belief is that with a little knowledge of hieroglyphs, we might be able to come to some conclusions about whether Exodus occurred.

Let's look at the Merneptah Stela to see what we can figure out. First, let's see how Israel's spelled. You can make it out. There's a reed, the bolt *z*, and other hieroglyphs we're familiar with. See, there's a mouth used for the *l*. But more important, if you look at all those countries Merneptah's talking about—Canaan, Ashkelon, Gezer—at the end of each of them is the determinative hieroglyph for a foreign land. It's the three mountains sign, ᴗᴗ. But when Merneptah refers to Israel, we don't have the three hills to designate a foreign country. Look closely at what we have. Can you figure out what the hieroglyphs are? It's not easy. They're roughly done, basically scratched into the stone. It's the hieroglyphs for people, a man and a woman,

.

In other words, at this point in time, Israel is not a place, not an established country. Why not? They're still wandering in the desert. So during the time of Merneptah, they have not yet established themselves as a nation. Now, if we count backwards from year five of Merneptah, when the Israelites were still wandering, we come to the reign of Ramses the Great. The Exodus must have happened during his reign.

The great Egyptologist and biblical scholar Kenneth Kitchen even suggests a year when the Exodus took place. Remember Amun-her-kepshef, Ramses's firstborn? We know from other records he died around the 20th year of his reign. So that may be when the Exodus occurred. The math isn't exact, but it's close enough to add credence to the Exodus story. It occurred during the reign of Ramses, and the Israelites were still wandering during the early years of Merneptah. So our knowledge of hieroglyphs helps support the idea that the Exodus probably was a historical event. It wasn't exactly as portrayed in the Bible, but something happened.

I'll see you next time.

Dependent Pronouns and the Passive Voice

This lecture starts of with some more work involving suffix pronouns. You'll see how they can be used to talk about oneself. Then we'll move on to a new kind of pronoun: dependent pronouns, which are able to stand alone, unlike a suffix. The lecture next covers the passive voice (not to be confused with the past tense) before moving on to look at a monumental expedition. Then the lecture describes the Chicago House, which is doing very important work today in the field of Egyptology.

Reflexivity

- Suffix pronouns can also be used to talk about oneself. This is called *reflexive*. In English we say, "myself," "herself," and "himself." They are used for emphasis: "I did it myself" carries more emphasis than "I did it."

- Egyptians didn't have special reflexive pronouns. Often they just repeated the suffix pronoun for emphasis. For example, look at this sentence: 𓋴𓂋.

  ○ The verb is *djed*, meaning "to say" or "speak," and we have the suffix pronoun viper, which is "he." So that's "He says."

  ○ Next we have the water sign, which is "to" for people. Now we have "He talks to" someone. Another viper makes that someone himself: "He talks to himself."

- Sometimes, to emphasize a reflexive, a special word is used, *djes*: 𓊪. Here's an example: 𓂋𓈖𓏤𓊪𓂋. *Ren* is "name" and the man sign is the suffix pronoun for "my." The folded cloth would give it the sense of "my own name," which is a bit more emphatic.

Dependent Pronouns

- Unlike suffix pronouns, dependent pronouns do not have to be added onto any other word in the sentence. They stand alone.

- Dependent pronouns are usually used as the object of the verb— the thing or person receiving the action. For example, "He sends me" has two pronouns: "he" and "me."

- Translating the "He sends" part is easy. It's 𓅓𓄿𓂝. But we haven't had the "me" dependent pronoun. It is written like 𓅱𓀀 and was pronounced *wi*. So, "He sends me" would be pronounced *Hab.f wi* and written 𓅓𓄿𓂝𓅱𓀀.

- "He sends you" needs a different dependent pronoun for "you." If it is a masculine "you" that "he" is sending, like his son, then we need the masculine dependent pronoun *tchu*: 𓏙𓏤. "He sends you" would be *Hab.f tchu*: 𓅓𓄿𓂝𓏙𓏤.

- If it is a female "you" who is being sent, then we need *tchen*: 𓏌 "He sends you" with a female "you" is 𓅓𓄿𓂝𓏌.

- For "him" or "it" masculine, it is *sew*: 𓊃𓏤. If someone is sending "him" it would look like this: 𓅓𓄿𓂝𓊃𓏤. For "her" or "it" feminine, it is *sey*, 𓏭. "He sends her" is 𓅓𓄿𓂝𓏭. The two strokes typically mean dual, but once in a while it is a dependent pronoun.

- To help the process, make a dependent pronoun chart of your own. You can find a model of one at the back of this book.

Plural Dependent Pronouns

- There are also dependent pronouns for plurals. They are the same as the suffix pronouns. So, for example, if we wanted to say "You ferry us across," we start with the verb, *dja,* 𓊦𓏲. Then we add the suffix pronoun for "you," which is the basket. ⌇🦅⏦ forms the "You ferry across" part.

- Now we add the dependent pronoun, which is the same as the suffix in this case. That's *tchen*, giving us ⌇🦅⏦☰. That's pronounced *Dja.k tchen*.

- If we wanted to say "They ferry you [plural] across," we'd start with the verb, "ferry across," ⌇🦅◁. Then it's time for the suffix pronoun for "they," which is *sen*, giving us ⌇🦅◁|||.

- That's the "They ferry across" part. Now we need the dependent pronoun for plural "you." It's the same as the suffix pronoun plural for "you." That's *tchen*, giving us ⌇🦅◁||| ||| ☰ as "They ferry you across."

Uses of Dependent Pronouns

- Dependent pronouns are very useful. They are often used after phrases of exclamation, like "Behold," which is *mek*: 🦉⏦.

- Sometimes the arm hieroglyph will be holding a rounded loaf in its hand: 🦉⏦. This has the same meaning, "Behold."

- Another exclamation that uses dependent pronouns is "Lo," which is *istch*, ||⏦.

- One grammatical note related to dependent pronouns: The ancient Egyptians never simply said something like "You are my scribe." They would use an owl *m* to say "You are *as* my scribe." The owl hieroglyph is the "as," and we can call it the owl of predication.

The Passive Voice

- Next, let's learn the passive voice. ⌁🦅𓀀 is in the active voice and translates as "I hear," pronounced *Sedjem.i*.

- If we insert a loaf and a quail chick between the verb and the subject, it would look like and sound like this: ⌁🦅◠𓀀,

Sedjem.tu.i. This insertion of the loaf and quail chick forms the passive voice; we translate it as "I am heard."

- Another example: ⌀🦉⌐ translates as "You hear." If we insert *tu*, the loaf and quail chick, between the verb and subject, we get ⌀🦉⌐🦆⌐, or "You are heard."

Rosellini's Expedition

- The first expedition to copy hieroglyphs that could actually read them was an all-star team composed of French and Tuscan scholars. The French were led by Jean-François Champollion and the Tuscans by Ippolito Rosellini.

- In 1824, Rosellini read Champollion's work on decipherment and fell in love with both Egypt and hieroglyphs. The two met in 1825 and quickly hit it off, with Rosellini happily taking the role of student.

- They visited each other frequently, with Rosellini helping Champollion catalog the Louvre's Egyptian collection. While there, Rosellini conceived the idea of a Tuscan expedition to Egypt to extend what the French had done with their *Description de l'Égypte*. Because his team could read hieroglyphs, he was convinced they could advance the study of Egyptology considerably.

- In 1827, Rosellini asked Grand Duke Leopold II to fund his expedition to Egypt. Leopold agreed. Champollion had never been to Egypt and enthusiastically agreed to join the expedition. He had some difficulty getting funding from King Charles X, but in the end prevailed.

- On July 31, 1828, the expedition sailed from Toulon for Egypt, almost exactly 30 years after Napoleon's savants left the same port for Alexandria. For 15 months, the dozen or so artists, Egyptologists, and scholars sailed up and down the Nile, recording everything.

- One of their goals was to validate Champollion's decipherment of hieroglyphs. In 1828, there were still linguists who doubted the validity of Champollion's translations, so the teams made a special effort to record inscriptions.

- When they returned, Champollion and Rosellini planned a joint publication, but it was not to be. Champollion died in 1832 at the age of 41. Champollion's elder brother, and executor, did not trust Rosellini with his brother's legacy. So in the end, each team produced its own publication.

- Because the two teams were working side by side at the same sites in Egypt, often sharing artists, the engravings produced by the Tuscans and French are often indistinguishable, but they have quite a different feel from the *Description de l'Égypte* engravings.

- Napoleon's men were mainly engineers and architects. The Franco-Tuscan expedition had professional artists. Another difference is that they could translate the hieroglyphs. They knew that an owl and a quail chick were not interchangeable. They spent days accurately copying lines and lines of hieroglyphs.

- This marvelous expedition set the ball rolling for the accurate and professional copying of hieroglyphic inscriptions.

The Epigraphic Survey

- The Epigraphic Survey of the University of Chicago's Oriental Institute has been copying hieroglyphic inscriptions for more than 75 years. It is a massive program, involving hundreds of extremely talented scholars.

- More than 100 years ago, the great American Egyptologist James Henry Breasted realized that the hieroglyphic inscriptions on temple walls were in danger of being lost to looting or decay.

- Breasted set out on a one-man campaign to translate every historical inscription in Egypt. He almost pulled it off. He ended up publishing a monumental five-volume set of his translations called *Ancient Records of Egypt*.

- Breasted convinced John D. Rockefeller that the temples of ancient Egypt were endangered and their inscriptions had to be accurately copied by a team of trained Egyptologists. Rockefeller agreed and provided money to build a compound in Luxor, Egypt, near the principal monuments, to house what would become known as the Epigraphic Survey.

- For more than 90 years, successive teams of scholars have lived at Chicago House, as the compound is called, recording inscriptions. Each epigrapher is both a talented artist and an Egyptologist who can translate hieroglyphs. Their painstaking recording method has become known as the Chicago House Method.

- The Epigraphic Survey chose the temple of Medinet Habu as its first major project. Medinet Habu, the mortuary temple of Ramses III (no relation to Ramses the Great), is the largest temple ever built by a single pharaoh.

Medinet Habu

- They began work in the late 1920s and published their first volume in 1934. Their work continues today. And their work has become urgent.

- Since the creation of the Aswan High Dam in 1970s, the water table in Luxor has risen considerably. This groundwater saturated the foundation stones of the temples and was wicked upward to the blocks higher up, causing the sandstone to crumble.

- This year the team has been aided by new digital technology. They are now able to photograph the walls, load the photographs onto a computer, and then "ink" the reliefs and hieroglyphs on the computer using a stylus. Then they digitally "bleach" the photo away, leaving the clean, clear drawing of the wall.

- All of Chicago House's work is available digitally on the Oriental Institute's website, and it's free. If you want a hard copy, the massive volumes are available for purchase.

Lecture 10's Homework Answers

Lecture 10's homework gave you two sentences to translate into hieroglyphs.

1. The first was "[Dual they] fare downstream to the city, together with her."

- We start with the verb, "to fare downstream." That's *khed*, . Next we attach our suffix pronoun for "they," which is the folded cloth, water sign, and two strokes for dual: .

- Now how do we say "together with?" That's *heneh, giving us* . Finally, it is with "her," so we can use the folded cloth suffix pronoun. We end up with , *pronounced Khed seny heneh.s.*

2. The second sentence was "This land is in joy when [dual you] are in the sky." Our verb is "is," so we start with *yew*, 𓇋𓅱. We next add the "land" ideogram, which was pronounced *ta*, giving us 𓇋𓅱𓏏𓄿.

   • We have to make sure we say that it is "this" land, so we need to add the correct "this." *Ta* doesn't end in a *t*, so it is masculine. That tells us to use *pen*, the masculine form for "this."

   • "This" follows the noun, so we add it after "land." Now we have 𓇋𓅱𓏏𓄿𓈖. The owl is the "in" and "joy" is *reshwet*, leaving us with: 𓇋𓅱𓏏𓄿𓈖𓅓𓂋𓈙𓅱𓏏.

Lecture 11's Homework

Translate these two sentences into hieroglyphs.

1. "You [singular feminine] send me to him."

2. "You [singular masculine] ferry her across to the city."

Translate these three sentences into English.

1. 𓊪𓅱𓂋𓈖𓊪𓀁𓁶𓂋𓈖𓊪𓈖. The word that starts with the field goal sign and ends with the man with the basket on his head is the determinative; it means "work" and was pronounced *kat*.

2. 𓅨𓂋𓏤𓃀𓂋𓏏𓀀

3. 𓏏𓊪𓄿𓏏𓏠𓆈𓅨𓅨𓂋𓏏

Translate these three sentences to hieroglyphs.

1. "I am sent to the city."

2. "They are seen in the river."

3. "His daughter is sent to the boat."

Dependent Pronouns and the Passive Voice

Welcome back. Last time I gave you two sentences to translate into hieroglyphs. Let's start with them. The first was "They—in the dual—fare downstream together with her." We all know by now that we start with the verb, "to fare downstream." That's *khed*,

.

Next, we attach our suffix pronoun for "they," which is the folded cloth, water sign ,and two strokes for the dual,

So, we have "them faring downstream." Now, how do we say "together with?" Well, that's *heneh*,

Finally, it's "with her," so we can use the folded cloth suffix pronoun,

And that's it. *Khed seny heneh.s*, "They fare downstream together with her." Good.

One more sentence from the homework. "This land is in joy when you—in the dual—are in the sky." Our verb is "is," so we start with *yew*,

Decoding the Secrets of Egyptian Hieroglyphs 235

Now it's the land that's in joy, so we next add the "land" ideogram, which was pronounced *ta*,

𓇋𓂋𓇾 I.

We have to make sure that we say that it's "this land," so we need to add the correct "this." *Ta* doesn't end in a *t*, so it's masculine. That tells us to use *pen*, the masculine form for "this." We also remember that "this" follows the noun, so we add it after "land,"

𓇋𓂋𓇾 I 𓂋𓈖.

The owl is the "in,"

𓇋𓂋𓇾 I 𓂋𓈖 𓅓.

And "joy" is *reshwet*,

𓇋𓂋𓇾 I 𓂋𓈖 𓅓 𓂋𓈙𓍯𓏏.

So now we have, "This land is in joy."

There was another way we could have translated that sentence with almost the same meaning. Can you figure out how? We could have used the verb, *resh*—"to rejoice"—and it would have been, "The land rejoices." Not exactly the same, but close. Next, we must do the second part of the sentence. The "when" is understood. So we need the verb "is,"

𓇋𓂋.

That's the "are." Now, we add the suffix pronoun for "you," in the dual; which is the same as "you" plural, but with two strokes rather than three—*techney*,

𓍿𓈖
𓏥 .

236   Lecture 11 Transcript • Dependent Pronouns and the Passive Voice

"In" is the owl,

{hieroglyphs}.

Good. And last is "sky," pronounced *pet*,

{hieroglyphs}.

And that's our sentence: "This land is in joy when you are in the sky," *Yew ta pen m reshewt yew techeny em pet*. Good.

Now, I'd like to do a little grammar with you, first involving suffix pronouns— those hieroglyphs added to nouns for possession or verbs to show who is doing the action, as in "He says," *djed.f*,

{hieroglyphs}.

Suffix pronouns can also be used another way—to talk about oneself. This is called reflexive. In English, we say "myself," "herself," "himself;" and they're used for emphasis. Rather than just saying, "I did it," I might say, "I did it myself" for emphasis. This is the primary use of the reflexive.

Egyptians didn't have special reflexive pronouns like we do. Often they just repeated the suffix pronoun for emphasis. For example, look at this sentence:

{hieroglyphs}.

You can translate that. The verb is *djed*, "to say" or "speak," and we have the suffix pronoun viper, which is "he." So that's "He says." Next, we have the water sign. What do you think it's doing? What does it mean? Well, it is "to" for people. So "He talks to." To whom? Another viper makes it, "He talks to himself." Sometimes, to emphasize a reflexive, a special word is used—*djes*,

{hieroglyph}.

That's used for all kinds of reflexive stuff. For example,

Ren is "name," and the man sign is the suffix pronoun for "my." So the serpent folded cloth would give it the sense of "My own name;" a bit more emphatic. Here's another one,

That would be "Re—the sun god—himself." "Re himself." Just remember that the serpent with the folded cloth is reflexive.

By now, you're somewhat comfortable with suffix pronouns. You know how to affix them to nouns for possession and how to tack them on to the ends of verbs for action. We've even seen that they can be used reflexively. Now I want to show you a different kind of pronoun, the dependent pronoun. Dependent pronouns do not have to be added onto any other word in the sentence. It's not a suffix; they stand alone. Dependent pronouns are usually used as the object of the verb—the thing or person receiving the action. For example, if I said, "He sends me," we have two pronouns in the sentence—two words that take the place of proper nouns. We have "he" and we have "me." Now the "He sends" part is easy; we've had that before. We start with our verb "to send," *hab*,

and then we add the "he" suffix pronoun, which is the horned viper, *hab.f*,

What we haven't had is the "me" pronoun. This is a dependent pronoun. It's written like this:

And as you would expect, it was pronounced *wi*. *Wi*. So, "He sends me" would be *hab.f wi*,

𓏠𓄿𓂺𓏤𓀀.

If I wanted to say "He sends you," I need a different dependent pronoun for "you." If it's a masculine "you" that he's sending, like his son, then I need the masculine dependent pronoun *tchu*,

𓏏𓅱.

So, "He sends you" would be *hab.f tchu*,

𓏠𓄿𓂧𓏏𓅱.

If it's a female "you" who's being sent, then we need *tchen*,

𓏏
𓈖.

"He sends you," but feminine,

𓏠𓄿𓂧𓏏𓈖.

For "him" or "it" masculine, it's *sew*,

𓋴𓅱.

So if I'm sending "him," it would look like this:

𓏠𓄿𓂧𓋴𓅱.

For "her" or "it" feminine, it would be *sey*,

𓊃𓏭.

So it would be *hab.f sey*, "He sends her,"

𓂋𓏤𓄿𓆑𓎛𓈖𓈖.

I know that when you see the two strokes now, you will think dual. Just remember that once in a while, it's a dependent pronoun.

I've been throwing a lot of pronouns at you. In the last minute, you've seen all the singular dependent pronouns there are. Don't be overwhelmed. You will get them. To help the process, make a dependent pronoun chart. Start with "I," "me,"

𓄿𓅱.

Add the way it's pronounced. Then add "you," masculine and feminine,

𓏏𓅱, 𓏏𓈖.

Tchu. For feminine, you can have *tchen.* Then we just need the third person, "he" and "she." "He" and "it" would be *sew,*

𓋴𓅱.

"She" and "it" would be *sey,*

𓇋𓈖𓈖.

These are your singular dependent pronouns. This is the kind of chart to use when doing your homework. Look it up.

There are also dependent pronouns for plurals. The good news is that they're the same as the suffix pronouns. So for example, If you wanted to say, "You ferry us across," we start with the verb *dja*—"to ferry across,

𓆓𓄿�barge.

Then we add the suffix pronoun for "you," which is the basket,

𓇋𓄿𓎡.

So that's the "you ferry across" part. Now we add the dependent pronoun, which is the same as the suffix, in this case, *tchen*,

𓇋𓄿𓎡𓍢𓏥.

Dja.k tchen. And that's "You ferry us across." If you wanted to say "They ferry you—in the plural—across?" How would you do that? Try it now. Take your time. Yes, you would start with the verb, "ferry across,"

𓇋𓄿𓊛.

Good. Then it's time for the suffix pronoun for "they," which is *sen*,

𓇋𓄿𓊛𓋴𓏥.

That's the "They ferry across" part. Now we need the dependent pronoun for "you," in the plural. It's the same as the suffix pronoun plural for "you." Well, that's *tchen*,

𓇋𓄿𓊛𓋴𓏥𓍢.

And that would be, "They ferry you across."

How would you translate the following sentence?

𓉔𓄿𓃀𓆑𓋴𓏥𓅓𓊛𓆑.

Well, there's sending going on. And we see the viper *f,* so he's sending. Now, whom is he sending? Yes, plural, "them." We have a bit more translation to go on. "In his boat," *Hab.f sen em depet.f.* Good.

Let me give you a few sentences for homework that involve dependent pronouns. There's a Dependent Pronoun Chart in our exercise book, but make your own chart for practice, just as we did for suffix pronouns to use for the homework. First sentence, translate into hieroglyphs: "You—singular feminine—send me to him." Next, try "You—singular masculine—ferry her across to the city." Good.

Dependent pronouns are very useful, and you'll see them often. They are also used after phrases of exclamation, like "Behold!" which is *mek*—that's the word for "behold,"

We should add this one to our dictionary. Sometimes the arm hieroglyph will be holding a rounded loaf in its hand,

It's the same meaning—"behold!" After "behold," you might see a dependent pronoun. Another, similar exclamation that uses dependent pronouns is "Lo!" which is *istch*,

. *Istch*.

I'll give you an example in a minute, but I want to show you something else, and then combine the two in one big example. The something else is a small grammatical note that's related to dependent pronouns. We have seen that the owl has many meanings—"from," "in." Let me show you one more important use. The ancient Egyptians never simply said something like, "You are my scribe." They would use an owl *m*—we call it the *m* of predication—to say, "You are as my scribe." The owl hieroglyph is the "as." So if we wanted to translate "You are my scribe," It would be *yew*,

,

which is the "are" part of the sentence. Then the suffix pronoun for "you" is the basket, if it's masculine singular,

.

I just picked that one. In English, "you" is ambiguous. It could be "you" feminine, our tethering ring; or it could be "you" masculine, our basket; or "you" plural,

𓏴𓏥.

We just don't know. That's the plural. In hieroglyphs, we have words for each. There is no ambiguity in Egyptian.

Now, for the moment of truth. We insert an owl. That's the "as" part,

𓆓𓂝𓅓.

Then we add the scribe hieroglyphs,

𓆓𓂝𓅓𓏌𓀀.

Next, we must add another man sign after scribe, because he's my scribe,

𓆓𓂝𓅓𓏌𓀀𓀀.

We don't translate the "as," we simply say: "You are my scribe." I view the owl of predication as an equals sign. What's on one side, "you," equals what's on the other side, "my scribe."

When the owl of predication is used after one of the exclamation particles like *mek,* "behold," you don't need the verb. For example, "Behold, you are my maidservant." We start with the "behold,"

𓅓𓂝.

Then we go straight to the dependent pronoun for "you," which is *tchen,* because "maidservant" is feminine, *baket,* 𓏴. Next is the *m* of predication, 𓅓.

Next comes "maidservant,"

𓀀𓏏𓏥𓀀𓁐𓏏𓏛.

Finally, "You are my maidservant," so I add the man suffix pronoun for the "my." *Mek! Tchen em baket.i,*

𓀀𓏏𓈖𓀀𓁐𓏏𓏛𓀭.

So it's really easy. It's, "Behold, you are as my maidservant."

Next, let's learn the passive voice; not to be confused with the past tense. It's passive voice. Let's look at a simple sentence that's active voice:

𓄿𓀀𓀭.

We would translate this sentence as "I hear," *Sdjem.i.* I'm doing something; I'm hearing. It's active voice. Now, if I insert a loaf and a quail chick between the verb and the subject, it would look like this: *Sedjem.tu.i,*

𓄿𓀀𓏏𓅱𓀭.

This insertion of the loaf and quail chick forms the passive voice, and we translate it as "I am heard." I'm not hearing; I'm heard.

Let's keep going with more examples; that's how you'll learn it.

𓄿𓀀𓏏,

we translate this as, "You hear." Let's insert the *tu*—the loaf and quail chick—between the verb and subject,

𓄿𓀀𓏏𓅱𓏏.

This is the passive voice, "You are heard." OK, now you do one. First, do the active voice. How would we say, "We hear"? We all know we start with the verb,

Then we add the suffix pronoun for "we," which is the water sign with three plural strokes,

That's "We hear." It's active voice; we're hearing. Now, form the passive voice; "We are heard." Same verb, same subject, we just insert loaf, quail chick,

And that's "We are heard." It's not difficult.

For homework, let me give you a few sentences to translate from hieroglyphs to English. Try this one:

It's a good one. This sentence has one word you haven't had yet. Can you pick it out? Yes, it's the one that begins with the arms up—the field goal sign—and ends with the man with the basket on his head. That's the determinative. The word means "work," the noun, and was pronounced *kat*. Now you'll be able to translate the sentence, and I think you'll enjoy it. Here's another:

One more hieroglyphs-to-English sentence, here it is:

Now, let's do three that are English-to-hieroglyphs. That's where we really learn it. "I am sent to the city;" start with that one. Next, "They are seen in the river." Next, "His daughter is sent to the boat." That should keep you out of trouble for a while. But wait, there's more—it's like the Ginsu steak knives.

We have been studying hieroglyphs for a while now, and I'm sure you all agree that hieroglyphs are important. They are part of our world cultural heritage and have been with us for more than 4,000 years. Early on in the course, we talked about how the ability to read hieroglyphs was lost. It was due to a combination of factors—there were foreign invasions, the literate priestly class was not supported, the dominant bureaucratic language of Egypt became Greek, Christianity replaced the old religion and the written script. So finally, the language was lost.

In the lectures that followed, we talked about how the language was rediscovered and the ability to read hieroglyphs reborn. We saw that a significant part of this rediscovery was due to Napoleon's Egyptian Campaign and the discovery of the famous Rosetta Stone. But Napoleon's artists and savants did far more than just discover the Rosetta Stone; they were copying inscriptions so that future scholars would be able to read them when the code was finally cracked. They were actively working towards the preservation and decipherment of hieroglyphs.

As you know, when they returned to France, they published the *Description de l'Égypte,* the both beautiful and encyclopedic history of Egypt that launched modern Egyptology. I want to show you an original page from that great work. They were making a table of all the hieroglyphs they encountered on the walls of the temples and tombs of Egypt. Now remember, no one could translate hieroglyphs when they were doing this; this was for future scholars. These were gifted artists and scholars working in the middle of a war—one they would lose. They were doing a remarkable job, but sometimes things aren't as they appear. Let me explain.

About 30 years ago, I was curator of an exhibition on "Napoleon in Egypt" at my University's museum. I thought it would be interesting if we created a reconstruction of an ancient Egyptian tomb based on one of the engravings in the *Description de l'Égypte*. I wanted one with hieroglyphs, so my students could participate in copying the hieroglyphs on the walls of the recreated tomb. Plate number 48 of Volume IV seemed perfect. It had a couple of figures in the front that were decorative and loads of hieroglyphs. The tomb was built, and my students began copying the inscriptions on the walls. Very soon, one girl came to me and said, "Doctor Brier, Doctor Brier, we can't translate this. It doesn't make sense." I went over to the wall and quickly saw what was wrong. The students had carefully copied what the savants had written, but it wasn't accurately copied in the first place.

So the bird hieroglyphs—now you can see there are plenty of bird hieroglyphs; vultures, falcons, ducks, et cetera. As you know, it's very important which bird you use. If you want to say "in" or "from," you better use the owl; the duck won't do. Or if you're writing Pharaoh's Golden Horus name, you had better not use a quail chick. But Napoleon's savants didn't know this. Decipherment was more than 20 years in the future, and they still believed it was picture writing. They figured a bird is a bird and just filled in a generic bird whenever there was a bird hieroglyph. After all, it was all picture writing, wasn't it? If they had been able to read the text, they would never have made that mistake. They did, however, begin a new discipline within Egyptology—epigraphy, the copying of inscriptions.

The first expedition to copy hieroglyphs that could actually read them was an all-star team composed of French and Tuscan scholars. The French were led by none other than Jean-François Champollion; the Tuscans by Ippolito Rosellini. Like Champollion, Rosellini was a linguistic genius, becoming a professor of Oriental languages at age 24. In 1824, Rosellini read Champollion's work on decipherment and fell in love with both Egypt and hieroglyphs.

The two met when in 1825, Champollion went to Italy to study an important collection of Egyptian antiquities in Turin. The two young men were kindred spirits and quickly hit it off, with Rosellini happily taking the role of the student. They visited each other frequently, with Rosellini helping Champollion catalogue the Louvre's Egyptian collection. While there, Rosellini conceived the idea of a Tuscan expedition to Egypt to extend what the French had done with their *Description de l'Égypte*. Because his team could read hieroglyphs, he was convinced they could advance the study of Egyptology considerably.

Because they couldn't translate hieroglyphs, Napoleon's savants concentrated on art and temple architecture, not really hieroglyphs. Often, they omitted the hieroglyphs, merely indicating where they'd been by two parallel lines. Remember the scene of Cleopatra giving birth to Caesarion? Well, that block that the savants copied is now lost to history. Wouldn't it be wonderful if they had copied the inscriptions that accompanied the scenes so we could read them today?

Rosellini realized all this and, in 1827, asked Grand Duke Leopold II to fund his expedition to Egypt. Leopold agreed. Rosellini was a great scholar in his own right, but wouldn't a joint Franco-Tuscan expedition be even better, with The Decipherer, as he called Champollion, leading the French team? Champollion had never been to Egypt and enthusiastically agreed to the combined expedition. He had some difficulty getting funding from King Charles X; but in the end, he prevailed. On July 31, 1828, the expedition sailed from Toulon for Egypt, almost exactly 30 years after Napoleon's savants left the same port for Alexandria, Egypt.

For 15 months, the dozen or so artists, Egyptologists, and scholars sailed up and down the Nile, recording everything. One of their goals was to validate Champollion's decipherment of hieroglyphs. You see, in 1828, there were still linguists who doubted the validity of Champollion's translations. So the teams made a special effort to record inscriptions.

When they returned, Champollion and Rosellini planned a joint publication, but it was not to be. Champollion died in 1832 at the age of 41. Champollion's elder brother and executor didn't trust Rosellini with his brother's legacy. So in the end, each team produced its own publication. Because the two teams were working side by side at the same sites in Egypt, often sharing artists, the engravings produced by the Tuscans and the French are often indistinguishable, but they're quite different from the *Description de l'Égypte* engravings.

Like the *Description*, they produced beautiful color plates of scenes. But they have a different feel. Napoleon's men were mainly engineers and architects; the Franco-Tuscan expedition had professional artists. Another difference is that these guys could translate the hieroglyphs. They knew that an owl and a quail chick were not interchangeable. They spent days accurately copying lines and lines of hieroglyphs, which can be read today as easily if you were in Egypt in front of the wall. This marvelous expedition set the ball rolling for accurate and professional copying of hieroglyphic inscriptions. Let me end by telling you about a remarkable program going on now to save hieroglyphic inscriptions on temple walls.

The Epigraphic Survey of the University of Chicago's Oriental Institute has been quietly copying hieroglyphic inscriptions for more than 75 years. It's a massive program involving hundreds of extremely talented scholars, and very few people know about their efforts. Let me tell you just what they're doing and how they're doing it.

More than 100 years ago, the great American Egyptologist, James Henry Breasted realized that the hieroglyphic inscriptions on temple walls were in danger of being lost. Inscribed temple blocks were being looted for local construction, some were stolen to sell on the illegal antiquities market, and some were just in poor condition and crumbling. Breasted set out on an incredible one-man campaign to translate every historical inscription in Egypt. It sounds like an overly ambitious plan, but he almost did it. For decades, he camped out at temples, translating the inscriptions on their walls. In the end, he published a monumental five-volume set of his translations called Ancient Records of Egypt. It's a remarkable legacy, but he left us even more.

Breasted convinced John D. Rockefeller that the temples of ancient Egypt were endangered and their inscriptions had to be accurately copied by a team of trained Egyptologists. Rockefeller agreed and provided money to build a compound in Luxor, Egypt, near the main monuments to house what would become known as the Epigraphic Survey.

For more than 90 years, successive teams of scholars have lived at "Chicago House," as the compound's called, recording inscriptions.

Everyone in Egyptology agrees that no one has ever made more accurate copies of hieroglyphic inscriptions than this team. The remarkable accuracy is due to a combination of their skills and the unique method they've developed over decades. Each epigrapher is both a talented artist and an Egyptologist who can translate hieroglyphs. Unlike Napoleon's savants, these people can read what they're copying. In addition, their exacting method almost guarantees accuracy.

First, the section of the wall that's being recorded is photographed with a large-format camera. Then enlargements are made on a special paper that can take an ink or pencil line. Next, the epigrapher takes the photograph to the temple wall and begins copying on top of the photograph all the carved details he sees on the wall. He copies what he sees onto the photograph because there are some details that can only be caught by the human eye and some that would be caught only by the camera.

This combination of photo and drawing is often confusing when first viewed. It contains not only the ancient carvings but also all the cracks and discolorations in the stone. Sometimes it's hard to differentiate between a carved line and a crack, especially if the block is damaged and eroded. But the next step takes care of that, and it's magic. The inked photograph is immersed in an iodine bath that dissolves away the photographic image, leaving just the inked drawing that has been made with the help of the photograph beneath it. This ink drawing of the wall is not the final product. It's now taken back to the wall for comparison, and corrections are made in pencil. A second epigrapher checks the corrections and the two come to a final agreement. An artist makes the final corrections, and this is shown to the Field Director, who checks it one more time at the wall.

The work of "Chicago House" team has become urgent. Since the creation of the new High Dam at Aswan in the 1970s, the water table in Luxor has risen considerably. This groundwater saturated the foundation stones of the temples and was being wicked upward by the blocks higher up, causing sandstone to crumble. In my lifetime, I've seen walls that I could read easily deteriorate so much that they're now unintelligible. The work of "Chicago House" is a race against time.

This year the team has been aided by new digital technology. They're now able to photograph the walls, load the photographs onto a computer, and then ink the reliefs and hieroglyphs on the computer using a stylus. Then they digitally bleach the photo away, leaving a clear, clean drawing of the wall. We're all benefiting in many ways from the work of this dedicated team. All of "Chicago House's" work is available digitally on the Oriental Institute's website, and it's free. If you want a hard copy, the massive volumes are available for purchase.

Some of the homework I've given you comes from the Oriental Institute's publications. Soon, we'll be translating a section of a wall at Medinet Habu. So when you do your homework today, think of "Chicago House" team, working at some temple wall in Luxor.

I'll see you next time.

LECTURE 12

Past Tense and Adjectives

This lecture will show you how to form the past tense. It is similar to the passive voice in that you tack something on to the verb. For the past tense, it is the water sign. Overall, it's an easy concept. After an introduction to the past tense, the lecture introduces some new biliterals that will let you expand your vocabulary. Then the lecture looks at how adjectives work before closing with an extensive homework section.

Introducing the Past Tense

- The past tense is extremely simple. For example, we know how to say "I see": 𓁻𓏏𓏭𓀀, pronounced *Maa.i*. The past tense, "I saw," is the same thing, just with a water sign inserted after the verb: 𓁻𓏏𓏭𓈖𓀀, pronounced *Maa.n.i*.

- "The vizier rejoices" translates as ⌒𓊤𓀾𓎡𓏏𓏭𓀀, *Resh.tchaty*. "The vizier rejoiced" is ⌒𓊤𓀾𓈖𓎡𓏏𓏭𓀀, *Resh.n.tchaty*.

"He was sent to town."

- We can even combine our passive voice with the past tense and say: "He was sent to town." We start with our verb, "send," which is *hab*, 𓎛𓃀𓂡𓆰.

- Now let's add the suffix pronoun for "he," which is the viper, 𓎛𓃀𓂡𓆑. But that's "He sends." We want passive voice in past tense, so we insert the loaf and quail chick for the passive, and the water sign for past tense.

- The past tense water sign comes before the passive voice loaf and chick. So, "He was sent" would be: 𓎛𓃀𓂡𓈖𓏏𓅱𓆑. Now we need to add "to town." The "to" will be the mouth *r* because it is to a place: 口𓅓𓆼𓏭𓂝𓏤𓂋.

- "Town" is *niwit*, so we add that and we have it. "He was sent to town" translates to 口𓅓𓆼𓏭𓂝𓏤𓂋𓈉.

New Biliterals

- This lecture's new biliteral family is the *w* family. They all end in the /w/ or /u/ sound.

- ○ is a small pot and is pronounced *new*. This is a very special pot, and we call it the "*new* pot." Very often you will see a pharaoh making offerings to the gods. In his hand he holds two *new* pots. He is offering beer.

- �𓎢 is pronounced *heket*. It has a little jug after it, so we know the word has something to do with a liquid. In this case, it's "beer."

- 𓇓 is a plant, which is pronounced *sew*. It is another very important one used in the word for king and even became a symbol of kingship.

- 𓆄 is a feather; it is pronounced *shew* and is yet another important hieroglyph in art.

- 𓈌 is the horizon hieroglyph; it is pronounced *djew*.

- 𓈗 is three water signs. It is pronounced *mew*. It is also used as a determinative, as at the end of river.

- There are other hieroglyphs in the *w*-family, but they are rarely used. For now, that's enough of the *w*-family.

Vocabulary Words

- Next we'll learn a few vocabulary words and see some of the new biliterals in action.

- ⌒𓏤𓅱 is pronounced *djew* and is the word for "evil" or "sad." The quail chick is the phonetic complement. It helps us remember the pronunciation of the biliteral. The little bird at the end often determines things that are negative.

- 𓏤𓅱 is the word for "empty." The feather is the *shew* biliteral, so the word was pronounced *shew.*

- 𓏃𓅱 is pronounced *bin,* and the word means "bad" or "miserable."

- 𓏤𓂝𓏤 is pronounced *iker* and means "excellent."

- 𓏠𓏤 is made up of a milk-jar carrier and a reed leaf. This hieroglyph was pronounced *mi,* and by itself it means "like" or "as" in the sense of comparison. The second hieroglyph, the reed leaf, is the phonetic complement *i.*

- 𓏠𓏤 is a noun version of the same word, pronounced *mitlet* and meaning "a likeness."

- 𓂝𓅱 looks just like the passive loaf chick but has a completely different meaning. Loaf chick also is an impersonal pronoun and means "one," as in "One always hopes for the best." So if you see 𓂝𓅱 and it doesn't make sense as a passive voice, think impersonal pronoun.

- 𓄤 is an adjective pronounced *nefer,* as in Nefertiti and Nefertari, two great queens. The word *nefer* has three different but related meanings: "happy," "good," and "beautiful."

- ▽ is a woven basket and was pronounced *neb.* It's a biliteral and means "all" or "every." It's an adjective.

- 𓎟 means "lord."

- 𓐍 is pronounced *khet* and means "thing."

Nefertiti

-  means "large" or "great."

- is a cone of incense being offered or given to the gods. It is the word for "give."

- is shorthand for "give," especially in prayers where offerings are being presented.

Using Adjectives

- Adjectives can be used in three different ways. The first way is the traditional way, modifying a noun. This is known as using an adjective as an epithet. The adjective comes after the noun and agrees with the noun's gender.

  ○ In the phrase "the evil plan" we would start with the noun "plan," which is *sekher*, . Then comes the word for "evil," *djew*, would come after: *sekher djew*, or .

  ○ If we wanted to say "the evil woman," we would write "woman" first, , and then follow with the adjective *djew*. But we would add a *t* at the end of the adjective because "woman" is feminine and the adjective has to agree in gender with the noun it modifies: .

- The second use is as a predicate in cases where we have the verb "to be." So instead of "miserable woman," we can use the adjective "miserable" as a predicate and say "The woman is miserable."

  ○ For this kind of use, the adjective begins the sentence and doesn't have to agree with the subject, much like a verb. So, "The woman is miserable" would look like this: ⟨hieroglyphs⟩. We don't need the *t* for the feminine form of *bin*. It's being used as a predicate, so we use the masculine form.

  ○ Let's try a second example, a sentence with a new ideogram: ⟨hieroglyphs⟩. The new ideogram is a heart. *Nefer* is at the beginning of the sentence, so it is a predicate, but we don't know yet if it is "beautiful," "good," or "happy."

  ○ "Heart," pronounced *ib*, comes next, and then we have a man sign, which is probably the suffix pronoun for "my." A reasonable translation is "My heart is happy." It could also be a moral statement: "My heart is good."

- The third use is slightly less common. It is an adjective used as a noun. Here it is just the adjective followed by a determinative. For example, here we have the determinative for "child": ⟨hieroglyphs⟩. That could be "the bad child." This third use can be confused with the predicate use sometimes, but will still result in basically the same meaning.

Lecture 11's Homework Answers
Lecture 11 asked you to translate these sentences to hieroglyphs.

1. "You [singular feminine] send me to him." We start with the verb *hab,* "to send," ⟨hieroglyphs⟩. Next we add the feminine singular suffix pronoun. That's the tethering ring, giving us ⟨hieroglyphs⟩.

- Next we need the "me," which is where we need the dependent pronoun *wi*. Now we have 𓂜𓆓𓏤𓊨𓏭. For the "to him" part, we use the water sign *n* for "to" and the dependent pronound *sw* for "him." In the end, we have 𓂜𓆓𓏤𓊨𓏭𓈖𓏤𓋴𓅱.

2. "You [singular masculine] ferry her across to the city." We begin with the verb, "to ferry across," which is *dja*, 𓂧𓆓𓂝. For the "you" we can use the basket suffix pronoun, and for "her" we use the dependent pronoun *sey*.

- This gives us 𓂧𓆓𓂝𓏤𓏭. Now we just need "to the city." The "to" has to be the *r* mouth hieroglyph because it is to a place. "City" is *niwit*. In the end, we have 𓂧𓆓𓂝𓏤𓏭𓊖.

To help you learn the passive voice, Lecture 11 asked you to translate these sentences to English.

1. 𓂜𓆓𓏤𓂋𓊨𓀀𓊖𓁷𓏤𓎡𓏏𓈖

- We start with the verb *hab*, "to send." Right after the verb is the passive indicator, *tu*, the loaf and quail chick. So we know something or someone is being sent. The manservant is being sent.

- Now we have the mouth *r* followed by the word for "town." The manservant is being sent to the town.

- Next is the face hieroglyph with a stroke. One meaning for the face hieroglyph, even with the stroke, is "concerning" or "because of." That makes sense because the next word, *kat*, means "work."

- At the end of *kat* is *ten* "this." It agrees with the noun "work," which is feminine. That's why it is *ten*, not *pen*, which is the one used for masculine nouns. Our complete sentence is "The manservant is sent to town concerning this work."

2. The next sentence was: [hieroglyphs]. The verb is clearly *yew*, "is," and we have a suffix pronoun (the tethering ring) attached to it. The makes "You [feminine] are."

   - Next is an owl. The owl could mean "in," "from," or something else. The rest of the sentence will have to help us decide.

   - The next word is "maidservant," *baket*. The owl is almost certainly the *m* of predication. After maidservant we have another suffix pronoun, which makes it "my maidservant." The sentence means: "You are my maidservant."

3. [hieroglyphs] was the last sentence. We have the verb *resh* and the noun *tchaty*, so it's a vizier rejoicing. This is followed by another verb, *maa*, to see. The suffix pronoun viper tells us "he" is seeing. What is he seeing? Well, this time it is "face."

   - If we take into account the suffix pronoun folded cloth attached to face, it is "her face" that the vizier is seeing. If we want to make it a smooth translation, we can add a "when." The final sentence: "The vizier rejoices when he sees her face."

Lecture 11's homework also had a few English-to-hieroglyphs sentences in the passive voice.

1. The first was "I am sent to the city." As always, we start with the verb, and in this case it is *hab*. The key is going to be that this is a passive voice sentence. We need to insert the loaf and quail chick that indicates passive voice. It attaches to the verb, so we can add that to *hab*, creating [hieroglyphs].

   - Since it is "I" who is being sent, we add the suffix pronoun for "I," which is the man hieroglyph. Next we add "to the city," which uses the mouth *r* for "to" and *niwit* for "city." Our final translation is [hieroglyphs].

2. "They are seen in the river" uses the verb *maa*, "to see." Since it is passive voice, we attach the loaf and chick to the verb: ⟨hieroglyphs⟩. The suffix pronoun for "they" is *sn*, so we add the folded cloth, water sign, and plural strokes: ⟨hieroglyphs⟩. Next we add the owl for "in" and the determinative of three stacked water signs for the "river." Our final sentence: ⟨hieroglyphs⟩.

3. "His daughter is sent to the boat." Start with the verb, *hab*, and add the loaf and quail chick because it is passive: ⟨hieroglyphs⟩. It's a daughter who is being sent so we add *sat*, "daughter." And since it is "his daughter" we add the suffix pronoun viper for "his" to the end of "daughter."

   • That creates ⟨hieroglyphs⟩. The "to the boat" part is easy. We add the mouth *r* for "to" because a boat is a thing. Last we just need the word for boat, *depet*. The final sentence: ⟨hieroglyphs⟩.

Lecture 12's Homework
Translate these sentences from English to hieroglyphs.

1. "She rejoiced when she saw his face."

2. "The town was miserable when the river was empty of water."

3. "They sent the beer to their father."

Translate these sentences from hieroglyphs to English.

1. [hieroglyphs]

   [hieroglyphs]

   [hieroglyphs]

2. [hieroglyphs]

3. [hieroglyphs]

Past Tense and Adjectives

Welcome back. Last time I gave you some sentences using our new dependent pronouns. Let's do those first. We started with "You—singular feminine—send me to him." Well, we start with the verb *hab,* "to send,

𓉔𓄿𓂡.

Next, we add the feminine singular suffix pronoun. That's the tethering ring,

𓉔𓄿𓏏;

that's "you send." Now we need the "me," which is where we need the dependent pronoun *wi,*

𓉔𓄿𓏏𓅱𓏭.

OK, "you send me." Now we have to get "me" to "him." Well, for the "to" we use the water sign *n*, which is the "to" for "people,

𓉔𓄿𓏏𓅱𓏭𓈖.

Last, for the "him," we use our dependent pronoun *sew,*

𓉔𓄿𓏏𓅱𓏭𓈖𓋴𓅱.

That's "You send me to him." Good.

We also had the sentence "You ferry her across to the city." As we all know, we begin with the verb, "to ferry across," which is *dja*,

𓊽 𓄿 𓈖 .

For the "you," we can use the basket suffix pronoun,

𓊽 𓄿 𓎡 .

Now comes our dependent pronoun *sey* for "her,"

𓊽 𓄿 𓎡 𓊃 .

Now we just need "to the city." The "to" has to be the mouth *r* hieroglyph because it's to a place,

𓊽 𓄿 𓎡 𓊃 𓂋 .

The last thing we need is "city," and that's our old friend *niwit*,

𓊽 𓄿 𓎡 𓊃 𓂋 𓊖 .

And that's, "You ferry her across to the city." Good.

Last time, we also learned the passive voice, and I gave you some sentences to translate as practice. Let's see how you did. Our first hieroglyphic sentence:

𓉐 𓄿 𓂝 𓃀 𓊪 𓀀 𓂋 𓊖 𓏏 𓊪 𓏤 𓈖 .

We know that our verb comes first, and we recognize that it's *hab*, "to send." Right after the verb is the passive indicator, *tu*, the loaf; the quail chick. So we know something or someone is being sent. Not sending, which would be active voice. Well, it looks like "The manservant is being sent." Now we have the mouth *r* followed by the word for "town." We know the *r* is for places, and that makes sense since town is a place. So, "The manservant is being sent to the town."

Next is the face hieroglyph with a stroke. When I see this, the first thing that comes to mind is "face." After all, it's a face with a stroke. It looks like it should be an ideogram, but that really doesn't fit. Another meaning for the face hieroglyph, even with the stroke, is "concerning" or "because of;" and that makes sense because the next word, *kat,* means "work." At the end of *kat* is *ten,* "this." I'm sure you noticed that it agrees with the noun, "work," which is feminine. That's why it's *ten,* not *pen,* which is the one used for masculine nouns. So our complete sentence is "The manservant is sent to town concerning this work." Good.

Our next sentence was this one:

The verb is clearly *yew,* "is." And we have a suffix pronoun attached to it—a tethering ring. So, it's "you" feminine. So, we have, "You are." Now, next is an owl. What is that owl saying? It could be a lot of things. The owl could mean "in," "from," or something else. The rest of the sentence will have to help us decide. The next word is "maidservant," *baket.* So, your owl is almost certainly the *m* of predication. After "maidservant" we have another suffix pronoun, which makes it "my maidservant." "You are my maidservant." Good.

We have one last hieroglyphs-to-English sentence:

Well, someone is rejoicing. That's our verb, *resh.* Next is "the vizier," *tchaty.* So, "The vizier rejoices." This is followed by another verb, *maa,* to see. The suffix pronoun viper tells us "he" is seeing. What is he seeing? Well, this time, it is "face." And if we take into account the suffix pronoun folded cloth attached to the face, it's "her face" that the vizier is seeing. If we want to make it a smooth translation, we can add a "when." "The vizier rejoices when he sees her face." Good.

We also had a few English-to-hieroglyphs sentences. Our first was: "I am sent to the city." As always, we start with the verb; and in this case, it's *hab*,

𓎛𓄿𓃀𓂻.

Now the key is going to be that this is a passive voice sentence—"I am sent." So we need to insert the loaf and quail chick that indicates passive voice. It attaches to the verb, so we can add that to *hab*,

𓎛𓄿𓃀𓂻𓏏𓅱.

Now, since it's "I" who is being sent, we add the suffix pronoun for "I," which is the man hieroglyph,

𓎛𓄿𓃀𓂻𓏏𓅱𓀀.

Now we just add "to the city." Since it's a place, we use the mouth *r* for the "to,"

𓎛𓄿𓃀𓂻𓏏𓅱𓀀𓂋.

And now we add "city," *niwit*, and we have it,

𓎛𓄿𓃀𓂻𓏏𓅱𓀀𓂋𓊖.

"I am sent to the city." Good, you're getting it.

I suspect this is getting even easy for you. Let's do our next sentence: "They are seen in the river"—it could be crocodiles. Again, a passive voice sentence. Our verb is *maa*, "to see,"

𓐝𓄿𓄿.

Since it's passive voice, we attach the loaf and the chick to the verb,

𓐝𓄿𓄿𓏏𓅱.

Now we have to remember what the suffix pronoun for "they" is. We can always look it up in our pronoun chart. It's *sen*, so we add the folded cloth, water sign, and plural strokes,

𓅯𓄿𓈖𓀀𓈖𓏥.

That's the "They are seen" part. "In the river" is easy. Our owl is the "in;" we always remember that,

𓅯𓄿𓈖𓀀𓈖𓏥𓅓.

And *iteru* is "river," with the determinative of three stacked water signs,

𓅯𓄿𓈖𓀀𓈖𓏥𓅓𓇋𓏏𓂋𓈗.

Good. So, we have that one right.

Now for our last sentence: "His daughter is sent to the boat." Start with our verb *hab*,

𓉔𓄿𓃀.

Then we add the loaf and quail chick because it's passive,

𓉔𓄿𓃀𓏏𓅱.

Good. It's a daughter who's being sent, so we add *sat*, "daughter,"

𓉔𓄿𓃀𓏏𓅱𓅭𓏏.

And since it's "his daughter," we add the suffix pronoun viper for "his" to the end of "daughter,"

𓉔𓄿𓃀𓏏𓅱𓅭𓏏𓆑.

That's the "His daughter is sent" part. "To the boat," again, it's easy. We've done that before. We add the mouth *r* for "to" because the boat's a thing. If it were a person, it would be the water sign, *n*,

🏠🦅🔧🐦🦆🐍〰️○.

Last, we just need the word for boat, and nobody ever forgets it; it's *depet*,

🏠🦅🔧🐦🦆🐍〰️○🚤.

And that completes our homework. Good.

Now for something new. Today I would like to show you how we form the past tense. It's similar to the passive voice in that we tack something on into the sentence, next to the verb. For the past tense, it's the water sign. So for example, we know how to say "I see,"

👁️🦅🦅🧍.

How would you pronounce it? That's right, something like *maa.i* Now, let's do the past tense, "I saw." Same as "I see," we just insert the water sign after the verb,

👁️🦅🦅〰️🧍.

Maa.n.i; That's "I saw." We can do this for any sentence we've had in the past lectures. "The vizier rejoices,"

🗣️🦅🪶🧍,

Resh.tchaty. To make it past tense, just insert the water sign,

🗣️🦅🪶〰️🪶🧍.

"The vizier rejoiced," *Resh.n.tchaty.*

It's really easy. If we want to get fancy, we can even combine our passive voice with the past tense and say: "He was sent to town." That's both passive voice and past. As always, we start with our verb, "send," which is *hab*,

𓎛𓃀𓃀𓂻.

Now let's add the suffix pronoun for "he," which is the viper,

𓎛𓃀𓃀𓆑.

We all remember that now. But that's "He sends;" we want passive voice. But we also want past tense. We know that we insert the loaf and quail chick for the passive,

𓎛𓃀𓂻𓏏𓅱𓆑.

But we also know that we insert the water sign for past tense,

𓎛𓃀𓃀𓆑𓈖.

But we're going to use both. Which comes first, the past tense or the passive voice? The answer is that the past tense water sign comes before the passive voice loaf and chick. So, "He was sent" would look like this:

𓎛𓃀𓂻𓈖𓏏𓅱𓆑.

Now we need to add "to town." The "to" will be the mouth *r* because it's a place,

𓎛𓃀𓂻𓈖𓏏𓅱𓆑𓂋.

"Town" is *niwit*, so we add the mouth and town, and we have it. "He was sent to town,"

𓎛𓃀𓂻𓈖𓏏𓅱𓆑𓂋𓊖.

Good.

I'll be giving you some past tense sentences for homework today, but first I want to show you another family of biliterals. This way we can have some new vocabulary words, and thus do some new and interesting sentences. One biliteral family we know already is the /a/-family—hieroglyphs that end in the sound /a/, like *ma*,

;

or *sa*,

;

or *ba*,

.

Well, the new biliteral family is the *w* family—they all end in the sound /w/ or *u* sound. Here's the first example:

○.

It's a small pot, and t's pronounced *new*. This is a very special pot, and we all call it the "new-pot." Very often, you will see a pharaoh making offerings to the gods. In his hands, he holds two *new*-pots. He's offering beer. Since I showed you the pot that held the beer, the *new*-pot, I might as well give you the word for "beer." It's pronounced *heket*,

.

It was a little jug after it, right? You see the jug? So we know the word has something to do with a liquid. In this case, it's "beer."

Another bilateral with a *w* at the end is the "plant," which was pronounced *sew*,

.

At the end of this lecture, I'll show you special uses for some hieroglyphs—so many were very, very important and used as symbols and all kinds of things, but I'll show you later. This feather is pronounced *shew*, and it's another important hieroglyph,

The "horizon" hieroglyph is pronounced *djew,*

◡.

Three water signs were pronounced *mew,*

〰
〰
〰.

It's also used as a determinative at the end of the word "river." There are other hieroglyphs in the *w*-family, but they're rarely used. If we come across one in a word later, we can talk about it. For now, that's enough of the *w*-family.

Now, let's learn a few words and see some of the new biliterals in action; that's the only way you're going to learn them. Many of our new words are going to be adjectives, and this will enable us to move closer to translating complex sentences. Our first adjective, the word for "evil" or "sad." It's pronounced *djew,*

◡ ⸚ ⸚.

The quail chick is the phonetic complement. It helps us remember the pronunciation of the biliteral. The little bird at the end often determines things that are negative, or not so good. For example, the word for "empty" is *shew,*

⸚ ⸚ ⸚.

The feather is *shew* biliteral, so the word's pronounced *shew*. I guess the reason the word for "empty" also has that little negative bird is because it's not so good to be empty.

Let me give you another word with the little bird. It doesn't involve our new biliterals, but it'll help us see the bad bird in action—I call him the bad bird.

How would you pronounce this word? Yes, *bin,* and the word means "bad" or "miserable." Since we have the word for "bad," I should give you the word for "excellent,"

How's it pronounced? Yes, *iker.* We've seen the *w*-family of biliterals. There are quite a few others, but I don't want you to try to learn the all at once; that would be too much. Just do what we've done.

Let me show you just one more word from the /i/-biliteral family that's quite important,

The first hieroglyph is a milk jar carrier. You know those net bags that some people use at supermarkets to carry light-weight things? Well, that was invented in ancient Egypt. We are looking at a net bag with a jar inside it; and the handle, the loop is on top. This hieroglyph was pronounced *mi*— like *m i*—and by itself, it means "like" or "as" in the sense of a comparison. The second hieroglyph, the reed leaf, is the phonetic compliment *i.* There was a famous vizier in the New Kingdom named Rechmire. *Rech* is "knowledge" —we've had that. The *mi* is "like," and the *Re* is the sun god. So his name means something like "Smart like Re!" That's something to live up to. There's another form of the word that's a noun,

This version, pronounced *mitet*, *mitet*, means "likeness."

One word we need for our homework looks like the passive voice quail chick, right? The loaf and the chick,

But it has a completely different meaning. I mentioned this when I did suffix pronouns. Loaf chick also is an impersonal pronoun and means "one," as in "One always hopes for the best." No specific person is intended. It's the ancient Egyptian equivalent of the French "on," as in "On dit"—"One says." So if you see it,

and it doesn't make sense as a passive voice, think impersonal pronoun. For example, how would you translate this one,

Yes, "One says." Sometimes this impersonal pronoun can follow the emphatics, like *mek*, "behold,"

It could also be written this way,

which still means "behold," but more literally—"Behold you!" Or "Look you!"

As I mentioned, many of our new vocabulary words for today are adjectives—words that modify nouns. Today, we learn how to use them. Adjectives can be used in three different ways. Knowing these three ways will give you considerably more translating power. The first way is the traditional way, modifying a noun. Sometimes this is called an "epithet;" it attributes some character or property to the thing—the noun—

being described. For example, "The evil plan." "Evil," the adjective, is the property being attributed to the noun, "plan." This is a traditional use of an adjective—"pretty woman," "sad child," "tall tree."

When used as epithets—which is their most common use—adjectives come after the noun and agree in gender with the noun. So the phrase, "The evil plan"—it's not a complete sentence, it's a phrase—would start with the noun "plan," which is *sekher*,

𓊪𓐠𓏌𓊪.

Then the word for "evil" would come after, *sekher djew*,

𓊪𓐠𓏌𓊪𓅓𓂃𓅆.

Now, if we wanted to say "The evil woman," we would write "woman" first,

𓏏𓁐,

and then follow with the adjective *djewt*. But we have to add a *t* at the end of the adjective because woman is feminine, and the adjective has to agree in gender with the noun it modifies,

𓏏𓁐𓅓𓂃𓏏.

Before we go on to the second way adjectives are used, let me give you a new adjective. It's so neat and important that I want to highlight it, rather than just add it to a list. The word is pronounced *nefer*. Yep, as in Nefertiti and Nefertari, two great queens. The hieroglyphs look like this:

𓄤𓂋.

The first hieroglyph represents the lungs and windpipe of an animal, and the hieroglyph itself is a triliteral. It represents three sounds, one after the other:

n, f, r—*nefer*. We fill in the *e*s so we can pronounce it, and it becomes *nefer*. The horned viper and the mouth hieroglyphs are phonetic complements. They're silent and just remind us of the sound of the triliteral. The word *nefer* has three different, but related, meanings: "happy," "good," and "beautiful." So if we wanted to say "The beautiful boat," we could start with "boat," *depet*,

,

and then add the *nefer*. But since *depet* ends in a *t*, it's thus feminine, we have to use *nefert*—the feminine form of the adjective, which includes the *t* loaf,

.

Good.

Now let's look at the second use of adjectives. The second use is as a predicate in cases where we have the verb "to be." So instead of "miserable woman," *bin*, we could use the adjective "miserable," *bin*, as a predicate and say "The woman is miserable." For this kind of use, the adjective begins the sentence, like a verb, and doesn't have to agree with the subject; again, like a verb. So, "The woman is miserable" would look like this:

.

Note, I don't need the *t* for the feminine form of *bin*. It's being used as a predicate, so we use the masculine form.

Let's try a second example, a sentence with an ideogram you haven't seen before. Can you guess what it is a picture of?

.

The ideogram that you haven't seen is a heart. How would you translate that sentence? Well, we can see that *nefer* is at the beginning of the sentence, so it's a predicate, but we don't know yet if it's "is beautiful," "is good," or "is happy." Which meaning it has will depend on the context determined by the words that follow it. "Heart" was pronounced *ib*; it comes next. And then we have a man sign, which is probably the suffix pronoun for "my." So a reasonable translation is "My heart is happy." It could also be a moral statement, "My heart is good."

Let me say something about the heart in ancient Egypt. The Egyptians believed that you thought with your heart. They didn't understand the function of the brain and during mummification, they removed it through the nose and threw it away. The idea was that you thought with your heart. This isn't crazy. Think about it. When you get excited, it's your heart that beats quickly, not your brain; as in, "Be still my foolish heart." A holdover of this Egyptian belief is that on Valentine's Day we give chocolate hearts. We really should be giving chocolate brains. Anyway, back to adjectives.

We now have seen two ways adjectives can be used. The most common way, as epithets, modifying a noun. And in this case, the adjective agrees with the noun it modifies. The second way is as a predicate, where the adjective begins the sentence but doesn't agree with the noun. Here the adjective acts as the verb. These two uses are quite common. The third use is slightly less common; it's an adjective used as a noun. Here, it's just the adjective followed by a determinative. So, for example, here we have the determinative for child,

That could be "the bad child." This third use can be confused with the predicate sometimes. But still, the result in basically the same meaning, so don't worry about it. The first two uses of adjectives is crucial.

I'm going to give you your homework in two stages. First, sentences to translate from English-to-hieroglyphs that will reinforce the past tense and some of our new biliterals. Try this one: "She rejoiced when she saw his face." Next, do "The town was miserable when the river was empty of water." "They sent the beer to their father;" let's try that one. Be careful to pay special attention to the tenses of these sentences.

Next, I want to give you some really great hieroglyphs-to-English sentences to translate, but you'll need a couple of more vocabulary words. The semicircle hieroglyph,

,

is a woven basket and was pronounced *neb*—it's a biliteral. It means "all" or "every." It's an adjective. If there's a man hieroglyph after it, it means "lord." Perhaps because the Lord has everything,

.

Next word, the word for "thing" is *khet*,

.

So if you wanted to say "everything," you can think of "thing" as the noun and "every" as the adjective. The adjective follows the noun and agrees with it, so we would write *khet nebet*, "everything,"

⊜▽
◠ ◠ .

It's *nebet* with the *t* because "thing" is feminine, and since it ends in a *t* and the adjective "every" has to agree with the noun. Good.

For our last adjective vocabulary word, I would like you to be able to say "large" or "great." We saw a version of this word when we talked about hieroglyphs in the Bible. Remember how the king was called *per ah* "pharaoh" by the Israelites, because he lived in the great house? Well, when the word for "great" is spelled out, it looks like this:

⊃▷🐦❘.

We've seen the first hieroglyph before, especially in our /a/-family biliterals. It's a column or a pillar and the *eha* biliteral. We usually pronounce it just *ah*, though. But look how it's used in the word. The arm phonetic compliment should come first, after all, it's the *eha* biliteral, not the *a-eh*. But for some unknown reason, it comes second. That's why I said you have to be flexible in ancient Egyptian.

One last word. It's an ideogram; it's a picture of what it means,

🔥.

This hieroglyph is a cone of incense, being offered or given to the gods. It's the word for "give," so it's a verb. Sometimes just the cone of incense is used for the word—it's pronounced *di*,

🔥.

Di, "to give." The cone by itself became a kind of shorthand for "give," especially in prayers where offerings are being presented. We will see that in later lectures. When we translate prayers on tomb, you'll see this hieroglyph.

Now, for your adjective homework assignment. They are all hieroglyphs-to-English, and I think you will like them. You now have lots of vocabulary, and we're well beyond the "See Spot run" phase. You can now translate real sentences from ancient Egyptian texts. And we're only halfway through the course. You're doing fine.

The first sentence is a maxim—advice to a young man. It's a long and complicated sentence; the most difficult thing we've had to do so far, but it's the real deal. My suggestion is to break it into words you know and then try to make sense of it. This one won't be so easy, but don't worry; we're going to go over it next time. Just do the best you can and have fun with it. I want you to experience the real thing and also some of the difficulties we encounter with ancient Egyptian translations. It's really long.

𓂋𓍿𓄿𓀁𓂝𓏤𓏤𓏏𓂋𓄿𓂋𓇋𓂋𓇋𓏏

𓏏𓇋𓂝𓏤𓏏𓄿𓍿𓏲𓄿𓏏𓏤𓇌𓏏𓎼

𓄿𓏏𓂋𓄿𓄿𓂋𓎛𓏏𓄿𓏤𓄿𓄿𓍿𓄿𓏴

Remember that it's a bit of wisdom, and that will help you figure out the meaning.

I know that we have done a lot today. We've learned new biliterals and also vocabulary words that include them. Then we went on to see three ways that adjectives can be used. Don't feel overwhelmed. It'll come with use. For the new biliterals, add them to a biliteral chart, and that will help recognize them when you see them. Same for the vocabulary words; add them to your dictionary. In the homework, you'll see lots of the adjectives, and that will help towards remembering how adjectives are used. For now, do your homework, and I'll see you next time.

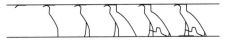

The Egyptian Alphabet

A   Egyptian vulture

B   Foot

Ch, Kh Placenta

D   Hand

E   Arm

F   Horned viper

G   Jar stand

H   Reed hut

H   Twisted flax

I   Flowering reed

J, Dj   Cobra

K   Basket

M   Owl

N   Water

P	Reed mat	
Q	Hill	
R	Mouth	
S	Folded cloth	
T	Loaf	

U, W	Quail chick
Y	Double reed
Z	Door bolt
Sh	Pool
Tch	Tethering ring

Some Difficult-to-Draw Hieroglyphs

Man

Seated woman

God

Face

Head

Pintail duck (*sa*)

Duckling (*tcha*)

Flying duck (*pa*)

Jabiru (*ba*)

Sparrow (small, bad, etc.)

Crocodile

Tadpole

Lizard

Rabbit

Bee

Sedge plant (*sew*)

Column (*eha*)

Column (*iwen*)

Boat

Chisel (*mer*, *ab*)

English	Hieroglyph	Pronunciation
Abydos		Abdju
alabaster		*shes*
all, every		*neb*
among		*khenu*
another		*ket* (f.)
another		*key* (m.)
answer		*usheb*
Anubis		*Inup*
appear		*kha*

are		*yew*
arise, stand up		ehe
Atum		Atum
bad, miserable		*bin*
beautiful		*nefer*
beer		*hket*
behold		*mek*
Black Land		*Kemet*
boat		*depet*
body		*khet*
Byblos		*Kopny*
clothing		*menkhet*

commoner, poor man		*nedjes*
companion		*semer*
concerning		*her*
counsel		*secher*
Crete		*Keftiu*
Crocodile		*mezeh*
cubit		*meh*
daughter		*sat*
day		*heru*
Dendera		*Iunut*
descend		*ha*
desert		*desheret*

Die, death		*met*
donkey		*eha*
Duametef		*Duametef*
east		*iabet*
Egypt, Black Land		*Kemet*
emergence, season of		*peret*
empty		*shew*
endure		*wah*
enter		*ahq*
eternity, forever		*djet*
every		*neb*
evil, sad		*djew*

excellent		*iker*
exist		*kheper*
face		*her*
fare downstream		*khed*
father		*it*
ferry across		*dja*
first		*tep*
foremost		*tep*
forever		*djet*
from		*em*
front		*hat*
Geb		*Geb*

give		*di*
glad		*resh*
go down, to descend		*ha*
go forth		*per*
god		*netcher*
gold		*nub*
good		*nefer*
grain, measure of		*heqat*
great, large		*eha*
hall, office		*kha*
happy		*nefer*
Hatti		*Khatti*

hear		*sedjem*
heart		*ib*
Heliopolis		*Iunu*
Hittites, land of		*Khatti*
horizon		akhet
hour		*wenut*
house		*per*
How!		*wey*
ignorant of, not to know		*khem*
in, from		*em*
interior, among		*khenu*
inundation		akhet

is		*yew*
Isis		*Ist*
Iunu, Heliopolis		*Iunu*
joy, gladness		*reshwet*
Ka-priest		*hem-ka*
Karnak Temple		*Ipet-Sewet*
know		*rekh*
Kush, ancient Nubia		*Kush*
lake		*she*
land		*ta*
life		*ankh*
like, as		*mi*

likeness		*mitet*
likeness		*teyet*
lord		*neb*
maid servant		*baket*
man		*z* also
man servant		*bak*
many		*esha*
Memphis		*Men-nefer*
miserable		*bin*
month		abed
moon		*yeah*
name		*ren*

Nephthys	𓏏𓆓	*Nephthys*
Netherworld	★ ⌂	*duat*
night	𓄿𓏏	*gereh*
north	⌐	*meh*
not to know	⊖𓅓	*khem*
Nubia	𓂝𓅓	*Kush*
Nut	○⌐	*Nut*
obelisk	⌐⊖𓊽	*tekhen*
office	𓄿𓅓𓊠	*kha*
one, sole	⌐	*weh*
Osiris	𓊨𓁹	*Ausir*
Overseer	𓅓 ⌐	*em-r*

Palestine		*Retchenu*
palm, a unit of length		*seshep*
People		*retchu*
place		*bew*
plan, counsel		*secher*
pleased, to set sun		*hotep*
plentiful, many		*esha*
pool, lake		*she*
poor man		*nedjes*
power		*was*
priest		*hem-netcher*
Ptah, god		*Ptah*

Punt	𓊪𓏏𓈉	*Punt*
pure	𓃂	*wab*
Re, sun god	𓂋𓏤𓀭	*Re*
rear	𓄖	*peh*
Red land, desert	𓌂𓂋𓏏𓈉	*Desheret*
rejoice, glad	𓂋𓈙𓀁	*resh*
remember	𓋴𓐍𓅢	*secha*
rich, plentiful, many	𓆷𓏭𓏪	*esha*
rise, shine	𓄊𓏏𓇳	*weben*
river	𓇋𓏏𓂋𓈗	*iteru*
road	𓈗𓅱𓏏𓊪	*wat*
rod, unit of length	𓏏𓈖𓏤	*khet*

sacred boat		*wia*
sacred, holy		*djeser*
sad		*djew*
scribe		*sesh*
secret		*seshta*
see		*maa*
seed		*peret*
send		*hab*
servant of the god, priest		*hem-netcher*
servant statue		*shabty*
Set		*Set*
set sun		*hotep*

shabti, servant statue	𓀉𓅭𓏛	*shabty*
shine, appear	𓈍𓏤	*kha*
Shu	𓆄𓃀𓀭	*Shu*
sight	𓁐	*her*
silent	𓊪𓀀	*ger*
sole	𓌙	*weh*
sky	𓏏𓊪	*pet*
son	𓅬𓏤𓀀	*sa*
soul	𓅭	*ba*
soul	𓅡	*ba*
Southern Heliopolis, Thebes	𓊨𓏤	*Iunu Sut*
sovereign	𓇋𓏏𓏤	*ity*

speak		*medu*
stability		*djed*
stand up, arise		*ehe*
summer		*shemu*
sun		*re*
sun, day		*re*
Syria, Palestine		*Retchenu*
Tefnut		*Tefnut*
temple		*per-netcher*
Thebes		*Waset*
Thebes		*Iunu Sut*
then		*ikh*

therein		*im*
thing		*khet*
this		*pen* m
this		*ten* f.
thousand		*kha*
to for people		*en*
to for place		*er*
to be, is, are, etc.		*yew*
together with		*heneh*
town		*niwi*t
truth		*maat*
upon		*her*

upon	☟	*tep*
vizier	🐫𝍱𝍱👤	tchaty
voice	☺𝍱👤	kheru
wab-priest	𝍱👤	wab
Wepwawet	𝍱𝍱	Wepwawet
West, the next world	𝍱	Iment
Woman	𝍱	zet
words, speak	𝍲	medu
year	𝍱	renpet
year, as in date	𝍱	hat-sep

Hieroglyph	Pronunciation	English

𓄿 - A

Hieroglyph	Pronunciation	English
	abed	month
	Abdju	Abydos
	ahq	to enter
	akhet	season of inundation
	akhet	horizon
	ankh	life
	Atum	Atum
	Ausir	Osiris

⌐ - B

🦅	*ba*	soul
🦅	*ba*	soul
🦅 ⌣ 🧎	*bak*	man servant
🦅 ⌣ 🧍	*baket*	maid servant
🦵🦅	*bin*	bad, miserable
🦵🦅	*bew*	place

⊜ - C, KH

⊜🧍🦅〰	*Khatti*	Hatti, land of Hittites
⊜〰	*khed*	to fare downstream
⊜🦉〰	*khem*	to be ignorant of, not to know
⊜🧍🦅	*kheru*	voice

	khet	thing
	kha	1,000
	kha	hall, office
	kha	shine, appear
	khenu	interior, among
	khet	body
	khet	a rod, unit of length

▭ - D

	depet	boat
	Desheret	the red land, desert
	di	to give
	Duametef	Duametef

★⌂□	*duat*	netherworld

⟞◗ – E

⟞◗ 𓅦 𓏭	*eha*	great, large
⟞ 𓃘	*eha*	donkey
𓊽 ⟞◗ ⟋	*ehe*	stand up, arise
𓏥	*esha*	rich, plentiful, many

◿ – G

𓅬 𓀭	*Geb*	Geb
𓇌 𓀉	*ger*	to be silent
𓇌 𓏏	*gereh*	night

	ha	to go down, to descend
	hab	to send
	hat	front
	hat-sep	year, as in a date
	hem-ka	Ka-priest
	hem-netcher	servant of the god, priest
	heneh	together with
	hotep	to be pleased, to set sun
	heqat	a unit of grain measure
	hket	beer
	her	face, sight, upon, concerning

𓉿𓄿𓇳	*heru*	day

𓏺 - |

𓍋	*iabet*	east
𓄣	*ib*	heart
𓇋𓏲𓎛	*yeah*	moon
𓇋𓏏	*ikh*	then
𓇋𓍯𓂋	*iker*	excellent
𓇋𓅓	*im*	therein
𓋀𓏏	*Iment*	the west, the next world
𓇋𓊪𓃣	*Inup*	Anubis
𓇋𓊪𓏏𓋬	*Ipet-Sewet*	Karnak Temple
𓊨𓏏	*Ist*	Isis

 𓇋𓏏𓀀	*it*	father
 𓇋𓏏𓃛𓈗	*iteru*	river
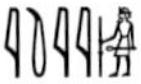 𓇋𓇋𓇋𓏏𓊪	*ity*	sovereign
𓉺𓊖	*Iunu*	Iunu, Heliopolis
𓉺𓏏𓈗𓊖	*Iunut*	Dendera
 𓉺𓊖𓏏	*Iunu Sut*	Southern Heliopolis, Thebes
𓅱𓏤	*yew*	to be is, are, etc.

𓄿 - 𓆓

 𓊌𓅱�	*dja*	to ferry across
𓊽	*djed*	stability
�	*djeser*	sacred, holy
𓆓𓏏	*djet*	eternity, forever

⌣𓅨𓏏	*djew*	evil, sad

⌣ - K

⌣𓅨𓎡	*Kush*	Kush, ancient Nubia
𓎡𓅨𓎡	*Keftiu*	Crete
𓆣 𓎡	*kheper*	to exist
𓎡𓅨⊗	*Kemet*	Egypt, the Black Land
𓎡 \\ 𓎡	*Kopny*	Byblos
𓎡	*ket f.*	another
⌣𓏭𓏭	*key m.*	another

𓅓 - M

𓅓	*em*	in, from
𓂹 𓅓𓅓	*maa*	to see

	maat	truth
	medu	words, speak
	meh	north
	meh	cubit
	mek	behold
	menkhet	clothing
	Men-nefer	Memphis
	em-r	overseer
	met	die, death
	mezeh	crocodile
	mi	like, as
	mitet	a likeness

~~	*en*	to for people
▽	*neb*	all, every
🏺	*neb*	lord
𓊮𓀏	*Nephthys*	Nephthys
𓋴𓄤	*nefer*	happy, good, beautiful
𓈖𓄿𓀒	*nedjes*	commoner, poor man
⊐	*netcher*	god
𓋞	*nub*	gold
⊗ ⌐|	*niwit*	town
𓇿	*Nut*	Nut

▷	*peh*	rear
▢ ﹏	*pen* m.	this
⊏⊐ ╷	*per*	house
⊏⊐ ◇∧	*per*	to go forth
⊓ ⊏⊐	*per-netcher*	temple
⊏⊐ ◇⊙	*peret*	season of emergence
⊏⊐ ◇◦	*peret*	seed
▢⊐ ⊏⊏	*pet*	sky
▢ ⅄ ⊿	*Ptah*	Ptah, god
▢ ﹏ ⊔	*Punt*	Punt

◯	*er*	to for place
◯⟋	*Re*	Re, sun god
◯⊙	*re*	sun
⊙	*re*	sun , day
◯	*rekh*	to know
◯	*ren*	name
⌐	*renpet*	year
◯	*resh*	to rejoice, to be glad
◯	*reshwet*	joy, gladness
◯	*Retchenu*	Syria, Palestine
	retchu	people

![- S

🦆	*sa*	son
🦆	*sat*	daughter
	secha	to remember
	secher	plan, counsel
	sedjem	to hear
	semer	companion
	sesh	scribe
	seshep	a palm, a unit of length
	seshta	secret
	Set	Set

▭ - SH

𓈙𓏤	*she*	pool, lake
𓈙𓅡𓏏𓏥	*shabty*	shabti, servant statue
▭𓈙𓇳	*shemu*	season of summer
𓎃	*shes*	alabaster
𓆄𓅱𓀭	*Shu*	Shu
𓆄𓅱	*shew*	empty

▢ - T

𓇾𓏤	*ta*	land
𓄤𓏏𓏭𓀭	*tchaty*	vizier
𓏏𓆑𓏏𓃭	*Tefnut*	Tefnut
𓏏𓐍𓈖𓋇	*tekhen*	obelisk

⌓	*ten f.*	this
🐦	*tep*	first, foremost, upon
⌒	*teyet*	likeness

𓏲 - U, W

𓏲 ⎯ × 🐦	*usheb*	to answer
𓏏𓏏𓏲	*wah*	endure
𓎛	*wab*	pure
𓎛 🐦	*wab*	wab-priest
𓌋	*was*	power
𓌋 ⌓	*Waset*	Thebes
𓅱 𓏲 ⌓	*wat*	road
𓅱 𓃀 ⊙	*weben*	rise, shine

⌐	*weh*	one, sole
🐍○★⊙	*wenut*	hour
𓎡	*Wepwawet*	Wepwawet
🦅ıı	*wey*	how!
🦅🦅⛵	*wia*	sacred boat

—•— - Z

🧍	*z*	man also 🧍ı
—•— ◠ 🧍	*zet*	woman

A family

🦤	*ba*
⚱	*dja*
⚊	*eha*
🌱	*ha*
∪	*ka*
⚑	*kha*
🔪	*ma*
🦅	*pa*
🦆	*sa*
〰	*sha*
⬭	*ta*
🦢	*tcha*
🪝	*wa*

B family

ab

neb

D family

djed

Eh family

weh

kheh

I family

mi

M family

gem

kem

tem

N family

𓃒	*hen*
𓏠	*men*
𓊃	*sen*
�	*shen*
𓅱	*wen*

P family

𓎡	*kep*
𓎺	*wep*

Q family

𓅘	*aq*

R family

𓁷	*her*
𓁹	*ir*
𓌳	*mer*
𓇋	*mer*
𓉐	*per*

S family

𓄟 *mes*

T family

𓅐 *met*

W family

𓈋 *djew*

𓏌 *new*

𓈗 *new*

𓇓 *sew*

𓆄 *shew*

†   *ankh*

        hotep

        kheper

        nefer

        sedjem

English	Hieroglyph	Pronunciation

Singular

English	Hieroglyph	Pronunciation
I, me		*wi*
you masculine		*tchu*
you feminine		*tchen*
he, him, it		*su*
she, her, it		*sey*

Plural

English	Hieroglyph	Pronunciation
we, us		*n*
you		*tchen*
they, them		*sen*

Suffix Pronouns

English	Hieroglyph	Pronunciation

Singular

English	Hieroglyph	Pronunciation
I, me, my	𓀀	i
you, your masculine	⌐	k
you, your feminine	⇨	tch
he, him, his, it, its	↼	f
she, her, it, its	𓏭	s

Plural

English	Hieroglyph	Pronunciation
we, us, our	⫴	n
you, your	⫶	tchen
they, them, their	⫶	sen

we two, our		ney
you two, your		tcheny
they two, their		seny

Hieroglyph	Pronunciation	English

Lecture 3 Vocabulary

Hieroglyph	Pronunciation	English
	bew	place
	khet (f.)	thing
	key (m.)	another
	ket (f.)	another
	im	therein
	em	in, from
	en	to (for people)
	pen (m.)	this
	pet	sky

⬯	*er*	to (for places)
⬯𓀭	*Re*	Re, sun god
⬯⊙	*Re*	sun
⊙	*re*	sun, day
⌒	*ten* (f.)	this
𓄿𓂋⊙	*weben*	rise, shine

Lecture 4 Vocabulary

⊖𓅓	*khem*	to be ignorant of, not to know
𓎼𓀀	*ger*	to be silent
𓎛	*heneh*	together with
𓇋𓅱	*yew*	to be is, are, etc.
▢𓊨	*Ptah*	Ptah, god
⬯⊖	*rekh*	to know

	ren	name
	retchu	people
	usheb	to answer
or	*z*	man
or	*zet*	woman

Lecture 5 Vocabulary

	depet	boat
	ha	to go down, to descend
	hab	to send
	khed	to fare downstream
	niwit	town
	sedjem	to hear
	reshwet	joy, gladness

	secher	plan, counsel
	tekhen	obelisk
	wia	sacred boat

Lecture 6 Vocabulary

	akhet	horizon
	gerh	night
	heru	day
	yeah	moon
	nedjes	commoner, poor man
	sesh	scribe
	she	pool
	ta	land

𓅭𓏺𓀀	*bak*	manservant
𓅭𓏭𓁐	*baket*	maidservant
𓇋𓅓𓉐	*cha*	hall, office
𓊃𓅓𓂻	*dja*	to ferry across
𓄿𓃘	*eha*	donkey
𓏠𓄿𓅓	*maa*	to see
𓏠𓄿𓏏	*maat*	truth
𓊃𓀀	*sa*	son
𓊃𓏏𓁐	*sat*	daughter
𓋴𓐍𓅓	*secha*	to remember
𓊪𓋴𓐍𓏏𓅓	*seshta*	secret
𓊹𓇋𓏭𓏭𓀀	*tchaty*	vizier

	wat	road

Lecture 8 Vocabulary

	ankh	life
	djed	stability
	her	face, sight, upon, concerning
	it	father
	iteru	river
	mezeh	crocodile
	er	mouth, magical spell
	resh	to rejoice, to be glad

Lecture 9 Vocabulary

	kheper	to exist

Lecture 10 Vocabulary
None

 𓀃𓂝𓏭	*mek*	behold

Lecture 12 Vocabulary

 𓂾𓄿𓅪	*bin*	bad, miserable
 �𓅱𓅪	*djew*	evil, sad
𓂝𓏭	*di*	to give
𓂞	*di*	to give
 𓂝𓅆𓏭	*eha*	great, large
 𓆼𓊪𓏏	*heket*	beer
𓄣𓏤	*ib*	heart
 𓇋𓊪𓏭	*iker*	excellent
𓏧𓏭	*mi*	like, as
𓏠𓏏𓏭	*mitet*	a likeness

⌣	*neb*	all, every
🏺	*neb*	lord
⚘	*nefer*	happy, good, beautiful
⟘⟘🦅	*shew*	empty

Lecture 13 Vocabulary

⚘	*ehe*	stand up, arise
⚘	*esha*	rich, plentiful, many
⚘	*kha*	shine, appear
⌐	*netcher*	god
⌇	*was*	power
⌇⊗	*waset*	Thebes/Luxor

Lecture 14 Vocabulary

𓇋𓐍	*ikh*	then
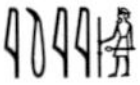 𓇋𓅱𓇋𓇋	*ity*	sovereign
𓎟	*neb*	gold
𓅨	*wey*	how!
𓏏𓊨	*wah*	endure

Lecture 15 Vocabulary

 �d𓏏𓎼𓏏	*heqat*	a unit of grain measure
𓆼	*kha*	1,000
𓯟	*meh*	cubit
 𓊠	*seshep*	a palm, a unit of length
𓄿	*khet*	a rod, unit of lengths

Lecture 16 Vocabulary

𓅓𓏏𓇹	*abed*	month
𓈊	*akhet*	season of inundation
𓉐𓏏𓇳	*peret*	season of emergence
𓆳	*renpet*	year
𓆷	*hat-sep*	year, as in a date
𓈊𓅆	*shabty*	ushabti/shabti, servant statue
𓈙𓇳	*shemu*	season of emergency
𓅨𓏏𓇳	*wenut*	hour

Lecture 17 Vocabulary

𓇋𓏏𓅓	*Atum*	Atum
𓅬𓃀	*Geb*	Geb
𓊨𓏏	*Ist*	Isis

𓏏𓅱	*Nebt*	Nephthys
𓏏𓇯	*Nut*	Nut
𓊨𓅱	*Ausir*	Osiris
𓄗𓅱	*Set*	Set/Seth
𓍱𓄿𓅱	*Shu*	Shu
𓏏𓆑	*Tefnut*	Tefnut

Lecture 18 Vocabulary

𓆓𓏏	*djet*	eternity, forever
★𓂧𓏏	*duat*	the next world
𓋀𓏏	*Iment*	the west, the next world
𓐍𓂋𓅱	*kheru*	voice
𓅓𓏏	*met*	die, death

Lecture 19 Vocabulary
None

Lecture 20 Vocabulary

𓁹𓂋𓎼	*Abdju*	Abydos
𓄛𓏏𓈉	*Desheret*	the red land, desert
𓉺𓏺𓊖	*Iunu*	On, Heliopolis
𓉺𓈖𓏏𓊖	*Iunut*	Dendera
𓉺𓏺𓏏	*Iunu Sut*	Southern Heliopolis, Thebes/Luxor
𓈎𓅓𓏏𓊖	*Kemet*	Egypt, the Black Land

Lecture 21 Vocabulary

𓊹𓅱	*hem-netcher*	servant of the god
𓎛𓂓	*hem-ka*	ka-priest
𓉻𓏏𓊪𓏏𓊖	*Ipet-sewet*	Karnak Temple
𓎡𓊪𓈖𓏭	*Kapny*	Byblos

𓈎𓄿𓈙	*Kush*	Kush, ancient Nubia
𓐍𓏏𓄿	*Khatti*	Hatti, land of the Hittites
𓎡𓆑𓍿	*Keftiu*	Crete
𓏠𓈖𓄤	*Men-nefer*	Memphis
𓉐𓊹	*per-netcher*	temple
𓎅	*menkhet*	clothing
𓊪𓈖𓏏	*Punt*	Punt
𓂋𓍿𓈖	*Retchenu*	Syria, Palestine
𓍱	*shes*	alabaster
𓃂	*wab*	pure
𓃂	*wab*	*wab*-priest

Lecture 22 Vocabulary

★🦅🦅⟶𓀀	*Duamutef*	Duamutef
𓊨▭𓃥	*Inup*	Anubis
🦅⌒	*em-r*	overseer
‖	*semer*	companion
𓁶	*tep*	first, foremost, upon
⟋	*weh*	one, sole
⋎📦𓃡	*Wepwawet*	Wepwawet

Lecture 23 Vocabulary

🦵	*hat*	front
⚘	*iabet*	east
🗝	*khet*	body
⌐	*meh*	north

![peh glyph]	*peh*	rear

Lecture 24 Vocabulary

	ahq	to enter
	ba	soul
	djeser	sacred, holy
	hotep	to be pleased, to set sun
	khenu	interior, among
	medu	words, speak
	peret	seed
	teyet	likeness

Aldred, Cyril. *Jewels of the Pharaohs*. New York: Praeger, 1971. Especially relevant to Lecture 19.

Allen, James P. *The Heqanakht Papyri*. New York: Metropolitan Museum of Art, 2002. The full story of the life of a *ka*-priest.

Andrews, Carol. *The British Museum Book of the Rosetta Stone*. New York: Dorset Press, 1994.

———. *Amulets of Ancient Egypt*. Austin: University of Texas Press, 1994. Especially relevant to Lectures 5 and 18.

Bernal, Martin. *Black Athena*. New Brunswick: Rutgers University Press, 1987. Especially relevant to Lecture 6.

Brier, Bob and Jean-Pierre Houdin. *The Secret of the Great Pyramid: How One Man's Obsession Led to the Solution of Ancient Egypt's Greatest Mystery*. New York: Smithsonian, 2008. Especially relevant to Lecture 22.

Buchwald, Jed and Diane Josefowicz. *The Zodiac of Paris*. Princeton: Princeton University Press, 2010. The full story of how the Dendera Zodiac came to France and the controversy it started. Especially relevant to Lecture 4.

Budge, E.A. Wallis. *The Egyptian Book of the Dead*. New York: Dover, 1967. Dated but useful for the hieroglyphic text. Especially relevant to Lecture 18.

Burleigh, Nina. *Mirage: Napoleon's Scientists and the Unveiling of Egypt*. New York: Harper/Collins, 2007. Especially relevant to Lecture 4.

Carter, Howard and A.C. Mace. *The Discovery of the Tomb of Tutankhamen*. New York: Dover, 1977. Reads like a novel because it was ghostwritten by Carter's novelist friend. Especially relevant to Lecture 23.

Clayton, Peter. *The Chronicle of the Pharaohs*. London: Thames & Hudson, 1995. Basic reference work on the chronology of Egypt. Well illustrated. Especially relevant to Lecture 3.

Description de l'Egypte. Cologne: Taschen, 2002. All the engravings done by Napoleon's artists. Especially relevant to Lecture 4.

Drower, Margaret. Flinders Petrie. *A Life in Archaeology*. London: Gollancz, 1985. Wonderful biography of the founder of modern Egyptology. Especially relevant to Lecture 19.

Eaton-Kraus, M. *The Sarcophagus in the Tomb of Tutankhamun*. Oxford: Griffith Institute, 1993. The basis of Lecture 24.

Fagan, Brian. *Rape of the Nile*. New York: Charles Scribner's Sons, 1975. Tells of the early adventurers in Egypt. Especially relevant to Lecture 6.

Faulkner, R. O. *The Ancient Egyptian Book of the Dead*. New York: Macmillan, 1985. Especially relevant to Lecture 18.

Findlen, Paula. *Athanasius Kircher: The Last Man Who Knew Everything*. London: Routledge, 2004. Nice account of Kircher's misguided attempt to translate hieroglyphs. Especially relevant to Lecture 5.

Fischer, Henry. *Ancient Egyptian Calligraphy*. New York: Metropolitan Museum of Art, 1988. How to draw the hieroglyphs. Especially relevant to Lecture 2.

Gardiner, Alan. *Egyptian Grammar*. Oxford: Griffith Institute, 1988. The bible of grammar. Especially relevant to Lecture 1.

Gaudet, John. *Papyrus*. New York: Pegasus, 2014. How papyrus was made in ancient Egypt and how it changed the world. Especially relevant to Lecture 9.

Gillings, R. J. *Mathematics in the Time of the Pharaohs*. New York: Dover, 1982. Especially relevant to Lecture 15.

James, T. G. H. *Howard Carter: The Path to Tutankhamen*. London: Tauris, 2001. Wonderful biography of Carter. Especially relevant to Lecture 23.

Kamrin, Janice. *Ancient Egyptian Hieroglyphs*. New York: Abrams, 2004. User-friendly way to learn hieroglyphs.

Lichtheim, Miriam. *Ancient Egyptian Literature*, vol. 2. Berkeley: University of California Press, 1976. Nice anthology of Egyptian writings. Especially relevant to Lecture 8.

Morokot, Robert G. *The Black Pharaohs*. London: Rubicon, 2000. Solid work on the Nubian kings. Especially relevant to Lecture 8.

Parkinson, Richard. *Cracking Codes: The Rosetta Stone and Decipherment*. Berkeley: University of California Press, 1999.

Quirke, Stephen. *Who Were the Pharaohs?* New York: Dover, 2002. Good reference work on the kings of Egypt. Especially relevant to Lecture 14.

Reeves, Nicholas. *The Complete Tutankhamen*. London: Thames & Hudson, 1990. Well-illustrated descriptions of the artifacts in Tutankhamen's tomb by the leading expert. Especially relevant to Lecture 23.

Remler, Pat. *Egyptian Mythology A to Z*. New York: Facts on File, 2000. Good, simple reference on all the gods. Especially relevant to Lecture 13.

Seyler, Dorothy. *The Obelisk and the Englishman*. Amherst: Prometheus, 2015. The story of William Bankes's contributions to decipherment. Especially relevant to Lecture 6.

Thompson, Jason. *Wonderful Things: A History of Egyptology*. Cairo: AUC Press, 2015. Especially relevant to Lecture 7.

Welsby, Derek. *The Kingdom of Kush: The Napatan and Meroitic Empires*. Princeton: Markus Wiener, 1996. Nice account of the Nubian Dynasty.

Williams, Caroline Ransom. *The Decoration of the Tomb of Per-Neb*. New York: Coachwhip Books, 2012. The basis of the translation in Lecture 22.

Image Credits

Page No.

i .... © Hoika Mikhail/Shutterstock..

iii .... © Artoptimum/Shutterstock.

4 .... © WitR/Shutterstoc.

5 .... © BasPhoto/Shutterstock.

22 .... © Pecold/Shutterstock.

25 .... © Francesco Ferla/Shutterstock.

26 .... © Fedor Selivanov/Shutterstock.

42 .... © WitR/Shutterstock.

44 .... © Rachelle Burnside/Shutterstock.

44 .... © Waj/Shutterstock.

45 .... © Kamira/Shutterstock.

46 .... © alessandro0770/Shutterstock.

66 .... © I. Pilon/Shutterstock.

87 .... © Everett – Art/Shutterstock.

110 .... © BasPhoto/Shutterstock.

134 .... © Jeff Dahl/Egypt Archive/Wikimedia Commons.

158 .... © Jeff Dahl /Wikimedia Commons/CC BY-SA 4.0.

180 .... © Vladimir Zadvinskii/Shutterstock.

182 .... © Marco Ossino/Shutterstock.

207 .... © Nicku/Shutterstock.

231 .... © GQ/Shutterstock.

255 .... © Vladimir Wrangel/Shutterstock.

Notes

Notes

Notes

Notes